Father Finn was born in Boston, Massachusetts, in 1881 and received his early education at the Boston Latin School. He then attended St. Charles College in Cantonsville, Maryland, and Catholic University. He was Magister Cantorum at the Vatican in 1912 and in 1914 received his LL.D. at Notre Dame. Father Finn was ordained to the priesthood in 1916. For five years he was an organist in Boston. In 1904 at St. Mary's Church in Chicago he founded the Paulist Choristers. In 1918 he moved the choir to St. Paul's Roman Catholic Church in New York and there acted as their organist and conductor until a few years ago. Father Finn is an accomplished musician and a composer of both choral and instrumental music.

From his long experience and observation as the founder and conductor of the Paulist Choristers, Father Finn has formed a number of firm convictions about choral direction. He answers here many of the questions of choirmasters, school musicians and conductors of choral groups. His is a book for both the choral conductor and the orchestral maestro, for he believes that choir and orchestra are twin instruments of expression. It is a book about the fundamentals of music and the controlling factors of musical performance, namely *tempo* and *dynamics*. Father Finn reaches down to the nature of music—the poetic fluency, the stresses and slacks of rhythmical accent, the psychology of speed, the strategy and tactics of dynamics, and the influence of pitch upon the temper of a melody—all the mystery of the upbeat.

He explains methods for getting the best out of music whether it be hymn tune or part song. In his own words he shows "how to take Palestrina out from under the notes and make his music sound beautiful in an age of vertical clashing and horizontal 'swinging.'" Although dealing with a subject of a highly technical nature Father Finn has written in a style that makes his book both instructive and readable and he has frequently illustrated his point with musical excerpts. *Leopold Stokowski has written the foreword.*

THE CONDUCTOR *RAISES* HIS BATON

The mystery of music is in the upbeat.

THE CONDUCTOR

RAISES HIS BATON

WILLIAM J. FINN

FOUNDER OF THE PAULIST CHORISTERS

WITH A FOREWORD BY LEOPOLD STOKOWSKI

HARPER & BROTHERS PUBLISHERS

New York and London

By the Same Author

EPITOME OF CHORAL TECHNIQUE
THE ART OF THE CHORAL CONDUCTOR

This book is complete and unabridged
in contents, and is manufactured in strict
conformity with Government regulations
for saving paper.

CONTENTS

FOREWORD

FATHER FINN has devoted a lifetime to music and conducting, particularly to the inspired *a cappella* music of the sixteenth century. His book on conducting is an important contribution to the widespread development of music which will enrich the future life of the United States.

Conducting is a many-sided art. One of its numerous functions is to give *unity* to groups of singers, as in the masses of Palestrina—to groups of instrumentalists, as in the symphonies of Brahms—to both singers and instrumentalists combined, as in the Ninth Symphony of Beethoven. Unity of rhythm, tempo, phrasing—unity of breathing for singers, woodwind and brass players—bowing for string players. Unity of quality, contrast, and balance of tone—in giving homophonic music prominence to its melody, and relative quietness to its underlying harmonies—in giving clarity to all the voices or instruments in polyphonic music, so that each melodic thread in the woven mesh of melodies has its due value. But above all, unity of expression, thought, emotion, imagination—in conveying to the listener the message which all great music has—the message that cannot be conveyed by words or painting or sculpture or any other of the arts—the message that, by its nature, can only be expressed by Music.

LEOPOLD STOKOWSKI

PREFACE

THIS is a book about certain aspects of interpretative conducting from which some conductors have been distracted. It concerns primarily the choral conductor but regards as well the orchestral maestro, for the chorus and orchestra are twin instruments of expression. The title of the book and the caption on the flyleaf indicate the trend of ensuing chapters. From the experience and observation of years many convictions and some positive tenets have crystallized. These are written here. Perhaps the data will not singly compel all the single conclusions derived, but the facts, theses, and proposals, in aggregate, should stimulate curiosity. Probably many musicians know that fundamental properties of music as both a *fine* and a *liberal* art are ignored on many podiums. I am inviting the reader to consider some of the fundamentals, not academically but in their relations with practical processes. Succinctly, this volume deals with the controlling factors of musical performance, *tempo* and *dynamics*, emphasizing the sovereign position of quantity ratios. Therefore rhythm, phrasing, the balancing of melody and harmony, the apposition of contrapuntal figures, the tension of canon and fugue, and the valid disclosure of that musty old academic mystery—*the horizontal line of polyphony*—comprise the subject matter.

It has not been easy to write this book. It was not difficult to write in other books of the physical technique required for choral virtuosity: how to rid voice lines of ugly encumbrances; how to balance parts; how to blend these in a unified agency; how to manage the alto line (this was not so easy!); how to make the von Bülow crescendo and diminuendo; how to beat time in public. These were all questions of burning interest to choirmasters, school musicians, and an occasional local conductor of a choral society. And these questions could be answered directly and simply from the experience of the rehearsal room and the concert platform. But the topics of this volume are of a different order. They reach down to the nature of music, involving an understanding and a control of its patent and latent forces. Poetic fluency, the stresses and slacks of rhythmical accentuation, the psychology of slowness and quickness, the strategy and tactics of effective dynamics, the acoustical influence of high low, and middle pitches upon the temper of melody, the simplification of contrapuntal presentations, the sacred secret of polyphonic performance—these are subjects which, offering no showcase technique (except in the items of counterpoint and *a cappella polyphony*), may leave the superficial student cold. The ennui with which some of our conductors have glanced at such a list of subjects suggests the willingness of musicians and student musicians to discount their importance.

In these pages I engage myself to set forth, as logically as I can, the procedures which I have found dependable (and indispensable) for directing the competence of highly trained units to their most convincing communicability: how to guarantee rhythmic sweep to lyric melodies; how to promote the *melos* of music; how to guide movements to their rhetorical climaxes; how to relieve homophony of distressing monotony; how to improve a hymn tune or part song; how to clarify the *aural* obscurities of counterpoint, canon, and fugue; how to take Palestrina out from under the notes and make his music sound beautiful in an age of vertical clashing and horizontal "swinging." The precepts strewn through the pages are pet corollaries to the premises standing sentinel at the heads of chapters.

If you think the pages about rhythm to be unimportant, turn to the chapters on dynamics, and you'll probably turn back to the "unimportant."

On each page I am asking the student reader this question: *Did you ever think of this before?* I wish that some old-timer had asked me the same question about the same items—when I was young.

WILLIAM J. FINN

THE CONDUCTOR *RAISES* HIS BATON

CHAPTER I

THE CONDUCTOR A RE-CREATOR

THE art of conducting has become within the past hundred years a highly specialized phase of musical expression. The modern conductor is the product of the latter half of the nineteenth century. His precursors were primarily preceptors who accomplished their tasks, without public acclaim, in rehearsal rooms. The earlier maestros taught the techniques of concerted music to their singers or players, unified and burnished the individual contributions to ensemble effect, and inculcated principles of interpretation so thoroughly as to preclude the need of public coaching. But the modern conductor, frequently outranking in popular appraisal the soloists and groups which he directs, is rated as a performing artist. His gesticulating presidency over choral or orchestral units is expected to bring aesthetic delight to the audience. Sometimes his actual contribution to a performance is overestimated. The conductor whose worth is measured by the unsafe criteria of publicity and stage manner is usually too highly prized. Nevertheless, the role of the choral and orchestral conductor is of real importance in these days of confusing musical idioms, even if gullibility is fashioning too many nimbus-disks around the heads of celebrities. Modern choral and orchestral music is involved and frequently difficult of execution. An analyst is needed to discover and reveal much that is obscure and even esoteric. The conductor assumes the responsibilities of the analyst.

The older music required no conducting in our current understanding of the function. There was no obscure material in Gregorian chant; the rhythm of this ancient style was free and largely textual, thus eliminating the necessity of time beating; the dynamic variations were gentle and indicated by the arses and theses of a simple melodic curve line. Nor was there need for the public directing of an interpretative conductor in the increasingly elaborate polyphonies during the era from the fourteenth to the early seventeenth centuries. Polyphony expounded itself; the cues to its proper per-

1

formance were few and as easily discernible as those in the Gregorian unisons from which it stemmed; the imitative contrapuntal figures and phrases were conjured up in the creative imaginations of the polyphonists as mosaics of horizontal melodies which, in actual performance, could be tessellated aesthetically into harmonic units with a simple technique.

The introduction of absolute time values in the polyphonic style developed the need of conveying to performers the precise length of notes and rests. Without a quasi-metronomic indication of note durations, polyphony would have been only heterophony. This need was filled by the "sol-fa," frequently a singer, who, making slight gestures with a scroll of parchment, was wont to establish the continuity of pulsations. In such a simple manner was the great music of the *a cappella* masters "conducted." Even through the following two and a half centuries conducting involved only the beating of the measures. Sometimes the player of harpsichord or pianoforte would strike a few extra notes to call the attention of performers to irregularities of tempo or intonation, and in Ragenet's *A Comparison between the French and Italian Musick and Operas,* one learns that the eighteenth-century "conductor" at the Paris Opera had "an elboe chair and desk plac'd on the stage, where, with the score in one hand, and a stick in the other, he beat time on a table put there for that purpose. . . ."

Time beating, which naturally included the setting of the tempo, was the only public prerogative and obligation of the *maestro di cappella* and the *chef d'orchestre.* Until about the middle of the nineteenth century, when the art of the interpretative leader began to take form, the attempted superimposition of personal concepts or fancies by an individual on a chorus or orchestra during a public rendition would have been regarded as not only superfluous and silly but arbitrary and presumptuous. Wagner, Mendelssohn, Manns, Halle, Richter, Berlioz, and von Bülow, with their colleagues and disciples, made the first comprehensive canvassing of the new field in which the virtuoso conductor was to develop; and their findings, especially those preserved in the monographs of Richard Wagner and Felix Weingartner, constitute the substratum of the modern art of interpretative conducting. The technique built upon this substratum is applicable to the chorus as well as to the orchestra, for the two ensemble units of expression, both requiring by their natural and analogous structures a fine interlacing of many parts and the correlating of many tonal colors, are twins and must be nurtured to aesthetic maturity by almost identical processes; the philosophy of interpretation of the chorophonic and symphonic conductors must be the same, at least in primary premises.

Mastery of the art of choral conducting implies scholarship and practical competence in two major phases of ensemble directing. The complete maestro is skilled in two roles: he is both a creator and a re-creator. The art to which he has devoted himself charges him with a twofold responsibility. First he is commissioned to create, for he must make and maintain in dependable proficiency a singing unit which will invariably function throughout the diapason of choral tonalities and timbres aesthetically and with convincing musicianship.

He is charged with the second duty of re-creating, reviving and reactivating at each performance compositions which between performances lie embalmed in printer's ink on library shelves. The mortality of sounds is speedier than that of melting snowflakes; each time a given succession of sounds recurs, a process of re-formation is involved. Thus, to bring to printed notes the vitality of a living art, the conductor must acquire consummate skill in the science of re-creating.

His twofold task requires a twofold technique. Chronologically he must fulfill his first obligation before he can successfully address the second. He must, of course, create a singing unit. If his chorus cannot sing properly (and I mean by properly, with such elegance and beauty of tone as is connoted by the very word *music*) his interpretative intentions will be no more than academic ideas, frustrate and valueless. General musicianship and authority with the baton are invaluable assets to the choral conductor, but they are inadequate for the training of a chorus.

It would be an affront to serious students to insist at length on the self-evident fact that the finely specialized technique required for eminence in both phases of chorophony must rest upon the solid plinth of a broad musicianship. It is not pedantic or superfluous, however, to urge the conviction that the information about the general principles of music dispensed in many conservatories is necessarily fragmentary. During a student's academic courses scarcely more than the mere fundamentals—a table of contents—of any art or science can be disclosed. The undergraduate must realize that only postgraduate studies, research, and experiments will provide a reliable background for his artistic undertakings. The need for supplementing his information will continue throughout his professional career. If he is not a consistent student, reading almost daily books and monographs on all subjects which are relevant to his art form, investigating the new points of view of professional colleagues, and maintaining a lively interest in the humanities, his musical perspective will become narrower with the years. The narrower the perspective, the less a custodian of any art form has to express. Therefore it is incumbent upon choral and orchestral conductors, who preside over such potentially great instruments of expression, to acquire a comprehensive musicianship and a philosophy of music which is based on history, psychology, and aesthetic criticism. If he is fortunate in having attained such musicianship, he may be assured that the precise craftsmanship required for his specialty will be easily learned and intelligently applied.

Choral musicianship is preeminently a specialty. As a creator and a re-creator, the *maestro di cappella* must be versed in much vocal and interpretative lore that is not appurtenant to other branches of musical exercise.

To produce a singing ensemble of musical value, he needs complete information about all the rudiments, all the refinements, and all the related acoustico-physiological elements of choral technique. He is grievously at a disadvantage if he enters the rehearsal room or steps upon the podium in the concert hall without so competent a measure of skill as to be able instantly to diagnose and remedy all symptoms of ineptitude or inertia in single choral lines and in the ensemble. If he is really intent upon reaching the true ideals of chorophony, he will circumvest himself with the mantle of Job. Patience—extraordinary patience—is a cardinal virtue in the choir hall, for the choirmaster constantly faces the tedium of rebuilding, reinstructing, and revitalizing the group over which he presides.[1]

In this volume, the canons of authentic interpretation and the criteria of artistic performance furnish the material for examination. There are to be considered, first, the capital resources of execution and expression which generally determine the aesthetic validity of rendition. Ensuing considerations deal with the distinctive idioms of sundry and particular schools of composition. These, severally,

---

[1] The minutiae of this technical procedure have been set forth comprehensively by this author in *The Art of the Choral Conductor* (Boston: Birchard, 1939).

demand specific treatment. Although practical skill is gradually acquired in the rehearsal room and at public performances, the principles of interpretation upon which the faithful delineation of composers' intentions depends must be mastered as the abstract principles of any science or art are mastered.

Broadly, there are two kinds of musical composition, the scholastic and the popular. Both need studied attention from the conductor, for in the scholastic style the scientifically ordered movements, being often worked out like algebraic equations, lack animation and color, while in the popular style there is feeling and abandon with little consistency or method. In the words of John Pyke Hullah, the great English choral authority (1812-1884), "The scholastic music has no art, the popular music no science." This epigram is obviously not an accurate appraisal of the two styles of composition, but it is clear that the scholastic style is characteristically academic and mathematical, and that the popular style often lacks the balanced contours of formal construction. It is therefore incumbent upon conductors to invigorate the classical forms with artistic fervor and to temper the major extravagances of mere sentimental expression.

Music is both a science and an art. To achieve its full potential effect all the factors which compose the synthesis must be revealed. Some conductors, reacting chiefly to its theoretical and acoustical features, present music in its mathematical and therefore colder aspects. Others, perhaps immoderately sensitive to its more subtle and emotive constitution, subordinate form, balance, phraseology, and symmetry of contours to theme, setting this forth with an excess of romantic imagery.

It is clear that conductors of either class can give only inadequate performances. The master conductor recognizes, is influenced by, and undertakes to reveal both the academic and the emotional factors. Real music is not evolved from sounds which are, on the one hand, only corollaries of mathematical formulae, or, on the other, mere stimuli to effervescence. The physics of sound, the accepted laws of harmony and composition, and all the canons of aesthetic performance must be exemplified together in well-balanced coordination if music is to sing in convincing accents.

The ultra-mathematical conductors (and composers) need more emotional elasticity. They seem to be restrained by a musical austerity which permits their imaginations only puritanical opportunity. Elaborating their performance technique upon academic premises altogether, they are severe, formal, scrupulously bookish, and inhospitable to blithesome episodes.

In a treatise on conducting, much emphasis must be given to the need of comprehending the complete functional nature of music and what is required of the conductor to guarantee it aesthetic efficacy.

Probably many of us have nodded through programs (restively, of course, because of the sequence of *mezzo-forte, forte,* and *fortissimo*) during which it was not quite clear just what the conductor had in mind; programs which might have been rehearsed in an acoustical frigidarium. If conductors are inordinately influenced by a sort of Pythagorean approach to music, they will probably fail to be moved by its spirituality. They will never find any fun in it; they miss altogether the humor and sundry delightful bits of drollery which hide like elves behind sharps and flats, vault over the high curve lines of melody, and invite the spirited flights of optimism. I recently came across this item in a letter from Chicago to the editor of the San Francisco *Chronicle* (November 25, 1940):

"FUN AT THE OPERA

"John Charles Thomas, celebrated baritone, who has been a stalwart contributor to the new order of opera in the West, added his voice to the insistence upon a broader latitude in opera, urging: 'Let's have fun at the opera; let's have entertainment we can understand.'

"It was likewise Thomas who, after a recent unfolding of Verdi's *Aida,* stood before a crowded house in the barbaric costume of the King of Ethiopia and sang 'Home on the Range,' to applause and cheers."

Music can hardly enjoy itself under stiff conductors. It becomes introvert and pessimistic. Many choral and orchestral conductors in high places are smugly satisfied to discover the arithmetical functions —tangents, cotangents, sines, and cosines—of music. Such men are not fulfilling their responsibilities; they fail to vitalize.

Sometimes they seem content to fabricate their figures in ice, hankering to muse in temperatures below zero, phrasing frozen notation with icicle-batons. From the arctics and antarctics which they explore, they bring a refrigeration that benumbs artistic sensibilities. Many an auditorium is converted into a "thrilling region of thick-ribbed ice," the loges and stalls becoming igloos of inadequate shelter during sequences of gelid motets, sleet-sheeted symphonies, and polar-cold oratorios.

Conductors in the other extreme class are worse offenders against the fundamental demands of art than the icemen of the profession.

These allegedly soul-stirring, electric, heart-expanding, ecstatic, and rapturous smatterers only toy with music, concentrating on no substantial properties of a great agency. Amateurish professionals, they generally hide behind "much ado about nothing" gestures. They are fond of non-essentials, deriving satisfaction in whim and caprice. They tend, often unwittingly, to alter beyond recognition the masterpieces of genius. Distortions of rhythm, grotesque tempos, extravagant *rubato,* dynamic contrasts to nerve-racking extremes, and cloying *fermatas* to languishing exhaustion comprise such conductors' approach to the interpretation of music.

The extent to which a conductor may properly be influenced by his own imagery in re-creating a composer's music is an interesting point for debate. The baton is certainly not a crayon to be used in revising another's composition, nor does the gratification accruing from an alleged improvement of the score absolve a conductor from the obligation of directing an authentic reading of the original. Fidelity to a composer's intentions, as far as they may be discerned, is the cornerstone of music ethics. And yet some conductors seem to be intent upon discovering elements in scores, which, though trivial, by undue stress will make their readings "different," possibly prospering their personal eminence with undiscriminating audiences.

"Sing my music and not yours," said Gugliemi (1727-1804) to singers who habitually substituted their own ornamentations in his operas, and Shakespeare admonished in the third act of *Hamlet*: "Let those that play your clowns speak no more than is set down for them." Even deacons in the early Church required restraint by ecclesiastical councils, for in their chanting of the *alleluias* it had became their pernicious custom to improvise long melismatic roulades which robbed the simple chant melodies of their authentic unity and continuity.

Certainly the quest for latent factors which by carefully balanced emphasis can enrich a performance is not to be disparaged; on the contrary, it is highly recommended. But the substitution of unwarranted effects for the honest revelation of the substantial contents of a composition must be dismissed as unqualified arrogance and charlatanism. The master conductor loves both theme and form. He coordinates these with devotion and so deftly that neither sacrifices a jot of its inherence in music.

In all well-written music, the aesthetic concepts of the composer will discover themselves to listeners, if given fair chance, without much importuning from the conductor.

Admittedly, however, the conductor must know how to accord the music its fair chance.

He must recognize the locale of the melody in the score as it migrates from one part to another, and be on the alert to subdue concomitant features lest they obscure its primacy. Melody is the soul of music, the vivifying, energizing principle of the art; and if it is allowed to retire into the shade of overreaching harmonies, dissonances, contrapuntal commentaries, and embellishments, its spirit soon takes flight, leaving an inept something in its place, a waxen manikin, impotent and without *raison d'être*.

Richard Wagner establishes as a primary duty of conductors the *finding of the melody*. The following paragraph from his monograph *On Conducting* is apropos: "I received a good lesson at Paris in 1839, when I heard the orchestra of the Conservatoire rehearse the enigmatical Ninth Symphony. The scales fell from my eyes; I came to understand the value of *correct* execution and the secret of a good performance. The orchestra had learnt to look for Beethoven's *melody* in every bar—that melody which the worthy Leipzig musicians had failed to discover; and the orchestra *sang* that melody. *This was the secret.*"[2]

Also, the concurrent harmony and the relationships of simultaneous melodies must be analyzed: the juxtapositions of contrapuntal imitation, the tension between fugal subject and countersubject, and the entanglements of canonical antecedents and consequents. Furthermore, the conductor needs to recognize the different reactions stimulated by rugged diatonic modality, the *musica ficta* of the first era of multiple polyphonic development (1445-1521), the more subtle *musica ficta* of the second period (1521-1595), and the candid use of chromatics and the perfect cadence of the third epoch (1595-1643).

The melodies of these several eras, which may fittingly be called the infancy, childhood, and adolescence of harmonized music, are

---

[2] Richard Wagner, *On Conducting,* translated from the German by Edward Dannreuther (2nd ed.; London: Reeves, 1897), p. 15.

derivatives of the music theory of the respective periods. A modern director, therefore, is required by the criteria of authenticity to present each melody with due consideration of the epoch of its origin. Otherwise, anachronisms will destroy its distinctive features. This means that the modification of modal or tonic homogeneity by accidentals must be effected only in the degree intended by the composer. Thus the appropriate influence of an alien semitone in a motet by Okeghem is slight, perhaps even negligible, whereas that of an accidental in later periods is intended to be more subversive of modality. Beginning not later than Wagner, sharps and flats have been stalking across the diatonic tetrachords with the unmistakable purpose of effecting chromatic metamorphoses. In the current era, the twelve semitones are the shock troops with which the polytonalists and their dismal kinsmen the atonalists assail the constitutional stronghold of traditional melody. This stronghold, since the Ambrosian scales first gave aesthetic form to occidental music, has been either modality or keynote tonality to which all modulations have made respectful obeisance.

The conductor's obligations and prerogatives, in the preparation and performance of programs, are identical. His office is to "accord the music its fair chance."

The prerequisite for aesthetic efficacy, a tonally and technically competent unit, is taken for granted in these pages. No attention is given to any items of choral or orchestral musicianship which relate to the vocal or instrumental aptness of an ensemble. Free discussion of the *interpretative* responsibilities of a conductor requires the assumption that his *chorus or orchestra is equipped to fulfill his interpretative intentions.*

His interpretative responsibilities include, broadly,

1. *The finding of the melody in every bar.*
2. *Its presentation with due care for its essential properties.*
3. *Its correlation with all associated integrants both manifest and implied.*

Certain inadvertences to some particulars comprised in these three major inclusions have weakened contemporary performances of concerted music. A widespread indifference to the inherences of musical structure is noted. An amazing insouciance prevails regarding those qualities of music which endow the art with its emotive force and which may be assembled under the caption *poetic motion.* This nonchalant unconcern (sometimes it seems smug) has permitted inadequacies and positive inaccuracies to lessen the effectiveness of many skilled groups. Virtuosity in execution may be only a superficial accomplishment; it may be altogether mechanical. Probably music that is written candidly for entertainment or technical display is prospered by brilliant rendition; but the art of bringing to light and life the thoughts, aspirations, and inspirations which impelled composers to write great music involves more than facile vocalism and neat dexterity. Aesthetics and psychology must be heeded if the reading of scores is validly to re-create the compositions of masters.

Music is a medium of expression requiring rhythmical balance as well as intervallic propriety. The current boast that rhythm was never before so thoroughly understood and emphasized is blustering gasconade. As unbiased review of many current performances of classical as well as popular music reveals a growing disregard for the fluency and undulation which are indispensable to metrical motion and which, if one be permitted to make conclusions from the implications of earlier scores, must have distinguished the *modus operandi* of past eras. I am not unmindful of the high standards of musicianship exemplified on many podiums, in asserting that the average conductor seems content with a meager minimum of rhythmical rectitude. He is satisfied if broad sweeping contours are outlined. The stresses and slacks of rhythmical activity and periodicity are quite generally unobserved. Time patterns are obscured and phraseology suffers. Hard prose or doggerel is substituted for lyric versification.

Tempo has a psychological affinity with rhythm. It is natural, therefore, for those who are inattentive to the scansion of melody to underestimate the influence of pace and its sundry modifications. The choice of a prevailing tempo for a number and applications of *rallentando* and *accelerando* seem often to be made at random. *Rubato* is frequently madcap caprice. The psychological aspects of quickness and slowness have not engaged the interest of the majority of conductors.

Furthermore, the signal importance of dynamics in the unfolding of a musical idea or plan has, lamentably, been unsuspected by too many leaders. Excessive loudness in performance has robbed many a composition of inherent beauty. The ratios of *crescendo* and *diminuendo* to appropriate quantity levels are often unwarranted. The primary importance of carefully appointed dynamic appositions in the exposition of contrapuntal figures is recognized by a mild minority. Not only are latent, subsurface qualities thus allowed to remain concealed, but obvious surface properties are smudged. Therefore many conductors fail to make true music out of printed canons, fugues, and polyphonic intricacies generally. The average performance of a choral fugue is clamorous jargon; the average *fuguing* orchestra disseminates more tonal confusion than the sum total of its timbres and decibel strength would supposedly generate. A concerted choral-orchestral fugue may generally be depended upon to lump great hunks of sound together in a monumental mass of chaotic intonations.

The data presented in the ensuing pages are offered in the hope that student conductors will address themselves seriously and systematically to an analysis of the principles of musical efficacy from which flow the general and specific resources of aesthetic interpretation. Tonal and technical shortcomings are certainly inhibitive of artistic effectiveness. But the performance of the best choruses and orchestras is unavailing if interpretative inadequacies and mistakes, the consequence of inattention to the items abridged in the immediately preceding paragraphs, neutralize their competency.

The finding of the melody in every bar has been marked as the first task of the interpreter. Melody is the basis of music. It is, then, of paramount importance that the conductor always be cognizant of its locale. Usually the site of a principal melody is unmistakably evident. In strict polyphony, each voice line furnishes a melody of its own. But in the *homophonic quasi-contrapuntal* styles characteristic of much music of the nineteenth and current centuries, the melody migrates almost stealthily from one part to another. Frequently a complete melodic period is compounded of small arcs distributed through the choral or orchestral lines. The continuity of a composition requires that these arcs be discovered and organized. Otherwise, involved music will be necessarily enigmatic. The pursuit of migrating melodic *morceaux* not only is an obligation of the conductor, it is a fascinating challenge to his artistic perspicacity.

Since my purpose throughout this volume is to be practical, I shall not direct attention to the purely musicological or abstract memoranda pertinent to a thorough study of this topic. It seems adequate here to point out that the short arcs (perhaps of a few notes) which appear throughout a choral or orchestral score are either parts of a migratory melody or little (obiter dicta) melodies themselves and require underlining in performance. This underlining must be accomplished in accord with principles which are discussed and applied in their appropriate relevance throughout the book. The reader is referred for specific data to the section on scale-consciousness in the Appendix.

Without further preamble, therefore, we address the second task of the conductor, *the presentation of the melody with due care for its essential properties.* The principal and least understood of these is rhythm.

CHAPTER II

RHYTHM

ANY dissertation purporting to treat of the intrinsic dependence of music on rhythm is apt to be prejudged as just another "weary, stale, flat, and unprofitable" rehash of trite platitudes. All likely subject matter, it is almost universally assumed, has long since been compressed into a few frayed clichés. The cavalcade of musicians has ridden hard through the centuries with hackneyed slogans conspicuous in its heraldry. Unless a discussion of rhythm promises by its caption to pay homage to irregularities—the spasms of chronic syncopation, swing, and other fitful anomalies—it has poor chance of winning attention.

Certain generalities bequeathed by the sires of the art are accepted unthinkingly as a natural legacy by sons and grandsons. Our inherited rhythmical creed is a compendium of sluggish commonplaces: "Rhythm is of the essence of music"; "It is not only a medium through which a phase of the art is disclosed, it is a constitutional property, an immanent attribute, a generative principle of music itself."

Unquestioning acceptance of these traditional dogmas indicates that one belongs by right of birth to an upper caste of lyrists. He is not required to examine their validity or implications. He does not have to study Lord Chesterfield to be a gentleman. But just as good manners and other social amenities are sometimes marks of a specious refinement, so a veneer of musical tenets can, in practice, cover an ineffectual if not an altogether counterfeit musicianship.

It is easy to stray from the straight line of logic. It is difficult faithfully to follow in action the clear conclusions of right thinking. *The more abstract the subject matter, the less interest it stimulates, and so basic principles of philosophy and art alike are frequently glimpsed with pathetic lethargy, and the practical gain which might have accrued to an understanding acquaintance is unmindfully forfeited.*

There are two circuits in which the flow of rhythm must be

discernible, the small arc of the single measure and the circumference of the entire movement of which each arc is a unit. Some
pedagogues might put the latter first. But the priority of the circuits
in importance is of academic interest only and is therefore not
debated here. It is evident enough, however, that a silver chain cannot be made of iron links, and that metrical fluency cannot accrue
to a whole if its parts are unmetrical. It is true that a glance at the
terrain of the music, i.e., the grouping of measures and phrases
and the balancing of sentences and periods, provides an easy reconnaissance of the rhythmical intention and scope of a movement. But
such reconnaissance is valuable only if it discloses the key to the
metrical code. Each phrase needs measuring (in modern music);
each measure needs unifying; and each unit must be studied in its
poetic affiliation with other units.

The rhythmical coverage of periods and movements and the
general metrical silhouette of numbers are probably not so dependent
upon the watchfulness of the conductor as the rhythmical flow of
single measures, the former being kept in fair focus by the phrasing
of the composer and the latter only indicated in the time signature.
The time symbol almost timidly tells of an inherence in the score
which cannot survive the inadvertence or indifference of performers.
(If the little device were printed in red, would its blush for slights
stir sympathy?) The broad sweeps may be hinted at, but the shades
of meaning and feeling—the chiaroscuro of the passing moments—
which are the silken articulations of music cannot be made manifest
if the conductor as well as the performers set no store by accentuation.

One rarely hears good phrasing (except when due to printed slurs
and rest marks) if the metrical implications of single measures are
ignored. Conductors, habitually reading 4/4 time as 2/4, show a
chronic weakness for "phrasing in two."

Certainly a keen sense of rhythm is a prerequisite of musicianship. If the thought of a tone-deaf conductor must be dismissed as
absurd, the concept of a conductor waving a wild wand over
unsensed sequences of binaries and ternaries must be excluded as
equally inane. Nevertheless, there are some accredited musicians who
brandish batons with equivalent insensibility (i.e., indifference) to
tone or time. This insensibility is not incurable obtuseness. It is a
very clear *signum quo*: a *sign by which* reasonably to conclude that
such conductors have failed to examine the specific inferences
necessarily deducible from primary principles.

The convertible value of our heritage of verbiage about rhythm has been decreasing. The undulation and smoothness of movement, which would characterize performances of music if the inherited commonplaces were taken seriously and applied in practice, seem to emphasize their desirability by the tantalizing strategy of absence. The fact of their absence cannot be successfully concealed from those who expect to find them, or compensated for even with those who unknowingly sustain a loss.

The derangement of rhythmical sequences in the modern exercise of the musical art is manifest in the distortions which develop from unstudied performances in general, and ensue specifically from piebald time patterns, designless accents, ill-chosen tempos, the misapplication of *rallentandos* and *accelerandos*, the frequent grotesqueness of *fermatas*, and the disturbance of continuity effected by baroque agogics and the phrasing of fragments.

Rhythm and tone antedate melody, which is a combination of these. Primitive man, according to anthropologists, was sensitive to the excitement of percussion instruments. "From them," writes Alfred Einstein, "he discovered the power of rhythm. . . . At the same time man may have acquired practice in the use of notes of definite pitch for signals in war. . . . To tone and rhythm was added primitive melody."[1] The chronological order in which the components of music reached the consciousness of the race is of interest here only as a reinforcement of the premise that without rhythm melody is like a hypothesis of the absurd. But the order in which a conductor addresses the constituents and connotations of a melody may be considered a safe hint as to his interpretative acumen. Prior to all the other needs of music which he must serve is the requirement of rhythmical fluency. Physics and psychology demand this—physics because rhythm is the logically extended application of the phenomenon of periodicity, and psychology because of the innate tendency of men to note the duration of sounds and the sequences in which they recur.

Melody is the poetry of rhythm, but rhythm is the poetry of sound; without the latter all music would be but alphabetical prose. The history of music shows melodic movement developing, progressively, in three broad rhythmical orders, each in its respective era producing a corresponding genus of musical organization. These

[1] Alfred Einstein, *A Short History of Music* (New York: Knopf, 1938), p. 4.

orders are, broadly, *free rhythm, Renaissance-mensural rhythm,* and *time and phrase pattern rhythm.*

Free rhythm is a mode of utterance independent of absolute time values and accent patterns. The grace of its stately and unhampered motion is felt in well-snug Gregorian chant and the recitatives of oratorio and opera.

Renaissance-mensural rhythm is the basis of the great *a cappella* polyphonic architecture. The freedom of this order is preserved by the horizontal independence of each choral line which expresses accentual autonomy in its own arrangement of syllables and notes. The mensurability was designed, of necessity, to maintain the several free lines of polyphony in a feasible relationship of vertical accord.

Time and phrase pattern rhythm is the genesis of the music that began to take shape after the polyphonic epoch. The character of this order of rhythm is established by the regular repetition of accented notes in binary or ternary periodicity. A regular recurrence of strong and weak beats tends to require an arithmetical balance in the total number of measures over which a melody is distributed. This arithmetical balance is one of the bases of the six classical forms of post-Renaissance composition.

The scope of the present field of inquiry is limited to the subject matter pertinent to this order of rhythm. *Free rhythm* is often encountered, usually in isolated passages, in modern music, but it is essentially a distinguishing property of plain song, and detailed examination of it is not relevant here. *Renaissance-mensural rhythm* is discussed in the later chapter on polyphony.

L. J. de Bekker[2] offers a simple definition of what I have designated as the third order of rhythm: "Rhythmus or Rhythm is the METRE of modern music. . . . The units of Rhythm are Measures, as the units of the Measure are long and short notes grouped according to Accent."

The prosody of meters in Greek and Latin poetry derived from the length of vowels (accentuation was a later criterion) and, according to the allocation of long and short syllables, the meter is scanned as iambic pentameter, dactylic hexameter, etc. But in post-Renaissance music the meter is determined by the regular sequence of strong and weak beats in each measure, and is parsed accordingly as simple double or compound binary or ternary rhythm. Measures of *mixed*

[2] L. J. de Bekker, *Stokes' Encyclopedia of Music and Musicians* (rev. ed.; New York: Stokes, 1909), pp. 538-539.

rhythms (*q.v.*) are divisible into units of two or three pulsations. The reiteration of strong beats—accents—at the same place in successive measures is the kinetic force of modern music. The influence of *accelerando, rallentando, fermatas,* and *agogics* on the regularity of this reiteration is directed toward moods, since only the pace and not the order of the repetitions is affected.

Evidently, therefore, accentuation, the art of correlating the strong and weak components of modern metrical construction, is a subject of primary importance to all musicians and a fortiori to conductors.

Notation preserves the aspects of rhythm that are visible to the eye, but accentuation, which should make it discernible to the ear, is so nonchalantly ignored that even sketchy metrical contours are often concealed. Listening to unfamiliar compositions on the air waves is a handy means of ascertaining the prevalent standards of rhythmical integrity. Sometimes one is hard pressed to offer a good guess at the rhythmical structure of the composition in progress. "What is the meter?" "Is it simple or double, two-four or four-four?" "Where precisely is the upbeat?" "Was that sequence of slow notes a series of divided beats (Percy Scholes calls them 'subbeats') or did each pulsation indicate a numerical unit of the measure?" "Is this sudden brisk animation due to a change of rhythm or merely to an acceleration of tempo?" "Was that prolonged tone or chord a *fermata,* a gratuitously interpolated agogic, or a duration of indicated length?" One might develop the guessing of radio rhythms into an after-dinner game if scores with the right answers were at hand!

Non-metrical pulsations are unsuccessfully substituted for rhythmical serials, the art of accentuation having been discarded as a principal virtue in performance. Fluency, elegance, and much aesthetic satisfaction are thus sacrificed. *Examination of the average solo or ensemble rendition will confirm the truth of this affirmation.* All the notes of a temporal sequence seem to clamor with equal insistence for equal importance. The parity of eminence accorded to each time unit is destructive *in toto* of undulation, that wave-like motion to and fro, which is essential to the lyric nature of music.

The student is invited here, before proceeding further, to appraise for himself the relative artistic values of any melody, first as delivered in the current equal-stress fashion and then conformably with the rhythmic stresses and slacks implied in the time signature. It has been my experience invariably to observe a reaction of amazement when, probably for the first time, students have adverted to the aesthetic disparity of the two deliveries. There's no fluency in the flow of "Sweet Afton" when the water must sputter at every second and third beat! (Cf. the section on *simple ternary rhythm*, page 36 *et seq.*)

Flow gen-tly, sweet Af-ton, a - mang thy green braes; Flow gen-tly, I'll

sing thee a   song in thy praise; My Ma-ry's a - sleep by thy

mur-mur-ing stream, Flow gen-tly, sweet Af-ton, dis - turb not her dream.

FIG. 1.

All trained musicians know, in the abstract, that time melody is more than a progression of intervals, that it is a continuity arranged in some definite sequence of stronger and weaker pulsations. The prevailing disregard of metrical emphasis is therefore difficult to explain. Nevertheless, it is a fact that our music walks on stilts. There's little grace in its gait; it stumps when it should glide, betaking itself along instead of proceeding!

Not only venial irregularities but major transgressions against metrical form are commonplace. Offsetting many interpretative excellences, these defects thwart the lyric aims of composers.

Hymn tunes, motets, anthems, glees, oratorio and cantata choruses; sacred music, concert music, school music; simple music, involved music; monody, homophony, polyphony; solo, choral, orchestral music—all styles and types are grievously weakened by the widespread undervaluation of essential rhythmical properties.

Beauty of tone, balance of colors, and other evidences of artistic sensitiveness are neutralized by any consistent failure to exemplify the metrical bases of a composition.

Accentuation means the timely use of *louder* and *softer*. In this sense rhythm is dependent upon dynamics. In passing, it is interesting to note that a conductor who is a poor strategist in one field is rarely better in the other.

The essence of time-pattern rhythm being the collocation in regular series of stronger and weaker sounds, it is permissible to conclude that the gratification it provides derives from a natural law. For, modally, physical forces act by processes of alternation. The alternation is not always a precise metronomic intermittence, but it is clear that natural functions proceed in a timed relationship (however various the timing) and that they depend for efficacy upon an equivalent of rise and recoil. Each major or positive impulsion creates enough momentum to carry vitality through a passive or negative sequel to its next repetition. The undulation of the waves is a good example of this phenomenon. In poetry, the long vowels push the short vowels along, and in music the accented beats are the energizing principle of each measure. The trochee and its inversion, the iambus, give vitality to poetical feet at every second vowel. The accentuation of every other beat in binary rhythm is the musical correspondent of the trochee-iambus pattern; the dactyl, with one long vowel followed by two short ones, set the *mise en scène* for our 3/2, 3/4, 3/8 norms eons before the day of time-pattern music.

The heavy spondee with its two long vowels is not a fluent poetic meter, except in connection with other rhythmical feet. A poem of spondees alone would be an epic indeed! It would be like a versification of monosyllables. And yet the spondee struts through whole measures and movements of music as though endowed with superlative fitness. Characteristically, today our measures of two time are neither trochaic nor iambic; they are definitely spondaic —therefore pompously inflated. The facile dactyl slipped out of the musical arena some decades ago, and its place has been taken over by a hybrid of three ponderously equal pulsations.

The restoration of metrical validity is a present duty to art incumbent upon all who occupy the preferred and responsible positions in the musical profession. Upon the faithful representation of their rhythmical particularities the three great genera of music rely for authenticity. The soul of the epoch in which each genus was born and reared sings through its rhythms; deprive it of these, and it cannot manifest itself. Gregorian melodies, chanted without the stress idiomatic to their syllabic or melismatic forms, are amorphous and misnamed. Polyphony, bereft of its ingratiating paradox of independent rhythmical dependence, is a sorry masquerade. Modern music, minus the oscillation of temporal accentuation, misrepresents its own rhythmical basis, i.e., the strict mensural regularities of the seventeenth century culminating in the code of Handel and Bach.

For rhythmical integrity, our music needs the easing-up of minor time beats.

This easing-up process will evolve only from an understanding of the need for *anacrusis* in every measure. The word anacrusis has heretofore been restrictively applied to the unaccented note or notes which precede the first downbeat of a movement. But the word is etymologically too instructive (*ana* = up + *krousis* = beat) and valuable to be wasted in so limited an application. Therefore anacrusis is hereafter considered as implying the philosophy of the upbeat and requiring the removal of weight (stress) wherever it would hamper mobility.

Here follows a survey of the metrical implications of the familiar rhythmical patterns:

Simple binary
Double binary
Simple ternary
Double ternary
Compound rhythm
Mixed and complex rhythm
Syncopation

Simple Binary Rhythm (2/2—2/4)

Simple binary rhythm requires anacrusis at the second count of each measure. It is the swaying of the arms to and fro while walking. An arm moves forward with a leg for the pressure of a step, and backwards when the weight is removed from a foot. The first beat is the forward exertion, the second is the moment of relaxation in which energy is being accumulated for a similar exertion in the ensuing measure. The fall of a foot means that it has been raised into position to fall.

The efficacy of a first-beat accent in simple binary forms depends upon its preparation at the second beat of the preceding measure.

In composition, anacrusis provides that the initial accent of a movement may be preceded by an unaccented preliminary beat or subbeat, the duration value of which is borrowed in advance from the final measure. It is curious, therefore, to find the implication of so commonplace a composer's propriety ignored in a conductor's general appraisal of rhythmical periodicity.

In Figs. 2-4, normal rhythmical procedure is grievously obstructed by the unpunctuated continuity of accents. It is unfortunate that

Fig. 2.

Fig. 3.

Fig. 4

these figures record a widespread indifference to or repudiation of anacrusis, for binary counts are quite generally made evenly *marcato*.

The rhythmical content in Fig. 5 cannot be altogether neutralized because of the structure of the measures, the time unit of the first

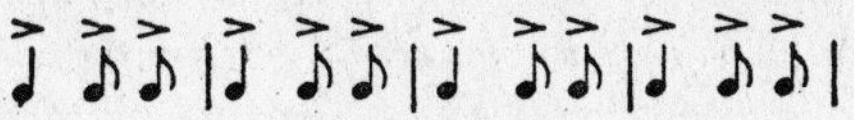

Fig. 5.

beat being followed by fractions in the second. Fig. 6, as far as

Fig. 6.

accentuation is involved in the average performance, might accurately be written in the ternary form shown in Fig. 7.

Fig. 7.

Without anacrusis, 2/2 and 2/4 time forfeit the to-and-fro symmetry that is the characteristic grace of binary movement. The fact that the "mystery of the upbeat" has eluded the consciousness of many conductors is attested by the rigidity of their baton technique, the lifting of the wand at the second beat being as energetic as the downstroke for the first.

The metrical undulations of 2/2 and 2/4 patterns are not mere oscillations of a pendulum or the tickings of a metronome; they are the alternation of bound and rebound, of pushing and coasting.

A young conductor is usually advised by veterans to develop an *authoritative downbeat*. This is good advice in the beginning; it serves his preliminary need of marking off the measures carefully and assuring the performers of his control. But, after a very short experience, he should learn that a downbeat will take care of itself, by the insistence of a sort of musical gravity. Having noted this fact, he should address himself to the much more difficult task of indicating the relative lightness of unaccented notes and especially of the upbeat.

I recently observed a truly great conductor at work. He was the guest conductor for a program by a well-known symphony orchestra. He immediately undertook, without much lecturing, to inculcate an appreciation of anacrusis, and presently the customary stilted pulsations of the unit were metamorphosed into real music. One of the numbers was written in 3/4 time. At first it sounded, accentually, as though it were in 1/4 pattern; but as the rehearsal developed, the weight on the second and third beats of the measures began to disappear, and in the performance the absence of unmodulated impacts created a poetic aura too seldom vouchsafed. Technically, he kept advising the players of the metrical form by moving his left elbow inward at second beats and raising his baton high with dangling looseness at the upbeats.

To revert to the accentuation of simple binary rhythm, it is obvious that the normal metrical pattern of two time is:

$$\overset{>}{\flat}\ \flat\ |\ \overset{>}{\flat}\ \flat\ |\ \overset{>}{\flat}\ \flat\ |\ \overset{>}{\flat}\ \flat\ |$$

Fig. 8.

The use of the stress signs over the notes in this figure must not be interpreted as signs denoting special stress; they are employed here merely to indicate the natural accent which marks the first count of a measure. Perhaps the portrayal in Fig. 9 is more serviceable since it invokes the procedure by which proper stressing is duly achieved.

Accentuation by diminuendo is the paradoxical formula for the procedure. It is not a question of what to do with accented beats; it is rather *what not to do with unaccented beats*. An unpardonable parody results from overstressing the accented counts.

Fig. 9.

Anacrusis implies only a very slight lessening of amplitude at the minor counts.

If the conductor and performers *think* the rhythmical sequence correctly, the thought will almost inevitably communicate itself to the actual sounds, and the less important beats will naturally assume their proper places in the metrical pattern. It is possible to *think through to reality* the contours of rhythmical movement even during the progress of a *crescendo* or a *diminuendo*.[3]

The physical technique for organizing any succession of stresses and slacks is (1) to avoid forceful impacts—as abhorrent as unnecessary—with first beats (see *subitos* and impacts, page 120) and (2) to supply no impetus to the minor beats.

The unaccented note in normal patterns should have the first consideration of the conductor.

If a composer has marked his music with signs calling for a temporary interruption of metrical conventions, the conductor must focus his attention on the special effects indicated, but the great volume of musical utterance is committed to the rule of accentual regularity.

Common Time. Double Binary Rhythm (4/2—4/4—4/8)

Common time, although described by some lexicographers as "having two beats or any multiple of two beats to a measure," is generally understood to designate the pattern of four counts to a measure. It is not written as the sequence of 2/4 proportions and therefore should not be so interpreted. The prevailing professional as well as popular use of the term, common time, however, is unwittingly more satirical than exact, for in practice it is perhaps the

[3] Cf. loop *crescendo*, in Finn, *The Art of the Choral Conductor* (Boston: Birchard, 1939), p. 213.

most uncommonly exemplified norm in the table of rhythmic group-ings.

The proper execution of 4/2, 4/4, 4/8 not only is rarely achieved, it is rarely undertaken. And yet a melodic sequence of alternately or equally stressed beats is certainly not identical with the same pro-gression of intervals accented in the rhythm of common time. A grouping of four counts in a measure is, theoretically, a combination of two simply binary sections, *the first conceived as stronger than the second*. Quite generally, both sections are accorded equal emphasis.

Leaving out of consideration the tendency of so many musicians to discount the worth of prosodic motion, we may conclude from the experience of listening that even the above-average conductor fails to differentiate between simple and double forms; one accentual plan suffices for both. Those who have been fortunate in sensing the rhythmical dependence of 2/4 time upon the unaccented second count should hasten to cultivate the further diagnostic perception of the reliance of 4/4 time on the lesser dynamic ratio of the second half of the measure. The reduction of 4/4 to 2/4 patterns by maestros whose insistence upon other criteria of musical excellence is highly applauded is an unaccountable whimsicality of current musicianship. There is a real difference between the dynamic intensities of simple and double groupings. The quick succession of equal accents characteristic of 2/4 time imparts a notched edge to metrical phrases. It tends to create monotony after the fashion of long phrases of *staccato* and *pizzicato*. Common time offers better opportunity for *metric-legato*. It provides in the second half of each measure an easy approach, a proceeding to an ensuing first half. Music seems to lose something of fluency when it trots long in 2/4 time.

Even in *alla breve* counting, an appreciable gain in elasticity is noted when the conductor so pairs the measures as to produce a serial of stronger and weaker bars, the accent of the latter being slightly less than that of the former.

The *running rhythm* of versification, i.e., the uninterrupted flow of alternate stresses and slacks, has been perhaps the most tepid and neutral prosody used by poets. *Sprung rhythm*, i.e., the diffusion of extra slack counts between the stresses and the varying of accentual sequences, is the richer scansion.[4]

Although the accentuations of poetry and music are necessarily

[4] Cf. Author's Preface, *Poems of Gerard Manley Hopkins,* edited by Robert Bridges (Oxford University Press, 1937).

proportioned to different designs, they are measured aurally and appraised psychologically by the same principles of equilibrium and canons of animation. Just as color and sound have a fundamental alliance, so poetry and music present phenomena which must be construed as parallel.

The psychic effect of running rhythm and of the simple binary or ternary measurings of music is equivalently the same. It is a leaping from crest to crest, the springing from one trochaic (2/4) or dactylic (3/4) stress to another. Sprung rhythm finds its musical counterpart in the assortment of stresses and slacks proffered by the double, compound, and mixed time forms.

Common time, being an improvement of 2/4, less monotonously *running*, demands alert and scrutinizing attention from conductors if, as true musicians, they would conserve to melody the true value of its resources.

The master composers' choice of simple binary rhythm for this episode and double for that cannot be explained by oblique hints at indifference or indetermination. Probably the time signatures with their definite metrical inferences influenced the growth of musical ideas in the minds of the craftsmen. The metrical appositions could hardly have been ignored and thought directed only to contrapuntal and harmonic structure. The great composers were meticulously careful in the construction of melodies, the rhythm of which is not an incidental detail but a prerequisite embryo. When Beethoven and Mozart wrote 2/4 time, they preconceived the alternation of down and up beats. When they composed in double binary time, they visualized a different sequence. If they had willed 4/4 to sound 2/4, they would have used the latter signature.

In the post-polyphonic epoch the symbols of both notation and time have had univocal meanings; it would be as likely for Mozart to be satisfied with E flat intoned in place of a written E natural as to approve of the substitution of one temporal form for another. There is no record of the polyphonic *musica ficta* essaying to extend its evasive elasticity to temporal forms during its sly sovereignty over semitones. A note might be raised or lowered from its notation pitch, but its prescribed duration value was unalterable. Accentuation was determined, in that era of charming intervallic disingenuousness, by textual indices, but any trifling with a rhythmical setup was gross disobedience to approved mandates. Such contumacy probably was penalized by exclusion from professional advantages. The naïve connivance of composers in the aberrations of singers from notation, on the one hand, and the prevalence of inexorable standards of rhy-mical relations, on the other, penned puzzling pages in the history of music.

The record of the factual phases of current music will furnish an equally enigmatic contradiction of precisions and easygoing for-bearances. Somewhere along the line (after Mozart, *please!*), exec-utant musicians began to develop a new *musica ficta*. This modern version is a reversal of the Renaissance whimseys, but it is not so *knowingly* inconsistent. Medieval and Renaissance maestros *knew* that they were strict and orthodox in rhythm but loose in intervallic conventions. The new *musica ficta* is unsuspected. It is not concerned with intervals; notes must be sounded in the printed series of large and small steps. In the historic *musica ficta*, time and accentuation were sacrosanct, only the interval being cunningly denied inalien-able rights. (The tritone was the one tonal leap rigorously and ubiquitously suppressed by the cinquecentist who feared Mephi-stopheles as much on the staff as in his other haunts.) But in the unacknowledged and unsuspected *musica ficta* of the current age, the interval finds inpregnable sanctuary (except from the uninten-tional assault of off-pitch intonation), and the estate of rhythm is left unconcernedly to the determination of rigid or flexible batons. Imperviousness to the truths of rhythm, or—this is worse—wanton disregard of them, is a result of the second *ficta*. Music is sacrificing immanent beauty to the license of thoughtless performers. Rhythm is a stream of sound, but it seems to matter little today whether it flows freely in ripples or is cradled into artificial watercourses, obstructed by dams, or otherwise impeded in its poetic purpose. Many musicians are interested in the exploitation of abnormal or cross rhythms but are singularly inattentive to normal forms.

If a rhythmical skeleton is sturdy enough to carry a tonnage of sharps and flats, it is serviceable and may be dismissed from con-sideration. If it is endowed with sufficient motive power to energize the tramping of a robot *da capo al fine*, why make much ado about it? If you are satisfied with the stiff inertia of the current character-istic musical performances, make no ado about it but smugly say with Pericles: "Come, gentlemen, we sit too long on trifles." But if you are dissatisfied, you must *habituate yourself to seeing, in every symbol of rhythmical measurement, a reminder of serial stresses.*

"Two quarter notes to the bar" is only a partial interpretation of the 2/4 signature. It is generally accepted as satisfactory, nevertheless, for its disregard of an important inclusion escapes notice. "Two quarter notes, or their equivalent, to the bar *with the stress normally on the first beat*" is the complete translation.

In order to speed the resuscitation of the erstwhile spirit of music and quickly to restore its essential grace, it is suggested here that inclusive but pithy formulae, interpreting all the time signatures, be made to supersede those current in the elementary schools, studios, and conservatories. Present translations suppress important information. They tell only of the number and kind of units to be found in ensuing measures. They should recall the place of accents; they should stress stress.

For instance, the present widespread understanding of common time is that it is a pattern of "four quarter notes to the bar." Its symbol, C or 4/4, does not carry an admonition to the average singer, player, or conductor. Therefore, if the duration values of notes are properly observed, although the fact that each measure includes two accents, the major on the first beat and the minor on the third, is ignored, the majority of performers enjoy a sense of righteousness attained.

The symmetry, fluency, and logical continuity which gracefully accrue to a piece of music well executed in common time are altogether inhibited by resolution into the two-four pattern. An example—a favorite of mine—of the smoothness lost by such conversion is the "Ave Verum" of Mozart. Although written with four counts to the bar, it is nonchalantly sung as though designed in simple binary rhythm.

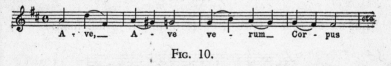
A - ve,— A - ve ve - rum— Cor - pus

Fig. 10.

With the lesser stress on the third beats, as prescribed in four-four time, the four measures in Fig. 10 glide along with unimpeded ease. There is no suggestion of restiveness in the phrase. On the contrary the tranquil peace of the Catholic contemplating the Eucharistic Mystery is clearly intimated, as the Catholic Mozart intended. But with the first and third beats sharing parity of accent, the melody loses its felicity; it no longer glides, it struts; the serene

exaltation and aesthetically spiritual communicability have vanished.
If written as sung, the popular misrepresentation would be:

A - ve,__   A - ve   ve - rum__   Cor - pus

FIG. 11.

I have gratuitously omitted placing stress marks on the upbeats of
these reconstructed measures, although fully aware that the average
conductor permits the singers this further disparaging indulgence.
Considering only the distortion effected by scalloping the generous
curvature of four-four with the little lobes of two-four, ignoring
the crass incomprehension displayed by sawing it into the jagged
notches of one-four, it is evident that the melody is forced out of
shape. Rhythm has greater influence than tonal succession upon
melodic personality, although neither can be altered without sacrifice of a characteristic trait.

Percy Scholes[5] gives such a convincing example of the transmuta-
tion of a melody by changing its rhythm that I submit it here: "So
important is it [rhythm], indeed, that recognition of a melody often
fails if its notes be reproduced in altered rhythm, whereas if the
bare rhythm be tapped it is often at once recognized.

"Many people would fail to recognize a certain well-known tune
played to them in the following form:

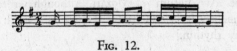

FIG. 12.

"But most would at once recognize it played in this form:

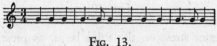

FIG. 13.

"The rhythmic organization of many fine melodies will be found,
on careful inspection, to be extraordinarily subtle."

Obviously, the rhythmical mutation caused by reincorporating

[5] Cf. *The Oxford Companion to Music* (London, New York, Toronto:
Oxford University Press, 1938), Melody: 4.

Mozart's notes in a two-four pattern is not so falsifying as the extravaganza on "God Save the King." This is an extreme example and is offered by Dr. Scholes as a striking and admirably rhetorical illustration of the import of rhythm to melodic conception. Dr. Scholes has altered both the duration of notes and their rhythmic plan. A new musical idea has resulted from the allocation of the same notes in a different sequence of spacing and meter.

Through rhythmical redesigning, the "Ave Verum" loses serenity. Probably the word *redesigning* is uncharitably chosen, for it implies a deliberate intention of alteration, and the majority of musicians do not deserve such imputation. Their offense is the offense of inadvertence. They knock things about and cause fine statuettes to crumble because they fail to look where they are going. But the results of their inattention are as destructive as if willed and prearranged. Somnambulant vandals!

Certainly, heedlessness or default never absolves from responsibility.

Disregard of the accentual organization of Mozart's measures not only encumbers the motion of the music, it suffers the syllabification of the poetic text to be distorted. Irreverence converts a trochaic tetrameter into spliced spondees. When both syllables of a duo-syllabic word are accorded equal emphasis, the strange effect of the second syllable seeming to carry a greater stress is created. This is due to the natural rhythmical sense of men which requires anacrusis, and in a series of spondees this is sure to be supplied instinctively. Therefore, equal accentuation of the first and third beats—an equivalent rewriting in 2/4 time—of the Mozart motet produces this textual disfigurement: *Avè verùm corpùs natùm.*

Furthermore, reduction of four-four to two-four doubles the number of bars to the verse, and, since true poetic motion frequently involves hemistich—caesural, halfway pause—the further ugliness of such phrasing as this results: *Avé, Avè‖verùm corpùs‖.* Not only is the verbal phonetic continuity of the verse unnecessarily interrupted, but the musical contiguity of cognate measures is summarily broken.

Here is a counsel that derives from the foregoing considerations: *Regard two- and four-count measures as different idiomatic forms of expression, in spite of the fact that they are, generically, aspects of one—the binary—principle.*

The unconsciously wayward interpretation of the Mozart number is sufficient witness to the prevailing proneness to ignore the psychological reaches of regular rhythmical routines. It is a sample of a general insensibility to the slacks of musical meter. Other examples are unnecessary. Nevertheless, students are recommended to investigate for themselves the *status quo* of rhythmical performance. They will doubtless be amazed by the widespread indifference which they will discover to be anesthetizing the consciousness of metric succession. They will observe that common time has been badly crippled by the jerkiness of the age. They will note that the wrong arithmetical process is unthinkingly applied, that quantity is *added to* instead of being *subtracted from* the minor beats. And unquestionably they will conclude that serious study of the correlation of rhythm and melody must be prescribed for musicians by and large, and especially for the fraternity of professional conductors.

Perhaps the surest and simplest method of developing what eventually will be a spontaneous sensing of rhythmical nuance is to read poetry aloud. Poetry and Latin hymnody are the richest sources of texts for musical settings. Latin hymns in excellent musical frames are available generally. In the process of reading the verses aloud and comparing the correspondence of the lines to the music, the psychic twinship of meters and measures becomes clear. The stresses and slacks of the poetry demand unisonance with major and minor musical accents. In the paralleling of the poetic and musical movements is the conductor's easy opportunity for increasing rhythmical sensitiveness. A professor of Latin has made this practical suggestion: "The ideal way to use these hymns is first to read them aloud sympathetically in the Latin, secondly to sing them to the ancient Gregorian melody, and thirdly to read the English metrical version with close comparison of the Latin."[6] To convey the metric feeling thus acquired to the more restricting and more difficult patterns of modern music, I recommend this modification of Professor Merrill's scheme:

> *Read aloud the Latin.*
> *Read aloud an English version in the same meter.*
> *Sing the Gregorian melody.*
> *Sing a modern setting.*

Careful fidelity to such a plan will be rewarded by an increase of perspicacity for metrical proportions, which in turn will promote response to all rhythmical intimations. It is unlikely that a conductor

[6] William A. Merrill, *Latin Hymns* (Boston: Sanborn, 1904), p. xii.

schooled by such an empirical course would allow the blind blunders
indicated to smudge the sheen of the Mozart number. Nor would he
be found insensible of the distortion which accompanies the transfer
of any double to a single form. The travesty of turning a 4/4 form
into ticking oscillations he would vehemently proscribe as *reductio
ad absurdum*.

Mozart and his contemporaries lived in an era which could not
have acknowledged squareness or angularity as properties of music.
There were still floating about too many gentle zephyrs of Renaissance rhythm stirred by the not far-off polyphonic currents to permit
the poetic sense to become arid. Lest the increasing constriction
of rhythm and its condensation in metronomic periods rob music
of resiliency, the eighteenth-century masters, perhaps unaware
of the real reason, developed the use of *fioriture*. The *fioriture* are
judged by many to have been music's frippery and tinsel in the days
of rococo courts and courtiers. It is true that many spangles were
stitched into the raiment of the art so that it might prettily sparkle
while satins swished, but the *fioriture* served the more substantial
purpose of preserving elasticity to music when the new forms
threatened rigidity.

Thus, to read Mozart's four-fours as two-fours is to misinterpret
his musical aesthetics altogether. The consequent manhandling of
associated texts is damaging enough. However, the poetry has more
than its metrical front to rely upon, since the essential impression
to be conveyed is the thought which persists independently of mere
syllabic rhythmicality. But with a wrong order of accents established in music, the sense of a composer's phrase is confused and
often totally lost. Poetry is a medium of expression with a vocabulary. Normally, vocabulary is direct and univocal; i.e., it conveys,
through the simple sensory experience of hearing, a definite concept
to the brain. Music has no vocabulary; it insinuates itself through
the imagination to the emotions not univocally but with allusive
meanings as diverse as the temperaments of those addressed. It is
stopped at the very entrance to the imagination if it is ungracefully
invested. The shibboleth required is its external attractiveness; it
may carry a message of import or it may be only a peddler of
divertissements, but it is denied audition if its contours are unin-
teresting. I do not mean to slander the art by dubbing it superficial
in the full meaning of this word. I mean only that its *strategy* for
winning attentive hearing is based upon a fortunate presentation of

surface qualities, traits that are immediately approved by the aesthetic feelings of average men. Its strategy is *melody*. Melody cannot function without rhythm. Rhythm is a mere Platonic abstraction, a diagram on paper as it were, unless its temporal, measurable qualities are immediately discernible and agreeable to the sense usually designated as aesthetic intuition.

"In music," writes D. W. Prall, "perfection of the sounding surface is the perfection of the music. In poetry, the sounding surface, important as it is, is only a comparatively slight, though essential, aspect of the beauty of even the verse as such."[7]

What a deprivation the delayed invention of the phonograph has been! Grateful as we are for its present benefactions, we cannot but regret that the music of the past, performed under the surveillance of its composers, has not been preserved in sound. In lieu of the physical verification which would authenticate principles of procedure, we must be satisfied with logical evidence from which to deduce canons of interpretation. There is plenty of such evidence in the parchments of the past. The stylus committing symbols to a score is not so peremptory an instrument as the needle on a gutta-percha disk, but the eye of a true student can discover from its notations at least an abstract of what the gramophone fills in for the ear. The student, having carefully conned the diagram, will, as a matter of course, also perceive the tactics required for translating its directions into acoustic reality.

A comprehensive examination of the readily available data concerning the probable criteria of rhythmical expression in various eras is beyond the purpose of this volume. The general history of the fine arts and the specific accounts of the development of poetry and drama as well as cyclopedias of musical information set forth the abundant evidence with which professional musicians should be familiar.

It is sufficient for the immediate purpose to insist that the arthritic stiffness which characterizes the present performance of double rhythmical patterns did not become epidemic until the chromaticism and the heavy-laden chordings of the later nineteenth century diverted attention from the metric melos of music. Mozart used 4/4 for the time symbol of his "Ave Verum." When he chose that symbol he assumed that it would be faithfully interpreted by his

[7] D. W. Prall, *Aesthetic Judgment* (New York: Crowell, 1929), pp. 202 *et seq.*

contemporaries. If he were composing now, seeking to assure the same melodic continuity, he would probably write the signature 2/2. César Franck, possibly fearing rhythmical distortion by singers, chose 2/2 for his celebrated three-part "Ave Maria." Perhaps many common-time pieces could profitably be reedited *alla breve*. The *alla breve* symbols 2/2 and ¢ are mnemonics about slack beats. They are like telegrams from composers urging conductors to respect the etiquette of precedence in the measures. The above-average conductor reacts to these symbols as the average man reacts to any telegraphed reminder—he becomes viligant, remembering. Such a conductor needs reminders to tone up his awareness, but the below-average conductor is too apathetic to react to anything but an anesthetic.

It has already been declared in these pages that the signs and symbols of musical notation are, on the whole, carelessly read. Accuracy in the execution of the directions supplied in scores is commonly transgressed. The new *musica ficta* safeguards the interval but extends the liberty of license to accentuation.

On the defensive, conductors may exclaim that broad spatial intimations of form are perfectly adequate for the purpose of rhythm in melody; that there are other signs of the temporal divisions of music besides the accent beat; that scrupulous punctiliousness in sculpturing the metrical minutiae of mere measures interferes with the circumferential sweep of an episode.

They would be justified, indeed, in expostulating, if it were true:

1. That broad spatial intimations constitute the totality of rhythmic value.

2. That the other indices of recurrence include the latent subtlety of stress and slack.

3. That the perfection of single measures can be accomplished only by straining their rectitude to an exaggerted self-sufficiency.

Rhythm is essentially a twofold intrinsic attribute. It is intrinsic to the succession of phrases, periods, movements as a whole, and it is intrinsic to the shorter but more insistent bar units which are *in se* metrical miniatures or directional indices of the complete succession. Rhythm requires not only a metrical arrangement of many time bars, establishing sense content with an over-all regularity; it demands, too, that each pair of measures qualify for the series by symmetrical balance. The over-all regularity can be intimated even when the measures differ in the modes of their division. Simple and double binaries, ternaries, and compound forms are frequently mixed by composers into a successful spatial design. The seven and five fours, if conceived as bases of a broad metrical sweep (cf. Tchaikovsky), eventuate as rhythmically acceptable. But the single measures must be prepared by individual treatment for the spatial design of which they are to be integrants. The passing moments must give a proper account of themselves as they pass. A quarter of an hour is pleasant because the constituent fifteen minutes of sixty seconds each have been singly pleasant. The same period would be judged unpleasant if something disagreeable had injected itself into a sufficient number of seconds to register its unpleasantness.

The subtlety—perhaps latency is the better word—of four-four time cannot be expressed in the phrasings of a movement, if an equal stressing of alternate beats marks the metrical pulse of single measures. It must *seep* through the interstices provided by anacrusis. There is gaiety in two-four time; gaiety is often satisfied with the surface of things. There are forthrightness and eagerness too in short rhythmical divisions, these qualities of utterance being prospered by the emphasis of *marcato* alternations. But the brightness of a gay two-four is too dazzling to tempt the *subsurface* content of serious music to come out into the open.

If there is any truly great emotional music in two-four notation, it is great in spite of its written form and because it is rendered with divided beats. The "feel" of subbeats actually converts a simple to a double pattern. *Alla breve—₵* in modern notation—is an *insistence* that there be less vigor in the second than in the first half of a 4/4 measure.

Other signs of metrical partitioning are not in themselves sufficient to convey the definite aesthetic impressions which accentuation and anacrusis guarantee. Rhythm provides not only perception of form but a response to it which is perception plus a felt experience. It is true that, with no accents whatever, successive patterns or

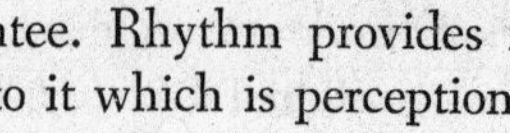

♪ ♪ ♪ ♪ ♩ ♩ |

FIG. 14.—Simple or Double Binary.

measures may be perceived to contain definite groupings of time beats. For instance, rhythm may be traced by regularly recurring higher or lower pitches, by regular changes in the direction, upward and downward, of a melody, or by regular repetitions of short and longer notes, the fractions identifying the integers as in Figs. 14 and 15. But such markings of the beginning and ending of groups are in reality only tracings, since no more than the general contours of each division are indicated. Silhouettes are inadequate portrayals

FIG. 15.—Simple or Double Ternary in Slow Tempo; Compound Rhythm in Fast Tempo.

of musical ideas, for they depict no moods whatsoever. From their shadowed outlines one cannot discover whether the thought is gay or heavyhearted, serene or agitated. A silhouette neither smiles nor frowns. The temper of the tune is unrevealed, and will thus remain until the proper sequence of accent and anacrusis makes it plain.

Sometimes one discovers a conductor hard at work on single measures; too hard, occasionally, for he seems to be straining to bring out the details in *physical* relief, and the net result of his effort is to defeat his own purpose. His "undercuts," in the parlance of sculptors, are deeper than necessary and his product is over-precise, leaving nothing to the imagination of an audience. But the portraying of the metrical qualities of the measure does not necessarily involve excessive undercuts or staid meticulousness. The deep-undercutting sculptor is apt to be more artisan than artist, his concern with the minutiae being more evident than his understanding of their relationship to a dominant idea. A *high relief* of rhythmical units is tediously a succession of prominent bosses and deep incisions. The shallow carving of *bas-relief* conveys the outlines of graceful motion.

I agree thoroughly with expostulators who decry rigid efforts as the basis for relaxation. Rhythm wants straight lines gently bent; they must be bent into a smooth curvature. If they are energetically bent they usually make angles. Angularity and rhythmicality are mutually exclusive ideas. The point of view sponsored here derives from the principle that spatial rhythm is musically convincing only when its constituent units are rhythmically established. The technique already suggested (cf. page 23) creates the well-balanced ratios demanded for rhythmic proportions. Accentuation is a delicate maneuvering of notes into metrical sequence, and the formula *accentuation by diminuendo* carries the probability that if the allocations are thought measurably, they will be sounded correctly.

The perfecting of single bars can readily be accomplished without affectations. The latter are a perilous hazard for any purpose to encounter. If the spatial sweep of music and its subsurface arcana are to be disclosed, the distance between each divisional marking must be traversed with poetic and symmetrical steps. The movement felt in the mind communicates itself to the feet. Ralph Waldo Emerson wrote: "The true poem is the poet's mind."

SIMPLE TERNARY RHYTHM (3/2-3/4-3/8)

The statements concerning simple and double binary time patterns are applicable substantially to the groupings of ternary and compound measures. In the ternary pattern an extra slack beat postpones the recurrence of stress. The period of coasting is thus lengthened, and so the movement of the ternary norm is felt to be smoother than that of the binary. Since the second and third beats of three-time are designed to follow in the wake of the accented beat, anacrusis has better opportunity to relax metrical effort. Poetic motion is impeded by stiffness but promoted by elasticity. Although an accented beat is not necessarily stiff in the strict, physical implication of the word, its authoritative position in the bar imparts a sense of firmness not duly expected from the unaccented units. Therefore, it may be insisted profitably, while poetic smoothness is not obstructed by recurrent accents, it is signally enhanced by as well as dependent upon anacrusis. The greater space between accents helps the very word *rhythm* to justify its etymology: from the Greek *rhythmos;* cf. *rheo*=flow. The tendency to shorten normally long vowels in Latin conversation and literature and prosody may be alleged as a proof of men's instinctive taste for anacrusis.[8]

Academically, the binary sequence seems to be the natural fundamental of rhythmical periodicity, the ternary being a ramification rather than a radix. I am aware that in the *free rhythm* of plain song the neumes of three notes may be said to impart a more mystic charm to its melismatic groupings. Nevertheless, the two-note neumes, not only in hymnal melodies but also in the settings

[8] Cf. W. M. Lindsay, *The Latin Language* (New York: Macmillan, 1900), "prosodical hiatus," pp. 132, 144 f., 209 f.; and *breves breviantes,* pp. 126, 129 f., 201 f., 210.

of the liturgical prose, greatly outnumber the three-note formations, and this notwithstanding the fact that there are four species of the former and seven of the latter.[9]

Similarly, although the ternary grouping was termed *perfectus* in the nomenclature[10] of late medieval rhythms—*mode, time, prolation*—the published works and extant manuscripts of the polyphonic masters show a notable choice of binary divisions. Three-dimensional divisibility was officially approved as the perfect medieval standard of rhythm. This approbation was almost necessary on account of the Schoolmen's axiom *omne trinum est perfectum* ("everything in three is perfect").

Binary rhythm is more direct and forthright. As the preponderance of usage indicates, it was more commonly employed than ternary. Chants and polyphony were intended to speak as directly as possible. When polyphony threatened to become excessively involved, the Church retaliated with the threat of interdict and embargo. The traditional rating of music as an accessory to the ritual was based upon its simple directness. With the later development of liturgical expression the field of musical intimation and allusion broadened, but rich opportunity for the dramatic properties of the art did not come until the revolution of Monteverdi was an acknowledged *fait accompli*. The ensuing vogue of time-pattern measures gave ternary time its good chance. The monotony of 2/2 and 4/4 was relieved more generally by the graceful fluency of 3/2 and 3/4.

The variation of measures of trochees or iambi by dactylic or anapestic groupings has found favor. Popular approbation of ternary time seems to have added something to music. Composers have flung themselves free of binary fetters and notation has become more hospitable to imagery and intimation. Perhaps an adumbration of liberty was sensed before the French Revolution in the freedom (very modernistic for those days) with which music glided in the easiness of the eighteenth-century waltz. Perhaps, too, the more generous anacrusis of ternary, compound, and mixed time opened the imaginations of composers to the aesthetic possibilities which were eventually realized in the romantic and impressionistic schools.

That the binary form of rhythm is more abrupt, more forcefully

[9] Cf. the *Liber Usualis* (with introduction and rubrics in English) New York: Fischer, 1938.

[10] Cf. Zoë Kendrick Pyne, *Palestrina* (New York: Dodd, Mead, 1922), pp. 222 *et seq.*

direct, and more in accord with natural processes generally is not debatable. But its very physical forthrightness makes it less persuasive of the more sensitive psychic reactions. The delayed recurrence of accents provided by the ternary pattern furnishes an *additional moment in each measure for music to bring something up from below the surface.*[11]

It follows from the foregoing that in three-time music the conductor must be actively sensible of the extra something, the hardly patent inkling and magic which lie in the second and third beats.

The student is referred again to the measures of "Flow Gently, Sweet Afton" (page 18) for experiment.

Double Ternary Rhythm (6/2-6/4)

The signatures 6/8 6/16 might be expected to be included in this classification, but they indicate usually a mixture of binary and ternary movement which is properly discussed in the next section on compound rhythm.

The 6/4 signature is more frequently encountered than 6/2, modern editors preferring the quarter- to the half-note symbol. If the tempo of a 6/4 is moderately fast, the composition is often nowadays re-edited as 6/8, for the metrical effect is that of compound rhythm. If the tempo is slow enough to require the counting-out of the six beats, or if the grouping is a sequence of three pairs to a measure, double ternary rhythm presents specific attributes and must be related to simple ternary as double is to simple binary.

The two forms of double ternary rhythm (*lento*) which must be examined for their metrical implications are shown in Figs. 16 and 17.

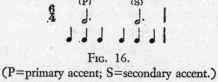

Fig. 16.
(P=primary accent; S=secondary accent.)

In the first figure a secondary accent is implied on the fourth beat. In the second there is normally no secondary accent.

[11] The *atempause* or slight delay on the third beat by Viennese conductors of the waltz is an interesting appreciation of this extra instant of anacrusis.

The division of the large notes into quarters finds the fourth note in different accentual positions in the two figures. It is placed for slight stress in the first, but for slack in the second. The anacrusis

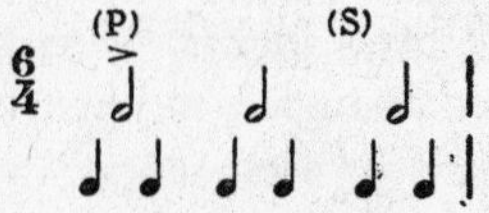

Fig. 17.

of five quarter notes imparts a long coasting range to the second grouping. The five notes must be sounded evenly (except for textual requirements).

The below-average conductor as a rule allows six equally accented pulsations in 6/4 patterns. His habit of ignoring metrical politesse leads him, as usual, by the nose. He should submit himself to control by his ears. The above-average conductor feels something of the suavity offered by the extended anacrusis, but he frequently concedes to the secondary accents the authority due only to the primary in Fig. 16; the couplet divisions of Fig. 17 readily deceive him. His readings therefore are sometimes equivalent to

Fig. 18.

Fig. 19.

Having fortunately reminded himself of the additional slacks implied in both patterns of 6/4 time, the alert conductor will devise a plan of baton technique which will suggest the necessity of protecting these to performers. Many directors indicate a 6/4 pattern with six equally vigorous gestures. This manner of conducting does not prosper anacrusis; it tends to endorse the indifference of singers and players. Professionals and amateurs alike, all participants in a concerted performance, need the mnemonic of prompting pantomime. The conductor himself is influenced subconsciously by his own gestures. If these are suggestive of metrical fluency, he reacts continually to the *idea* of rhythm, but if they are haphazard, without accentual hints, his consciousness of rhythmical grace becomes increasingly languid.

The surest means, in public performance, of inculcating the metrical relations of the beats in Fig. 16 is the sketching with the baton of two obtruncated triangles, the first larger than the second, as in Fig. 20.

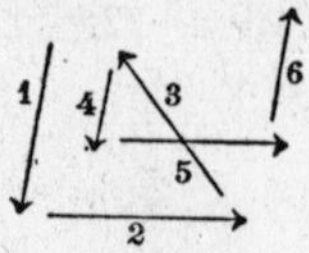

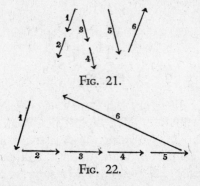

Fig. 20.

The line showing the primary accent is long and authoritative, the horizontal and ascending lines are signals for anacrusis on the second and third beats; in the second triangle, the fourth (secondary accent), fifth, and sixth beats are similarly indicated *in a smaller scale.* Thus performers are aided in envisioning the accentual ratios of the measure.

In Fig. 17 care must be exercised to avoid impressing upon the performers a sense of alternate accents and slacks. It is reasonable to suppose that composers in the time-pattern style would have supplied the stress marks if they intended the measure to proceed

Fig. 21.

Fig. 22.

in a series of three impacts. If a conductor uses the diagram shown in Fig. 21, he will probably fail to avert interpolated stresses. The six beats will phrase themselves, without undue accents, by reason of their intervallic or harmonic affinity, *if the conductor merely protects the anacrusis,* as in Fig. 22.

Habitual solicitude for the ease of unaccented beats in double ternary rhythm is usually repaid by a notable increase of sensitiveness to all metrical appositions.

Compound Rhythm (6/8-12/4-12/8) (9/4-9/8)

All symmetrical arrangements of time patterns are binary in their spatial effect, the total number of measures in any movement normally being a multiple of two. Duple and triple allocation of beats has each its characteristic traits which must be made discernible in the single bars of compound time. Although the circumferential survey shows binary divisions, the single segments reveal ternary structure.

It has already been noted that simple binary rhythm is so direct as to be often abrupt, that double binary is less terse, and that both forms are succinct rather than diffuse. Simple ternary norms are more lyric, except when the hard-hitting hammering of giddy-paced tempos builds each measure into a monostyle. Double ternary tends to insinuate composure of mind by the composure of its movement. But diffusion of momentum and ease in expressing are most palpable in the mixtures of *compound rhythm* where the alliance of twos and threes makes for over-all suavity. Diverse arithmetical elements are here combined in happy consonance. A contradiction of impulses is not even implied.

(Contradiction of rhythmical conventions is the basis of syncopation. When there is a multiplicity of contradictions or a great variety of metrical integers sounded simultaneously, one identifies the coalescence as the *counterpoint of rhythms*. This counterpoint is known to occidentals chiefly through the rhythmical independence of the Palestrinesque and later contrapuntal lines, but travelers to oriental lands have heard and been amazed by the intricate yet symmetrical pulses drummed out by tribesmen.)

Rhythmic counterpoint is complicated, but *compound rhythm* is only ingenuous ingenuity. It is frank and warrants no psychoanalysis, but the present neglect of its metrical needs has deprived it of grace.

In the first species of compound rhythm, the alternation of primary and secondary tends to fill the aesthetic sense with satisfaction, the division of the integers of a duple measure into ternary fractions giving melody a stout urbanity. It is the application to music of the old Latin counsel, *fortiter in re, suaviter in modo* (doing what is to be done with firmness but in the pleasantest manner possible). Theoreticians might debate the priority of effects in compound rhythm, whether the binary recurrence of stress or the ternary organization of the subbeats manifests itself more forcefully, but since such discussion is properly a topic for the seminar I shall not take time to weigh their arguments. Empirically—and this concerns the conductor—simple or double binary rhythm is heavier than ternary. In combination, the latter subtracts weight from the former. Since fluency is an essential quality of music, and in view of the fact that whenever weight is allowed to persist music loses fluency, *it must be logically concluded that the fractions in a compound measure have the greater responsibility*. In a binary pattern, the stress on an accented count lasts through the full time of the beat, whereas the subdividing of compound rhythm allows the accent to rest only on the first fraction of the beat, as shown in Fig. 23.

FIG. 23.

(The sign > is not to be understood here literally as a *diminuendo* but as indicating anacrusis.)

In the double form the additional number of slack moments provided by compound time is evident, as in Fig. 24.

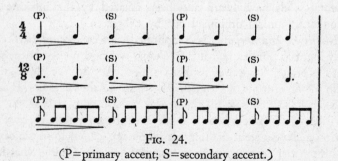

FIG. 24.

(P=primary accent; S=secondary accent.)

Since these time patterns—at brisk tempos—are respectively indicated with two or four gestures, the student is referred to relevant sections already presented.

Compound rhythm of the second species, 9/4-9/8, free of binary suggestion, imposes the obligation of avoiding all stress after the first fraction of the first beat. See Fig. 25.

FIG. 25.

The fact that there is notably so little of planned accentual weight in measures of compound rhythm recommends this form as specially worthy of study and profitable to practice. The triplet groupings which make up the temporal value of single beats offer students rich opportunity for becoming sensitive to the nuances of rhythm, to stress and slack, to anacrusis, and to the basic urge of metrical motion which is, of course, poetic undulation.

MIXED AND COMPLEX RHYTHM

Mixed and complex rhythm are not necessarily topsy-turvy or untidy derangements of metrical organization. Sometimes, it is true, they plague the aesthetic sense. Unskillful composers, or those who burn incense before the fetish of the unusual, succeed too well in making their irregular rhythms a test of tolerance. It is rather a bore to listen to music that suggests a restless gadding about or the pursuit of whimseys for their own sake. Skillful composers often make detours from regular routes with purposeful intent, their fancies not only bringing order out of disorder but gracefully expounding the more esoteric principles of rhythm.

Mixed rhythm is a conceded poetic license, an extension of the "measure's worth" (Scoles), latitude, to music.[12]

[12] The ear is pleased sometimes with the strange condiment of a regular series of metrical beats beginning in the middle or end rather than at the

Measures skillfully constructed of assorted sequences impart no impression of disarray or awkwardness, if the anacrusis is properly applied. *If, however, the anacrusis is ignored or misapplied, the resulting continuity will be necessarily stiff, disorderly, and offensive to the major canons of poetic motion.*

An artistic counterplay of well-ordered binaries and ternaries is most arresting. Mixed rhythm has, indeed, a piquant personality. It is par excellence individualistic, but its temperamentalness must be tamed. Otherwise it irks as the *enfant terrible* of music. If allowed to make mischief, it may grow into a fearsome rhythm-eating something, like the ogre who prowls in the fastnesses of neurotic modernistic scores, slaying helpless dactyls and trochees with trumpets, trombones, and timpani.

There are other causes, remote and proximate, which can reasonably be alleged to have contributed to the crumbling of sculptured rhythm, but I am convinced that the discard of anacrusis, at first unwitting, and the substitution of persistent accentuation for the undulation of stress and slack prepared the minds of composers and the disposition of conductors for the epidemic of violence now current in the practice of music.

Violence, although sometimes unavoidable, as in the cataclysms of nature, is always abhorrent to spiritually sensitive natures. Of course, men whose souls are laid away in layers of pachydermatous

---

start of a bar. Percy Scoles selects the gavotte and the *bourreé* to illustrate this point. I suggest the "Kyrie" double fugue in Mozart's "Requiem" as an enlightening example. The principal subject of the fugue begins on the first beat, but the answer enters at the third beat. Obviously, the metrical sequence set forth in the subject must be maintained throughout the exposition else the composition loses its mathematical contours. Therefore the answer, in the soprano and later in the tenor, must be read with the primary accent on the third and the secondary accent on the first beat. Why not consider the fugue as conceived in simple binary and thus avoid the mental adjustment required by the different written positions of subject and answer? Because it is clear that both the melody and the text require the anacrusis of 4/4 times as prescribed in the announcement of the theme by the bass line. If the subject were to be intoned in 2/4 time, the melody would chop itself into short *staccato* measures, and the fugue would sacrifice its *legato* consistency, sufficiently jeopardized by the short-note character of the second subject (*Christe*). The accentual syllabification would be unnecessarily impaired by the stress falling on unaccented final syllables, Kyrié eleisón. It is evident therefore that rhythmical serials cannot always be accurately indicated between bar lines, but they can always be accurately sounded if performers and conductors make note of the rearrangement of stress and slack beats involved.

cuticle do not suffer excessively from spiritual nerves, but the great majority of civilized peoples instinctively recoil from gratuitous furies and outbursts. Classes of people, however, can become gradually inured to violence and unfortunately, as in the case of ultra-modernistic musical composition and performance, grow to expect and accept it quite passively.

Nevertheless, continued or casual violence is antagonistic to the nature of music. A consistent ease of movement is essential to normal efficacy. Vehement, turbulent accentuation substitutes fitfulness for the regularities of music, disorder for its symmetries. Anacrusis preserves the proper disposition of its rhythmical properties.

Mixed rhythm strews its clusters along the horizontal lines of melody. Complex rhythm throws differently organized melodic rhythms into a vertical competition. Here one finds two or more rival patterns vying for pre-eminence. The contest can be either a *divertissement poétique* or a real conflict. For example, a cross-rhythm phrase of three bars of 4/4 in the treble against four bars of 3/4 in the bass, if not used persistently, may add a convincing savor to the harmonic relations and progression. The duration of the contraposed twelve units in 4/4 and 3/4 being temporally the same, the co-ordination of the measures into a satisfactory phrase is easily accomplished. Except in passages conceived to depict struggle or confused excitation, the conflicting measure norms must be set forth delicately, i.e., *with less than the normal stress on the first beats*. Rhythmical accommodation is further prospered by the *addition of an almost imperceptible stress to the third beats of the 3/4 bars*. Such a cross rhythm does not necessarily suggest a cross-purpose in the mind of the composer. It is frequently the clever exposition simultaneously of a musical idea from two points of approach. A simple example of the efficacy of the complex form is the popular "Angelus" of Sir Edward Elgar.

SYNCOPATION

Syncopation is a bold species of complex rhythm. It is a sort of metrical inversion. "Syncopation is that particular sort of crossing or conflict in rhythm that is produced by a shift of the accent to what was previously unaccented in the rhythmic pattern."[13] It calls

[13] Cf. D. W. Prall, *Aesthetic Judgment* (New York: Crowell, 1929), pp. 160 *et seq.*

attention to the single measures more emphatically than regular metrical organization. The sequence of standard recurrences of stress and slack establishes a subconscious throb which persists mechanically, soon ceasing to draw attention to itself. A sudden change in the unminded routine of the throb is certain to stimulate the reaction of surprise. Therefore, syncopation involves the unexpected and indicates the need of careful presentation.

Ragtime, the popular apotheosis of syncopation, is so regular a synthesis of metrical irregularities as to establish its own eccentric pulse which merely replaces the throb of normal patterns. Traditional recurrence of accents would be the surprise here. There is nothing unexpected, after it gets going, in the jazz type of syncopation. It is a sort of wild freedom from inhibitions. Its wildness is its asset. Therefore, the wilder the better! Students are referred to specialists for the tricks of managing its galvanic idiosyncrasies.

Another style of syncopation—the building of whole movements on *afterbeats,* as in Emmanuel Chabrier's *España*—is dismissed from consideration since it is relatively rare and frequently sounds, to those unfamiliar with the notation, like a normal if slightly fanciful procedure.

The syncopation in classical music can be gracefully executed with a simple technique by conductors well versed in the lore of the implications of rhythm. The procedure involves three steps which are written here as practical precepts.

1. (a) Maintain the throb of the regular pattern with special care in the measures immediately preceding and following the syncopated measure or measures. (b) If the syncopation is not assigned to all the choral lines, make the regular recurrences of stress *marcato* in the non-syncopated parts.

2. Study the syncopated measures for the *logical* places to apply anacrusis; no sequence, regular or irregular, is rhythmically right without anacrusis.

3. Don't overemphasize the intrusive cross accents; many conductors treat all alien stresses as *sforzandos;* an irregular accent needs no reinforcement to capture attention.

It is probably clear to the reader that I am disposed to safeguard all the principal processes of rhythmical conducting under the aegis of the slack beats. Admittedly, there is no single recipe which will assure the creating or re-creating of artistic entities, but the strategy and temper of a technique can be convincingly implied in a slogan. Just as *pianissimo* has been established as the slogan for effective chorus training, I propose anacrusis as the watchword for rhythmical rectitude.

In concluding this survey of time-pattern-rhythm, I am conscious that much is left unwritten. The scope of this book, however, has permitted only an abridged and suggestive discussion of salient material. Students are urged to undertake personal research in the field of psychology and poetry. When and in what degree to accent? The instinctive reactions of men to poetic motion in its diverse forms require study by musicians who would successfully answer this question. The correlation of mood and meter, of tune and time, of the sensory and supersensory is an insistent demand made by aesthetics upon every conductor.

Variations of rhythm, fast and slow tempos, graduation of dynamic intensities, and other subtleties that make up the mystic maze of music must be related to intuitions deep in the organism that is a man's mind.[14]

Otherwise there is no order in music. Where there is no order there is no science. Without science there can be no art, for art is the application of the inferences of science.

[14] D. E. Phillips, *An Elementary Psychology* (Boston: Ginn), pp. 105 *et seq.*

CHAPTER III

TEMPO

OBVIOUSLY, the delivery of a melody "with due care for its essential properties" requires that it be set forth at an appropriate pace. The influence of any musical sequence is necessarily affected by the degree of speed with which it is unfolded. The reactions to patterns *presto* and to the same patterns *adagio* are different. Aesthetic inherences can be so changed by incompatible tempos as to be altogether diverted from a composer's purpose. The telling effect of any metrical arrangement is dependent upon tempo. Although pace and rhythmical structure are linked in a cognate relationship, both having to do with recurrence, the rate of velocity of the recurrent patterns defines the trend of a movement even more clearly than the metrical arrangement. Quickness and slowness modify melody more substantially than consonance and dissonance, more conclusively than major and minor harmony. The prevailing tempo of a movement must be consistent with the character breathed into it by the composer. The conductor needs to recognize that character and to sense the degree of motion suitable, in given circumstances, for its exposition. Carelessness in the setting of a tempo is a major offense against musicianship. Furthermore, variations of a prevailing tempo by *rallentando, accelerando,* etc., must be applied according to criteria of psychology and artistry which commend themselves to discriminating judgment. Whimsicality in the choice of pace levels or in the application of tempo modifications imperils the form and substance while affronting the integrity of music. Tempo and dynamics—these are the sharp tools with which a conductor must work, and "there is no jesting with edge tools!"

It is, indeed, essential to true musicianship that conductors understand how to correlate tempo with the other phases of musical motion. One degree too slow? A glad melody swathes itself in cerements. One degree too fast? Solemn music derides its dignity. Sluggish sauntering or hectic hurrying can unfit a perfect sequence for any aesthetic design.

Richard Wagner is as querulous as forceful in referring to the importance of correct tempos.[1] In spite of chromatic satire and the failure to suggest criteria for a logical choice of tempos, his monograph is invaluable. He focuses the attention of conductors on points about which there is too little professional curiosity. Of course the master of music drama stretches platitudes across his pages. But one expects resonant enharmonics from Wagner, and with patience the student can modulate to tonic simplicities.

On page 19 he writes: "The right comprehension of the *melos* (melody in all its aspects) is the sole guide to the right tempo; the one implies and qualifies the other." And on page 20: "The whole duty of a conductor is comprised in his ability to indicate the right *tempo*. His choice of *tempi* will show whether he understands the piece or not."

These two statements are more rhetorical than accurate. Certainly the proper understanding of melody in all its aspects will dispose a conductor to choose the appropriate tempo, and probably, if he chooses the wrong tempo, it may be argued that he has not understood the composition. But Wagner does not list the aspects of melody covered by the word *melos*. It would be interesting to have learned his inclusions.[2]

Even though one must disagree with Wagner that the "comprehension of the melos is the sole guide to tempo" and that "the whole duty of a conductor is comprised in his ability to indicate the right tempo" (presumably after having located the melody in every bar), his words must be taken as an earnest admonition to conductors to set themselves right in the matter of tempo.

Precepts cannot reasonably be proposed nor formulae advanced to assure, under all circumstances, a felicitous choice of tempos, an artistic use of the major modifications *rallentando* and *accelerando*, or an effective application of the finer nuances of *rubato*. Too many

[1] Richard Wagner, *On Conducting,* translated from the German by Edward Dannreuther (2nd ed.; London: Reeves, 1897), pp. 19 *et seq*.

[2] I find *sixteen* aspects of melodic structure and relations involved in a comprehensive study of *melos* as it concerns the conductor. These aspects are the substratum of the present treatise: (1) Rhythm. (2) Melodic inherences and tempo. (3) Dependence on dynamics. (4) Curve line. (5) *Tessitura*. (6) Melody in homophony. (7) Tension and dissonance. (8) Melody in polyphony. (9) Melody in repetitions. (10) Modality. (11) Timbre. (12) Melody in choral and orchestral combinations. (13) Melody and tune. (14) The locale of melody in involved movements. (15) The modifying effect of accidentals. (16) Ornamentation. Cf. the index.

considerations of divers sorts are involved to warrant more than suggestive memoranda from which a student may work out a system for dealing with these items on a logical basis.

It seems convenient to arrange some pertinent notes as follows:

1. The inherences of the music itself.
2. The influence of various circumstances surrounding a performance.
3. The psychology involved in the modification of tempos.

The Inherences of the Music Itself

It is abundantly clear that the principal guide to the proper tempo is the intrinsicality of the score. The basic character of a composition cannot be revealed except through the notation. Many subleties— subsurface properties—may not be manifest on the staves because of the obvious limitations of notation symbols, but the melodic and harmonic implications are patent there. Only on the staves can the scholastic data which will attest the fitness of one or another tempo be discovered. Even traditional readings and the honored interpretations of master conductors should be subjected to critical and experimental analysis if they seem to be at variance with the score.

Although the written *melos* may neither academically nor expediently be established as "the sole guide to the right tempo," it is, indeed, the only key to the emotive concepts of a composer in *absolute* music, and an important corroborative indication in *program* and vocal music. It is reasonable to conclude that the organic implications of musical structure are intended to evoke definite moods. Separate movements of a composition may be designed to incite sundry sympathies serially. The temper of tunes, as revealed not only by innuendo in the sequence of intervals and rhythmical order, but manifestly in the modality of harmonic encompassment,[3] must be discriminatingly identified if the conductor means to disclose the aesthetic aims of the composer. The allusions woven into counterpoint need searching and sorting, lest the *truth* of the music lie latent and fainéant, wistfully peering through the lattice frames

[3] The three interpretative responsibilities of a conductor (cf. page 9) being closely conjoined, and melody being only one, although the primary element of music, it is advantageous casually to refer to integrants which are considered specifically in other pages.

of its notation staves, unrecognized by insouciant smatterers and
snubbed by strange spurious sounds.

Sometimes one is surprised by a lack of affinity between the
musical constitution and textual or titular connotation. Instances
of confused orientation, however, are rare in good music and, when
encountered, are best resolved in the direction of the topical inferences.

The genus and species to which a composition must be ascribed,
by its structure or title, are the primary and immediately discernible
guides to the approximate pace grades which are stylistically suitable.
A Gregorian prose chant approves the tempo of public declamation;
a Gregorian sequence or breviary hymn finds its metrical motion
prospered at a slightly quicker pace. Polyphony, syllabically, is
slower moving than most plain-song settings, since its textual utterance is delayed by ornate figuration (hockets) and notes exceeding
in temporal value the Gregorian *puncta*. Therefore the shorter
time units of polyphony should be sung faster than the *puncta*,
else the textual purpose of this honored style will be defeated.
Generically, all medieval and Renaissance polyphony presents
idiomatic characteristics; its movement, even in the *stile famigliare*,
is horizontal; its contrapuntal conformations, often complex, are
clearly coded. Therefore some conductors conclude that all *a cappella* polyphony of the era 1300-1650 should be paced at one *archaic*
(and therefore pedantically unmoving) tempo. Specifically, there
are two distinct classes of polyphonic music, the sacred and the
secular, the mass, motet and the madrigal schools. Structurally they
are identical. Psychologically, they are agencies to different ends.
Obviously the masses and motets should move at a slower pace than
the jesting sallies and satires which must merrily amuse Diana or the
donnas of Mantua. The *Madrigali spiritali* (e.g., "O Soave il Morir,"
Palestrina) are in effect motets with meditative but non-liturgical
texts. Exhuberant motets like Palestrina's and Sweelick's settings of
"Hodie Christus Natus Est, Nöe! Nöe!" are obviously so effervescently
rich with the thought of Christmas making the world all right that a
good brisk tempo is of the essence. Pavans, minuets, saltarellos,
waltzes, pageants, marches, funeral marches, etc., suggest by their
titles the tempos which they respectively require.

Form, binary or ternary, is not a valuable index of tempo; but the
category of a piece and the prevailing disposition of short notes seldom
fail to afford some clue to interpretative compatibilities. Thus a fugal

theme of quarter and eighth notes may reasonably be assumed, other things being equal, to intimate a faster pace than a canonical theme with similar temporal notation. A fugue literally connotes the idea of a *chase*, which of course implies dispatch if not always precipitate velocity, whereas a canon is probably prospered by a more sedate progress in keeping with its titular meaning: *formal imitation by standard or rule*. A fugue rides more ground than a canon; it deals with more factors; it seems keen to follow the hounds through the "cover" and whip on to get a good "brush" in the *stretto*. A canon is satisfied to stay indoors and expound truth with dignity. The light "rounds," diagrammed as canons, suggest pedantic professors on a picnic.

Short notes which are obviously *fioriture* designate a faster tempo than short notes singly pertinent to a melodic substance. Thus the sixteenth notes of the "Kyrie" ("Requiem") of Mozart imply more movement than the sixteenth notes of the "Benedictus" in the same Mass. The functional office assigned to short notes may readily indicate their importance, advising, if they are the rhythmical integers or are conspicuous in the temporal design, the speed at which the functional office will best be fulfilled. Thus, it seems to me, the triplet rosettes in the "Sanctus" (B minor Mass) of Bach imply a slow pace for eighth notes. The rosettes are entwined among binary units evidently with purposeful pains, to make up a striking bouquet of complex rhythm. The impressive octave steps of the vocal basses, emphasized by orchestral movement, set forth a deliberate double-binary *maestoso*. The pattern is evidently important to Bach, for the intervals are wide. Down an octave, a syncopated *tremolando* marking the descent, and up a bold major seventh! Obviously Bach has sought to create an unmistakably binary rhythmical effect. But he ties up contrapuntal eighth notes in threes from start to finish! Just as obviously, thus, he has provided a concurrent ternary atmosphere. The juxtaposition is therefore not to be understimated. The *Trisagion* is to resound before the Throne in a duality of rhythms. Therefore the eighth notes must have enough of eternal time to chant their apotheosis. The eighth notes in the "Hosanna in Excelsis" have no such exalted role nor so profound a responsibility. Here they are the little pivots around which sixteenth notes quiver to make prismatic caroling out of learned counterpoints. The Largo of the "Sanctus" and the Allegro of the "Hosanna" would be urged, it seems, by the eighth notes themselves, even if there were no text to confirm, and if the modern editor had neglected to supply a tempo recommendation.

Logical analysis of movements and measures will divulge the thoughts written into lines and spaces. The majority of composers have not thought with invisible ink. Nor are the contours of notation mere silhouettes of witless scribbling. *A sane idea is the substratum of each musical invention.* The conductor must seek to find and to recognize that idea. If the prompting thoughts of a composition are too obscure for certain identification, he must undertake to construe *some* likely notional or emotional purport. Otherwise, the tempos which he chooses, and the degrees and appositions of intensities will be necessarily adventitious and unconvincing.

Functional logic applied to musical structures often makes plain the salient features which suggest a definite tempo. With equal frequency, however, the more probing inquiry of experimental logic must be employed.

A surface examination sometimes provides sufficient clues to the proper pace. For instance: if long notes are the prevailing symbols in the melodic lines or arcs; if the style is heavily contrapuntal, sustained dissonances abounding; if the harmonic aura is mournfully minor; if the curve line (cf. following pages) of the principal themes intimates emotional stress, obviously, a gay tripping tempo is incongruous. Conversely, with equal clarity, a short-note design of homophonic fancy or in silken lace counterpoints, dissonances being only teasing passing notes, the harmony smelling of sunrise and the curve line swinging nimbly about without preoccupation, would be altogether frustrated in the somber pace of a lamentation. Logic need not always scratch beneath the surface for rational recommendations. If the music is fairly modern and bears a limitative tempo-indication (*Largo, Adagio, Allegro con fuoco, Presto*), the data offered by the notation are conclusively corroborated.

Experimental examination is necessary when the tempo proprieties are not patent; the composer's signs—*Moderato, Andante, Allegretto* —are dubiously enlightening. Probably any sequence of sixteen, thirty-two, or sixty-four bars of passably written non-idiomatic music will make some kind of grammatical sense at all except extreme tempos. Even the ubiquitous and unavoidable connoisseurs can be hoodwinked by syntax sense, if unfamiliar strains are parsed with a bit of exhibitionism by the conductor. But good conductors are not satisfied to be music-grammarians. They are artists, impelled by honest eagerness to discover and expound the real, intended, aesthetic import of every measure in the score.

The tepid, oft insipid, neutrality of much concerted music cannot be always charged against the readings of the gentlemen on the podium. There is little sap in some trees. One should not be judged a censorious iconoclast because he suggests that there is less vitality in much familiar music than a credulous society assumes. It is neither pertinent to the purpose of this volume nor profitable to sift the evidence prompting such a suggestion. Young conductors, if they have open minds, will learn to recognize a mere skeleton in many a program item, and perforce be content to keep the bones from too loosely rattling.

The art of interpretative conducting is too new to have accumulated an adequate bibliography. Nor has there been sufficient time for the development of a comprehensive pedagogy in the institutes of musical learning. The other major phases of musical exercise may be learned, at least in their basic outlines, at schools around the corner. The theory and practice of playing instruments, of singing songs, of composition, and of orchestration are taught in all the towns. But whither may an ambitious student direct his steps to find inclusive instruction in the plurality of topics which are gradually being seen as essential to authoritative conductorship? Professors are available everywhere to teach the *ways* of conducting. A tyro need not journey to metropolitan centers to learn pantomime; how to hold a wooden wand; how to cleave the air for twos and to swish it in triangles for threes; how to sense the sound of notation for transposing instruments; where to make cuts in this oratorio, that symphony, or any opera; where Maestro Gloriosissimo made a *grand succés* with *fermatas, accelerandos, grande pause; whens and wheres to do whats.* But like a nomad he must wander about from studio to studio seeking the *why* of each *what.* Monographs on conducting have addressed themselves chiefly to physical phases. The psychological and poetic *principia,* upon which aesthetic expression moves and upon which authentic interpretation correspondingly depends, are only beginning to be reassembled. No wonder, then, that an aspiring youth seeks in vain from practicing pedagogues a complete education in the arcana of the intimations of music.

The study of the *melos* as the guide to the proper tempo is inadequate and therefore futile if it fails to include an intelligent cognizance of the principia. This means, succinctly, that the mere shape of a melody, its lean or corpulent harmonization, and its modal fashion are often insufficient to furnish indisputable a priori grounds for selecting a particular pace.

With the current lack of codified and simplified formulae for the recognition of the subtle principia of music as a discouraging handicap, the young conductor must cultivate the custom of experimenting (more in private than in public) with puzzling scores. Not uncommonly, perseverance is rewarded by an inkling of what was probably uppermost in a composer's subconsciousness. Like so many of my colleagues, I have pored over pages and played pages persistently on the piano at various paces, analyzing, synthesizing, relating, correlating. This bulky fugue, that enigmatic canon, these polyphonic labyrinths, those esoteric dissonances! At what tempo and in which dynamic panel as a prevailing background[4] will they be artistically communicative? At $\downarrow$ = 70 in panel No. 3? No, there they seem inexplicably awkward. In No. 2 at the same pace? Better, but unconvincing. At 75 and 2? Yes! Why? Because, thus, they say something definite to my aesthetic sensitiveness naturally and with ease. I have examined the meaning of the musical sentences empirically and patiently; have I caught their gist? Inflections alter the significance of speech; have I finally heard the right inflections? At last I think I understand, and, if I make the adjustments indicated by the extrinsic criteria of tempo (cf. page 60 *et seq.*), *salvis salvandis* my rendering will probably convey the notional and emotional ideas of the composer. But I must persevere in my experimenting until the fugue has lost excessive bulk, until the canon has emerged from concealment, and until the polyphonies and dissonances have shown a felicitous and purposeful concordance.

Gradually a young conductor may hope to acquire, by the habit of experimenting with tempos, a reassuring facility in sensing subsurface elements. Until a great library of books has been written on the art of the conductor, each aspirant to the office of *maestro di cappella* or *chef d'orchestre* must seek mastery chiefly in his personal application of the simple processes of experimental logic.

The expedient of playing a complete melody by itself sometimes discloses a musico-psychological idea which accompanying chords may tend to obscure. One is easily distracted from the candor of simple melody by a Lorelei luring with confusing harmony. A

[4] See Diagram of dynamics in the index.

straightforward unison will often reveal the drift of a piece. On the other hand, sometimes concentration on the chordal progressions is more profitable, especially when complete melodies or their component arcs are trite or tepid. An inconsiderable theme may serve as an easel for a significant harmonic picture. Sometimes the enlivening, sometimes the sombre, approach of one triad to another will provide a hint of mood. The restlessness or tranquillity of interior parts; modulations by textbook clichés to nearby environments or non-textbook jerky jumps to alien tonalities; conjunct or disjunct, contrary or parallel motion; sly dissonances impinging wantonly on consonances, or passing notes traversing them uneventfully; stable temper or fitfulness—these are some of the vanes of harmony which show the trend of a piece and thus furnish clues to the appropriate tempo.

Excessively chromatic and modernistic harmonies should be unfolded more slowly, as a rule, than the simplicities of diatonic and near-diatonic progressions. At least, this is my personal conjecture. The ear has not yet become facile in translating polychrome and untunable sequences. If a modernistic number seems to depend for cataclysmic effects upon the overthrow of traditional harmonies, like Stravinsky's "The Rite of Spring," conservative and considerate tempos and intensities would be unfairly inhibitive. Similarly the stirring intensities of a Gershwin *Porgy and Bess* frequently demand speedy explosive utterance. But there is much in the fast-growing modernistic repertoire which is not concerned with startling revelations; this, for me, is prospered by slower rather than by faster presentation. Superposed consecutive fourths—a strange reappearance of medieval crudities—are sufficiently mysterious to be treated warily as new fads. Most listeners can take in, at a fairly speedy trot, the progressions that give some hint of some relationship to some tonic, but we slow down perceptibly when C F sharp B flat, E A D and other equally esoteric formulae establish the tonality.

E contra: the current diversion of skiing over corduroy lyrics on parallel tritones (or whatever augumented or diminished intervals the new music-skis are made of) is so giddy a downhill sport that great velocity is desirable. The quicker the skiers arrive at the bottom the sooner the dread is dispelled—temporarily—that the art of music is sliding ingloriously to a fatal turn.

It is opportune here to note the almost universal proneness to adopt a slow, solemnly awesome tempo for ritualistic music. The tendency seems to extend, perhaps less generally, to all sacred music. *Natural* tempos are intuitively judged unsuitable when discoursing of the *supernatural*. Thus the art of music undertakes to pay homage to religion with the dignified, respectful propriety of stately motion. Basically, such reverence must be acclaimed as the tribute of aesthetics to the spiritual. But tempo often pays its homage too ponderously with unwitting affectation. In the effort to exercise its liturgical privilege with decorum, music sometimes inhibits its own freedom to serve. An extravagantly exaggerated *adagio* may be a pious caricature of religious obeisance. Emphasized slowness suggests a sanctimonious manner; it is often platitudinous and pompous; it always defeats the Church's purpose for inducting music into the Sanctuary. This primary purpose is, obviously, to enliven the religious percipiency and the otherworldly emotions of the people. Animation and ardor are the qualities most instrumental in keeping the spiritual senses keen. Stodgy plodding slowness is only a degree removed from inertia, which is of course antipathetic to both religion and music. The penumbra of sepulchral gloom seems to hover over chancel stalls, waiting to embrace in its shadowy reach naves, triforiums, and transepts. Sacrifice of vitality and vigor to mistaken estimates of reverence is sheer waste. Music must be performed with becoming dignity in the House of God, but dignity does not hide in the heaviness of *Adagio pesante*. Why sing motets, inspired to praise God, as doleful threnodies? Why revere the eager spiritual aspirations of men in measures heavy-laden with fear or disappointment? Are alleluias tears shed by angels for the utter futility of human endeavor?

Early in my formative days I heard two heroic chanters, stiffly starched in pleated cottas, sobbing the versicle of an Introit: *Laetatus sum in his quae dicta sunt mihi* ("I rejoiced at the things that were said to me"). It was *Laetare Sunday* and the Church was urging men to find happiness in religion. The chant was in the cheerful fifth (Lydian) mode, but each Gregorian *punctum* was projected plaintively; it marched slowly, alone, and *marcato* through the basilica, unsuspectingly robbing the versicle of the joy proclaimed by the Psalmist. Music with grandiose satire frustrating spiritual appeal, and dignity gone obese! When the choir responded, it was unreasonable to think about the text for it might more properly have been one of the Good Friday *Reproaches*. The tempo had frowned the lightsomeness even out of the gay Rose Window.

After many years' opportunities to observe the strange processes of men's minds, I find the indeliberate travesty of groaning the praises and promises of Jehovah an inexplicable phenomenon, a species of spiritual hypochondria seeking alleviation in the hemp leaves of pious torpor.

There is a note of dread reluctance in creeping chants which is almost as ruinous to religious rites as the extravagantly agitated *prestos* with which occasional triflers and neurotics affront the ceremonial music. One extreme is as bad as the other, although many might suffer the sluggishness who could not tolerate the scampering. I have been unable to discover any valid reason for abandoning natural modes of expression when addressing religious subject matter. *Coeli enarrant gloriam Dei* ("The heavens show forth the glory of God") by following defined orbits. Sunrise and sunset are the same on weekdays as on Sundays. Christmas is Christmas in the snow or in the tropics. Architects, sculptors, painters, and poets have successfully portrayed sacred and secular themes with one technique. The concepts depicted are of different orders, entailing corresponding modifications in execution, but they reach the comprehension of the people through the same physio-psychological media. If perspective is badly drafted, the out-of-focus is inartistic, it matters little whether saints or sinners are distorted. Gaudy daubs of vermilion violence against yellow-ocher supineness make icons and idols equally grotesque. Ashen gray deletes the bloom from any picture, pious or pagan. Neither eternal nor temporal impressions can be effectively conveyed by any art if any externals of the treatment are offensive to aesthetic instincts. Tempo must be as naturally chosen for sacred motets as for Tudor madrigals. It is not musically fitting or psychologically expedient always to slow down Maëlzel for the former or to goad him for the latter.

The efficacy of music as an accessory of public worship does not depend only on the fitness of a particular form of composition or the historical associations of a particular style. Official approbation of certain types by critical censors does not guarantee more than a potential value. Actually, the efficacy of all music, sacred and secular alike, depends upon the manner in which appropriately written numbers are rendered. If the canons of aesthetics must be followed in the performance of profane music, a fortiori they should be exemplified in church music.

There is genuine drama in the Liturgy. There is movement to great histrionic climaxes in oratorio. Otherwise the Liturgy and the *Laudi Spiritali* would be ineffective. The most solemn mysteries of Christian devotion are enacted in the sanctuary with a correlation of dramatic rites which, in their purely dramatic aspects, parallel the technical procedure of the great theatrical dramaturgists. Music is endowed with properties which can most effectively enhance the power of pageantry and the richness of ritual.

Gregorian chant and polyphony are accommodated most admirably to ecclesiastical ends by the textual character of their rhythmical movement and (presumably) by the absence of chromaticism. Each in its own era of dominance was less exclusively spiritual in its intimations than we, who have become inured to vertical effects, time-pattern-rhythms, and pungent accidentalism, are wont to idealize. The chants were compounded by monks and Levites, it is true, but contemporary minstrels used the same modes and melodic patterns. The masters of polyphony designed their music chiefly for spiritual purposes, but "Diana," "Matona Lovely Maiden," and many another comely demoiselle were extolled and serenaded from Naples to Northumberland by Latins and Nordics with the same counterpoints, canons, and consonances.

Noting the excessive influence of romanticism on current repertoires of church music, we are probably well advised in judging the diatonic chant and horizontal polyphony to be more in accord with religious detachment. But one should not make the mistake of fancying that plain song and polyphony are essentially and necessarily *in se* uplifting.

A discussion of all the criteria by which to judge of the suitability of music to accompany Divine Services is irrelevant here. These criteria would, as usual, stimulate furious debate, and, also as usual, the "liberal" debater would come out second best. My aim in casting a passing glance at the harassed subject was not to vex it more, but to make this practical conclusion: *If the natural requirements of aesthetic expression are ignored or misunderstood, no art can serve a spiritual purpose with the full complement of its resources.*

Thus, in choosing tempos for Masses, motets, hymns, and anthems, conductors are warned not to fall into the pietistic error of slowing up their heartbeats "for the glory of God."

The Influence of Various Circumstances Surrounding a Performance

A synthesis of the data offered by notation would provide the apodictic criterion for selecting tempos, *if only purely musical factors were involved*. But suggestions from (1) psychology, (2) phyletics, (3) physiology, and (4) physics must be considered as well. The "circumstances" referred to here are the *variables* springing from these four sources which I designate hereafter *the serial of the four P's*.

Psychology must be minded because the psychic penchants of composers, conductors, and listeners are stimulated and manifested at strikingly different rates of speed. *Festina lente* ("Make haste slowly") or *Chi va presto va sano* ("Who goes quickly goes sanely"). Temperaments have long "agreed to differ." To slow-lighting imaginations quickness is hurry and unseemly agitation; to ardent eagerness slowness is inactivity and languor. *Sostenuto* demands delaying to some conductors. They therefore, to be at ease, should select a slightly more lingering pace than their colleagues who do not sense this insistence. On the other hand, *allegro* connotes *vivace* to many and without an extra degree of briskness these feel the tempo to be lacking in verve. It is usually a question of only a degree or two faster or slower, and, within this conservative compass, it is good sense for conductors to favor their personal susceptibilities. It is good psychology to avoid as far as feasible whatever tends to promote self-consciousness. The effort to adjust oneself to a pace uncongenial to one's predispositions induces stiffness which in turn prevents aesthetic freedom. The right tempo for one conductor may be unsuitable for another. Certainly the latitude within which it is advantageous to apply this consideration is limited. If a conductor cannot freely accustom himself to the tempo indicated by the inherences and important facts of acoustics, he should eliminate the composition from his repertoire. Else how can he be artistically honest? But, restrained by reverence for all the criteria involved in the selection of a tempo, a conductor will prosper a performance by temperately indulging his own predilections.

Furthermore, if a conductor is fond of clarity of detail, he will probably favor a slower tempo than a colleague who is attracted by the broader style with its modicum of delineation.[5] It is so easy, how-

[5] *The Oxford Companion to Music* (London, New York, Toronto: Oxford University Press, 1938), p. 928.

ever, to be influenced by unstudied preferences in this matter that a bona fide artist will first assure himself that the structural properties of a composition permit a choice between greater or less clarity in expounding the minutiae. Certain types of composition depend for efficacy, primarily, upon the dynamic and metrical appositions of single notes (cf. rhythm, tension, ornamentation, fugue; see index), whereas others (e.g., short dramatic episodes, marches on the double, and walking dances) may be well interpreted on the basis of the "measure's worth."[6]

It is interesting to note, in passing, the preoccupation of some conductors with very fast and very slow paces who show naïve unconcern for the precise degrees of speed appropriate to medium tempos. Not infrequently a maestro is observed in a dither about his *allegros* and *adagios* but complacently ignoring the *super* and *sub* ticks of the metronome which may turn *moderato* into tantamount immoderation. One needs to be steady in his understanding of the middle paces before concentrating upon extreme rates of movement. It is incumbent upon musicians to develop a sense of responsibility for *moderato* and *andante*. These are the designations for the majority of compositions. At what speed will the quiddity of a *moderato* piece be best manifested? At Maëlzel 110, 120, 130, 140, or 150? There is a range of at least forty degrees of velocity in which to set a so-called medium tempo. Under varying conditions what adjustments should be made lest temperate music lose its character? A conductor will find the right answer only after personal study of all the factors involved.

Long observation of the perplexing approaches of many conductors to this matter of tempo elicits the following recommendation: if you would cultivate control of well-balanced *allegros* and *adagios*, first become master of the implications of *moderato*. This recommendation[7] takes a logical place in the series of simplicities which my experience has shown to be the basis of an effective schema for successful conducting.

Conductors who are ruled by their idiosyncrasies to the extent of ignoring the susceptibilities of an audience are poor psychologists. Publicly to superimpose a personal bias against the sympathy of listeners is sententious folly. A tempo signally out of step with their

[6] *Ibid.*, p. 798, § 9.
[7] It shares importance with such recommendations as: *study piano for a good forte, staccato for legato, diminuendo for crescendo, anacrusis for accentuation, indirect attack for sforzando*, etc.

expectancy impedes *for them* the aesthetic communicability of a piece of music. Obviously, the effect of tempo is ultimately upon the audience and the influences by which the major part of this is likely to be moved must be duly pondered.

Furthermore, the circumstances in which compositions are rendered may engender different reactions in performers and listeners alike. A single predetermined tempo may therefore be unsuited for all occasions. A funeral march accompanying a cortege to the cemetery is probably effective at a slightly faster tempo than when given as a concert piece. In the first case the march should be at the pace of mourners actually walking along; there is, of course, no need for the music to create a mood. In the second case the slower pace helps to conjure up thoughts about the solemnity of death. A military march is more appropriate at lively speed in a bandstand than on a parade ground when weary platoons are trying to step rhythmically in neat columns. A waltz for dancers is more correct at a slower and stricter tempo than a purely musical waltz which is lightened by velocity and heightened by *rubato*. The "Miserere" of Allegri with its celebrated *abbellimenti* needs less *rallentando* and *accelerando* as a psalm at *Tenebrae* in church where the drama is supplied by the Liturgy, than as a straightforward musical item on an *a cappella* program.

Surroundings often create moods unexpectedly. I remember a striking instance of this fact when I was impelled subconsciously to allow the tempos of a whole program to readjust themselves. I was conducting on a high mountain under a five-thousand-year-old sequoia tree. The giant had looked out over the ravines below for three thousand years before the coming of Christ and had listened to the mighty intonations of storms and the ballads of zephyrs long before modality, meters, or measures began to manage music. The waves of the distant Pacific had, eons ago, left paleolithic secrets on the mesa where chorus and orchestra were symphonizing. I had planned, naturally, to set the approximate tempos of the indoors rehearsal. But I discovered quickly that any strictly metronomic tempo would be an irreverence amid such phenomena, "The eternal landscape of the past" would suggest the movement. Academic standards were less valuable than a dragoman to a Persian seer. And so I tossed my baton to the sequoia tree.

Phyletics (traditions may be included here) are often a guide in determining suitable speed. Racial characteristics are expressions of the temperament of a people. Broadly, these may be listed among the psychological factors to be noted before deciding upon the propriety of a tempo. It seems profitable to isolate them, however, and consider them as special influences. Racial predispositions function uniformly and may be relied upon to provide dependable clues. For races—genealogical stocks—are differentiated from one another by recognized temperamental traits. The traits are disclosed in characteristic modes of thinking and living and in corresponding manners of expression.

Without making an unnecessary digression into the field of ethnology, attention may safely be called to this salient fact: as a rule the tempo of Nordic enterprise is less spirited than that of the Latins. I do not imply, on the one hand, that Scandinavians, Finns, Teutons, British, etc., are duller or nervously less sensitive to all stimuli than Italians, French, Spanish, or Portuguese, or, on the other, that the latter group lacks the intellectual or emotional depth of the former. I mean simply that Latins are generally supposed to encounter, to experience, and to express impressions and sensations more on the instant than those others whose fancies are fanned by northern breezes. Quite unconsciously French, Spanish, and Italian conductors are urged by faster tempos than their German colleagues. Perhaps long residence, during student days, at Vienna, Berlin, Leipzig, Copenhagen, etc., brakes the speed of Latin impetuosity, and perhaps one may find a transplanted Parisian or Milanese actually delaying the progress of a Teutonic *largo*. Conversely, too, a Saxon, having shed his severity near the Étoile or south of the Pyrenees or Como may sometimes be observed outstripping the pace of tripping cisalpine tempos. Probably many a Dutch youth returned from Castile with a love for the swiftness of clicking Iberian castanets. It is true that cosmopolitan influences may reorientate journeymen tyros. These may acquire a foreign accent, but representative composers, conductors, and the people never lose their cradle lisps.

Nordic music usually suggests slower tempos than Latin music. A Frenchman conducting *Tannhäuser* at Dresden must have a care lest his Gallican urgency rob Wagner of sedateness and the people of the leisure (Cicero's *otium cum dignitate*) with which they want to listen. The astute conductor tries to correlate the racial temperaments of the composer, the listeners, and himself. Perhaps these are all at variance. A Latin conducting Latin music for Latins has no racial considerations to ponder before embarking upon a tempo. Nor has a German offering German music to Germans. But a Latin, undertaking to interpret German music for Germans or German music for Latins must weigh carefully the temperamental background of the score, the predispositions of the auditors toward velocity of utterance, and his own racial urge. A German in parallel circumstances should make a similar survey. The Bizet "Habañera" is seductive at different tempos at Biarritz and Bonn. Appropriate paces for music purporting to characterize Slavonic, other central European, and Balkan races can be determined only by study of their several distinctive traits. I can insist on the value of this counsel by the authority of humiliating experience, having once been rebuked, backstage, by a celebrated Russian composer who with French finesse thanked me for performing his favorite composition, "even though its sense was clouded by the wrong tempo." I learned on that occasion that there is more to this matter of setting a pace than meets the eye in the pages of a score.

Customary tempos and traditional interpretations generally are regarded as sacrosanct by the delightful dilettanti. The origin of the traditions or the authenticity which the holy term implies are rarely questioned. Usually an untraditional conductor is judged to be a trifler and condemned as an iconoclast, unless he is highly publicized or an expensive insurgent. The safe uneventful plan is to move along in the rut without curiosity as to when or by whom it was furrowed. Frequently, traditional readings leave much to be desired. Sometimes a musicologist is tempted to wonder if perchance an early bellwether led the sheep astray. Traditions, however, are important guides, if not always to the best reading of a musical piece, at least to the manner of performance which attained respectable acceptability. Traditions, like all conventions, enjoy the dignity and authority of usage. Contravention of them without irrefutable proof of their unfitness or inadequacy is rightly dubbed eccentricity. Effective exercise of the fine arts is reasonably presumed to depend upon certain regularities which custom has approved. But, obviously, excessive conservatism is never good or reasonable. In the matter of traditional interpretations, especially in the details of tempo and *rubato*, the tyrants of the concert hall (and those who lurk in sacristies!) have decreed such inflexible standards that an unendorsed *accelerando*, a furtive *fermata*, or an inconsequential resetting of the metronome is seized upon immediately as a sly and insidious attack on orthodoxy. Many conductors, frankly fearing for fees, adjust themselves supinely to the toryism of dictated conducting.

There is no doubt about the value of following established traditions if they are found to reflect the spontaneous creative intentions of composers. Conductors are urged, however, to refuse to be shackled by traditions if these are in conflict with what diligent unbiased analysis of scores discloses to intelligent study. One should not be afraid to investigate the history of a tradition. Such procedure is neither disrespectful to sires nor cavalier to colleagues. An accepted mode of presentation may be well founded in the intrinsic properties of a composition, or it may be only a *laissez-faire* continuation of an interpretation which originated in the exigencies of early performances or developed from the whims of signally individualistic conductors. Perhaps Beethoven, Handel, Haydn, etc., have not yet been freed from all the fetters forged in early smithies.

I was trained to interpret Gregorian notation first according to Parisian traditions which were alleged to be teeming with authenticity. Presently I was weaned from these by the more scholarly representations and claims of the Ratisbon school, only to recognize fatigue and futility when the Solesmes investigators published the pandect, now officially recognized, which, challenging the accuracy, set at naught many findings of France, Bavaria, Mechlin, and Montreal. Traditions profit by examination. Many illusions about the correct interpretation of *a cappella* polyphonic music have come down the generations, successfully concealing the aesthetic spirituality of Palestrina, Vittoria, *et al.*; but these subversive traditions, having been thinned out, are gradually losing prestige, and presently they will expire in belated desuetude.

Phyletics and traditions unquestionably merit consideration in the important matter of choosing tempos. The precise extent to which these factors should be permitted to influence the pace is not easily defined. Nevertheless, scholarly musicians take adequate cognizance of them and weigh them in the balance with other extrinsic factors as well as with the intrinsic elements of each musical structure.

Physiology—the physical *status quo* of singers and players—is not disregarded by astute conductors in setting a tempo. An admirably effective pace in some circumstances can be distressingly unsatisfactory in others.

If singers are fatigued, customary tempos for slow *sostenuto* movements need acceleration and *allegros* need slackening. Weariness prejudices the physical ease with which the vocal apparatus should respond to mental control. An overworked chorus, in spite of willingness and normal ability to vocalize freely, is grievously inhibited by tired minds and muscles. Somnolent singers inevitably try to force their intonations until they lose awareness altogether of quality and pitch. Tenseness develops in the delicate mechanism of the larynx and lessens the vitality of tone colors and imperils accuracy of intonation. Reliable choral technique is contingent upon the unencumbered reflex action of the vocal organs. The fatigue consequent to much unwise rehearsing, to many consecutive performances, to long dallying with dangerous dynamics, or to tiring touring "on the road" is sure to manifest itself in vocal languor. By the same token, all singers recognize the folly of eating heartily before a performance. Drowsiness impedes alacrity.

Ponderous tempos tend to promote dawdling and delaying. Therefore, a conductor is well advised to consider physiological symptoms. If the signs indicate lassitude in the chorus, he must undertake to stimulate the flagging powers. Perhaps he will decide to alter some details of his usual interpretations. A compromise may be required between the theoretical rights of a score and the propriety of always respecting them. Occasional adjustment of academic procedure to here-and-now exigencies is not necessarily a compromise between principle and expediency. It may be only a prudent effort to make the best of a situation. *The true musician always reveres the intrinsic right of all music to be always aesthetically vital.* Some modifications of interpretative regularity may logically be expected under his baton.

Allegros lazily vocalized lack definition and neatness to the extent of being slovenly. A worn-out choral unit is not sufficiently alert to manage a speedy continuity. Fast-moving sixteenth notes require more instant co-ordination between brain and vocal cords than tired singers can induce. Marked velocity is a precarious hazard because it is beyond the accomplishment of a torpid technique. Marked slowness must be avoided when the chorus is physically sluggish lest it add to the prevailing heaviness.

Players of wind instruments, and especially of the brass instruments, merit the same consideration as singers. String players, too, are influenced by fatigue, but their technique is independent of breath control and more mechanical than that of their aeolian colleagues. Horns, trumpets, trombones, and tubas cannot be addressed "with a good lip" nor can the notes of their harmonic series be previewed precisely if the players are played out.

The tempo should be accommodated to their temporary capacity. Breath control must not be overtaxed by long-drawn-out tones nor embouchure made altogether flabby by inconsiderate speed. Let an orchestra rehearse in the morning, play a matinee, and undertake *Die Walküre* in the evening! If the tempo of the "Ride" is not slightly retarded, the spluttering of "persimmon" lips in the brass section will inevitably mar the rendition. I have often found changes of tempo demanded, for passable performances of choral-orchestral works, by the muscular ennui of players.

During my many years of public conducting I have come to fear two *a cappella* motets if they must be sung by a wearied choir: the six-part setting of "Crucifixus" by Lotti, and the final movement of "Singet den Herren" by Bach. If I neglect to set a faster than normal tempo for the former, the *etiam* figure is sure to be so inert as to invalidate the performance almost at the outset. If, however, I indicate the customary brisk pace for the Bach fugue, the tired basses invariably smear the presentation of the subject, and I am hard pressed to prevent the entire exposition from becoming opaque and viscous.

Some conductors are wont to challenge such strategy, adhering inexorably to the dogma that, come what may, the tempo should always be that most probably intended by the composer. Prescinding from the likelihood of unanimity as to what the composer's intentions might have been in any given case, I agree heartily that it is a primary duty of all conductors to disclose his evident intentions as far as possible. But possibility does not always connote feasibility. Details of performance are only means to a visualized end. Stubborn absorption in the means may readily thwart this end, and conductors who insist on always conducting "by the book" should insert in their manuals this important protocol: *the whole aesthetic concept of a composition, its* raison d'être, *may be destroyed by a rigorous, pietistic insistence on any detail of interpretation which is unsuited to the physical circumstances of a particular performance.*

The details of interpretation which frequently require modification in order faithfully to portray the subsurface content of a composer's creation are pre-eminently the tempo and the application of dynamic intensities.

The *physics* of sound—acoustics—often gives invaluable hints as to the practicability of paces. Not infrequently a conductor is embarrassed in realizing, too late, that a tempo approved by all other tests is unmanageable in the existing circumstances. Conditions surrounding performances have trying mannerisms. They plague perspicacity by varying not only in bold outline but quite often in details which slyly secrete their significance.

All conductors know that the architectural contours of churches and concert halls influence acoustical properties; but, in the midst of a plentitude of things to worry about, they too often fail to note the many other features of buildings which affect clarity and resonance of sounds. Similarly, no maestro of much experience needs to be reminded that performances indoors and out-of-doors must be adapted respectively to different acoustical conditions. He is fully aware that the contingencies likely in one situation are unlikely in the other. But he is apt to forget that the agencies of audibility and vitality of sound are neither more nor less stable under the dome of the sky than under an arching apse, a playhouse proscenium, or the ceiling of a *salon*. Added to the major facts which differentiate the acoustical aspects of music in the blue serene and music in the aisles, there are factors which make some alfresco concerts more perplexing than others.

Here follow some notes pertinent to tempos indoors and out-of-doors.

Tempos Indoors.—The design and proportions of a hall, the relation of chancel, choir loft, or stage to the auditorium, the materials used in the construction of interior surfaces, and certain minutiae of decoration all have relevancy to the circumfusion of tonal vibrations. In wide, short halls tones spread and thus lose resonance; in long, narrow naves the pulsations seem to converge on a focal point, thus attaining a spearhead acuteness. Domes, cupolas, and transepts usually transform resonance into reverberation. Echo can convert comely concord into defacing discord. Commodious open spaces backstage, postapsidal Lady chapels and chantries tend to restrain sounds from floating frontwards in full diapason. Lofty vaults invite overtones to soar, while low flat coverings depress them to dreadful dullness. Loges with velvet valances and stalls in the plushy softness of now outmoded odeons have drained many a semibreve of the savor meant for their occupants. Funereal fronds flanking a chorus have often prepared an advance obituary of its efficacy. Zealots appointed by women's clubs to arrange appropriate stage settings for visiting choirs have converted many an advertised concert into a "Flower Show with Music." Attar of roses and essence of music, are they not the aroma of aesthetics? If one may not sense the song of sopranos, let him scent the perfume of petals!

It used to amuse me "on the road," when I was not overvexed, to count the palm branches on the stage and mentally to make a trial balance of these with the treble choristers. There was a sardonic satisfaction in conjecturing the strength of the interference interposed by the floral encumbrances. Disagreeable experience had taught that each frond would neutralize a soprano, unless I raised the pitch of *a cappella* numbers out of the waving reach of the palms and hurried the gait through the grove.

Ventilation and temperature influence the buoyancy and carrying power of tones. The dread of drafts has caused many an auditorium to be without sufficient ozone to exhilarate even a *staccato* sixteenth note. *A cappella* polyphony in the stagnancy of an unventilated assembly room has little chance of adhering to pitch and less of inspiriting listeners with the sparkle of its counterpoint.

A master conductor will wisely keep together on a mental shelf barometer, thermometer, metronome, and baton.

Although my first purpose in presenting the foregoing data was merely to draw attention to the influence of acoustics in general on the proprieties of tempo, some specific inferences of practical import may be drawn from them.

One aim of the alert conductor is always to establish the highest feasible degree of compatibility between his tonal forces and the acoustical properties of the place of the performance. Dynamics, pitch, and tempo are the means adjustable to this end. If the acoustical temperament of a hall is sluggish, one or all of these resources must be invoked to invigorate the air waves. An oft-reiterated premise of this treatise is that music and inertia are fated foes. Melody accrues from motion, and whatever impedes the natural fluency of sound waves is, therefore, an obstacle to be overcome. The non-resonance of a "dead" hall is such an obstacle, its negativeness being, paradoxically, a positive encumbrance. Some conductors seek to hurdle this hazard by increasing the decibels of quantity; but quantity, itself endued with an analogous weightiness, adds a quantum to the already encumbered environment.

Many directors of *a cappella* units have learned that the elevation of the pitch, by the very fact of increased vibrations per second in all the parts, helps to compensate for the lassitude of lazy acoustics.

But we are concerned here with tempo. It is clear that a fast-moving series of tonal impulses contributes a verve needed to offset the languor of a non-resonant room. The added verve is not always so enlivening as adequately to energize the muffled oscillations, but it is sufficiently refreshing to justify application. It is akin to taking the *sordini* off the strings.

Per contra, if the acoustical disposition of an auditorium is signally lively, the tempo may often be retarded with advantage. In an over-resonant room, speed tends to create the impression of agitation. This presently cedes candidly to confusion which turns the *melos* into sonorous shivaree or tintinnabulation. Unfortunately no architectural designs or specifications have been offered which guarantee satis-factory acoustics; the whereabouts of a building, its relation to neighboring structures, and the geological nature of its site exercise an influence which can only be conjectured. For the most part, how-ever, long halls of lofty lines seem to provide easy trackage and headroom for sound waves where normal tempos can be effective, whereas amphitheatrical and low-ceiled structures are likely to be found wanting in these assets. In the latter types of building accelerated tempos help to rally tones to concentration points, while slow tempos permit them to succumb to the already spread supine-ness of reluctant rooms. There are many concert halls throughout this country whose ratios of length to breadth to height are so unacousti-cally proportioned as to require an increase of motion in movements normally convincing at an impressive *largo* or *adagio*. On the other hand, much-traveled conductors know of many concert arenas whose spatial contours induce such keen vitality as to demand decreased speed in *allegros* and *prestos*.

If such a notable degree of acceleration or slackening as would take a composition out of character is indicated, the expedient of adjusting tempos to acoustical properties is, in a manner of speak-ing, malfeasance. In this circumstance, the conductor is well advised to make a substitution in the program. This easy exit from an uneasy situation being often barred, the perplexed maestro is frequently forced to rely upon astute use of the structural factors of a composi-tion—perhaps on the underlining of helpful harmonic relations in the interior parts—as well as upon the strategic interpolation of

agogics, *fermatas,* and *staccato* phrases, to establish an entente between the music and the surroundings.

Usually, however, a slight increase or decrease of pace is sufficient
to secure an adequate compatibility between musical and acoustical
features. Just as the raising or lowering of the pitch by a semitone
generally adjusts an *a cappella* motet agreeably to prevailing conditions, so the setting of the regulator a few degrees up or down the
Maëlzel pendulum will effect a working compromise between the
aesthetic proprieties of a number and the phonic characteristics of
the place where it is performed.

My personal experience has brought me into many diversely
designed churches and concert halls, and I have come to realize that,
for a happy choice of tempos in notably fast or slow, gossamer or
cumbrous movements, it is necessary to take cognizance of the
architectural lineaments of an auditorium at the outset, and *during
the progress of the initial number to study the effect upon resonance
of accelerandos, rallentandos, dynamic variations, and tessitura-
rilievos.* Before the conclusion of the opening number, an experienced
conductor should be able to judge reasonably as to the rates of speed
most suitable for the ensuing numbers.

Franz Kneisel, founder of the Kneisel Quartet, first turned my
thoughts in the direction of such procedure. He was an artist of
extraordinary talent and achievement who sublimated his art by
explaining its bases to interested inquirers. One phase of his greatness was his sensibility to the influence of acoustics on the persua-
siveness of music. He sought understanding of the subtle relationships of pitch and tempo to the temperament of an auditorium. For
many years he had noted, systematically in a little book, memoranda
concerning acoustical facts of the halls in which he gave concerts.
Thus he had the data from which to conclude that, in a certain
auditorium at Chicago, he should avoid the key of B flat and
dragging *maestosos*; at Boston, that the key of E natural would ring
with metallic clink and that lively *allegros* would be madcap races;
at Cincinnati, that an F minor *adagio* at traditional tempo would
overload an atmosphere already weighted with threnody, etc. He
urged me *to concentrate on the acoustical rather than on the artistic
effect of the starting number,* thus opening for me a new vista of
musical thought. Very soon I inaugurated the custom of beginning all
miscellaneous choral programs with an *acoustics finder* which was

programmed simply "Invocation Motet."[8] By marking the greater or less resonance of the extreme (soprano and bass) parts, the clarity or muddiness of the choral axis (alto and tenor parts), the continuance or lessening of buoyancy in *rallentandos* and low *relievos*, the effect of *accelerandos* on blend and balance in ascending chordal progressions, the result of attempted *animandos* both *con* and *senza crescendo*, and of *diminuendos con* and *senza rallentando*, I was enabled to acquire information of paramount importance to the success of the concert. It became easy to discern, with safe certainty, the *overtonic* quality of a room and to organize the tactical plan of maneuvers with tempo, pitch, and dynamics best suited to its acoustical conformation. Intelligent obedience to hints offered by an acoustics finder is a dependable guarantee of freedom from the furtive interference of elements which so often concur to frustrate artistic purpose.

Arthur Nikisch is said to have replied to a concertmaster's query as to whether he would distribute the beat of a certain *andante*: "Wait until I reach it; look then and you will find out." Probably the great Leipzig conductor could have informed the concertmaster after the opening number. Personally, since my indoctrination with the Kneisel notions, I have never tried to determine exact tempos or dynamic scales until the conclusion of the "Invocation Motet." And many an accompanist, over the years, has been distrait before concerts because I declined to specify the pitch for *a cappella* numbers. It was strategy to wait until the situation could be appraised from Kneisel's belvedere. When the character of the program does not permit the graceful inclusion of the "Invocation Motet," I habitually use the first movement of the first number as the range finder. After the soundings have been made I feel confident in unfolding the purely musical aspects of the program. On the occasion of the silver jubilee concert of my choristers at the Metropolitan Opera House, New York, yielding to the suggestion that the opening selection be a unison Gregorian chant (sung by men's voices), I sacrificed the benefits of the "Invocation Motet" to which I had been so long accustomed, and unfortunately chose the wrong tempo, the wrong pitch, and the wrong dynamic compass for the great "Ascendo ad Patrem" of Palestrina. Eventually, as the concert proceeded, I made

[8] The number has become popular among conductors through this country for its usefulness in this connection as well as for its intrinsic worth: "Emitte Spiritum Tuum" ("Send Forth Thy Spirit") by Fr. Jos. Schuetky, C. C. Birchard, Boston.

the proper readjustments, but too late to redeem the most significant features of the highly publicized program. An extensive velvet curtain hung behind the choristers. This of course sapped much of the vitality of their intonations. The "Invocation Motet," offering rich opportunity for experimenting, would have revealed immediately that the light volatile timbre of the soprano boys needed high pitch and brisk tempo to neutralize the unfriendliness of that furry fabric.

The late Cleofonte Campanini, distinguished conductor at La Scala, Covent Garden, Manhattan Opera House, and Chicago Auditorium, being aware of the choral ideals I was struggling to promote, once advised me to cancel an advertised concert in a great city of the Mississippi Valley. The concert was announced to be presented in a horse-show arena. Sig. Campanini had just returned with the Chicago Opera Company from a tour including that city. With much feeling he exclaimed that his experiences there were the most disheartening of his career. In the vast spaces where I was announced for an *a cappella* concert, he had heard the ten-count in a conflict with unfriendly acoustics. Echo and reecho, farrago and jumble, medley and muddle had metamorphosed his splendid music into cluttering and chaotic clatter. A facile interpreter said that the maestro warned, eloquently: "You will be very unhappy if you try to conduct your motets in that misshapen cavern. It is the hiding place of ogres who hate music. They will swoop down from high girders and snatch away your loveliest effects. They will emerge from front and back and sides, and dig tearing talons into your harmonies. Flutes will sound like trombones, and trombones like city noises. I could hardly remember if I were conducting the *Jewels* or *Louise*." He was probably amazed at my American and adolescent nonchalance when, thanking him for his solicitude, I declared myself free of fear of any combination of acoustical phenomena (except the dread deadness of low-ceiled rooms) because I had found a scheme for correlating tempos, dynamics, and acoustics. This scheme stemmed, of course, to the seed sown by Dr. Kneisel. Sig. Campanini, having heard later of the successful performance of the concert, applauded the validity of the Kneisel idea. The auditorium in which he and the opera company had found disappointment and where I had only to be cautious to be happy, was indeed an ugly amorphous enclosure. It was the sort of arena where sounds seemed inevitably doomed to chase one another around, colliding madly and disastrously; where eight notes could make a double fugue in entirety—exposition, episodes, and *stretto!*

The "Invocation Motet" challenged the old barn, casting a disclosing beam on the aeries of the ogres and lighting up dark, dangerous spots in the acoustical loft. The strategy it revealed to be both necessary and adequate was slower tempos; lowered pitches (except in pieces dominantly in the minor mode); prepared dynamics, i.e., no *sforzandos* or *subito pianissimos*; resumption of *a tempo* gradually after *fermatas*, i.e., the first few ensuing beats purposefully slower; the use of *staccato* in the interior and bass parts occasionally to permit greater definition amid possibly entangling reverberation, etc.

The choice of the slow tempos is the only item of the strategy strictly relevant here; but the aim of the conductor being so to correlate his performance and the acoustics as to assure an *aesthetic* vitality to the music, and such animation being affected by pitch and volume as well as by pace, the modifications required in those circumstances have been included.[9] That particular auditorium was so violently over-animated by structural urgencies that it was necessary to inject an anti-spasmodic sedative into the tone currents. To speed one noisy sound after another through such a ravine would indeed be to invite confusion: Wolf-Ferrari and Charpentier, Palestrina and John Philip Sousa, John Sebastian Bach and Shostakovich could easily interlace their lute strings.

Although it is evident that no general prescription may be offered for adjusting tempos to the particular personalities of all rooms even of similar design and dimensions, it has been my experience to find the more animated tempos desirable in the moderately sized auditorium which accommodates approximately fifteen hundred people. If a larger hall, a Roman dome, Byzantine or Romanesque arches, or Gothic vertices have prearranged a notable and repercussive verve, a less active pace is more suitable. Metronomic marks may not always be observed with successful safety. A composer is wont naturally and unsuspectingly to indicate the Maëlzel tempo of a piece that has satisfied him in his composing studio. This latter is usually a small room with little overhead spacing and a minimum of resonance. A tempo appropriate in such surroundings is almost certain to be unsatisfactory in a basilica or a great concert hall. Beethoven is recorded as having expressed amazement at the startling ineffec-

---

[9] Cf. dynamics and pitch in the index.

tiveness of a piece when he rehearsed it in a theater *because he set the tempo which he had deliberately chosen at home*. I remember the chagrin and sense of futility I experienced listening to a radio performance of an orchestral arrangement of mine conducted by a distinguished and gracious maestro who paid me the unfortunate compliment of following my metronomic recommendation. Probably $\flat$ = 52 had approved itself in my resonant choir hall; $\flat$ = 70 might have averted the lingering death suffered by the opus in a small broadcasting studio.

Some critics feel the gorge rise when a conductor disregards the tempo markings, just as they are wont to arch musicological eyebrows when the pitch is raised or lowered for *a cappella* numbers. Of course one does not conduct a concert with a fountain pen or portray musical effects with scrivener's ink; but the majority of conductors, being artistically sincere and therefore open-minded, welcome constructive criticisms of tempos, etc., if it is evident that the fluent reviewer has sensed the conductor's purpose and needs in his readjustments. Naturally we don't like to be called wantonly naughty when we are trying hard to be very good. I have ascertained personally from many professional reviewers that they had never adverted to the fact that the surroundings in which a composition was created and first trued and the surroundings in which it must be re-created and vitalized in public performances are widely and influentially different. *The task of the conductor is to bring life to printed notes.* Each performance is a resuscitation. The circumstances of single performances vary. Therefore, to accomplish his primary purpose, the conductor must justly be conceded the right of bringing interpretative tactics into accord with the variations. Music is not pantomime; the same gestures are not always or equally effective. Notes are not mere marionettes manageable as Punch and Judy. They are symbols of the aesthetic vitality which the composer sought in composing. He found this vitality in certain pace panels and at particular pitches at his desk or piano. Perhaps these particular pace panels and pitches are too vital or not vital enough for the spaces where the conductor finds acoustical influences of which the composer was probably unmindful.

The effects of varying acoustical properties upon the validity of a performance are so signal as to warrant reiteration of the necessity of studying them before embarking on a notably fast or a notably slow tempo. Perhaps the lassitude of a hall will be countervailed by slight acceleration, and extravagant resonance by slight retardation.

The position of the performing forces on the stage is sometimes an important item to be considered in determining a pace. If they are so assembled as to be at a disadvantage tonally, an extra degree of speed in a *largo* will often engender needed encouragement, and the reining of racing fugues will temper the fear of impending errors and disaster. Singers are accustomed to rehearse on flat platforms without any impression of disadvantage, probably because the practice rooms usually have low ceilings. But on the concert stage, especially in theaters which have extensive areas off and above stage, raised tiers are assets. If the tenors and basses, singing usually behind and approximately with half the pitch vibrations of the upper voices (therefore with less definition) are elevated to vantage positions, the singers in front are more secure in their intonations. The acoustical relations of the singing unit must be coordinated on the stage before projecting the result beyond the proscenium if the conductor is to be free to deal with other acoustical factors. Otherwise he must resort to compensating processes to render the group ready for resonance. Modification of tempos and dynamics is his most dependable resource here as in so many cross-grained circumstances. Unsatisfactory grouping arrangements tend to rob a performance of vitality, if for no other reason than because they superinduce the feeling of awkwardness in the participants. Sometimes the resulting insufficient animation can be supplemented by invigorating the tempo. The acoustics finder will report the acoustical *status quo* on stage as faithfully as it will disclose the temperament of the auditorium.

Tempos Out-of-doors.—Making "merrie musik" out-of-doors is not always a merry experience. Favorite features of indoor interpretation must frequently be abandoned. Ears must be reached without the aid of pent-up resonances. The strangely inhibitive freedom of the air must be carefully assayed lest the majesty and cruelty of space ridicule the lesser majesty and the urbaneness of music. The wand that mesmerizes magic modulations in Carnegie Hall, New York, may, a few blocks away in Central Park, be only a silly stub of a stick stalking sounds that steal into the heavens.

A conductor needs to feel some reality in the notes he is trying to revivify from the inked score. If he receives no sensory impression of success, he must rely upon the tepid suasions of mechanical calculation and cool determination for confidence to continue. It is difficult, indeed, to ignite and more difficult to keep aglow the aesthetic material of music that is blowing about in the open air.

No matter how strained and meager its acoustical hospitality, an enclosed arena at least acknowledges the activity of sounds. The conductor knows that the intonations he has evoked are concentrated within definite dimensions; he is sure that they have not emigrated into the far wastes beyond audibility; he feels physically *en rapport* with the listeners who under the same roof sense the same tonal repercussions. A painter, preferring a northern light, can function even if the windowpane has chosen a southern sill, but without dismal doubts he cannot fashion apt contours, distribute tints and shades, or impress meaning upon a canvas in the dark. Similarly, a conductor, happier if a kindly architecture has limned the sound tracks, can produce music with some certainty of artistry even when a dome or flat ceiling variously interferes or a stray triforium or a pall of plush has fallen across ·the tracks, but he can sense only by agnostic guessing how to balance melody and harmony before releasing them to uncharted spaces of the ether. Sometimes, standing on an outdoor podium, one feels as though each carefully wrought phrase were lifted and borne away by a helium balloon. In the open, a conductor is quite likely to feel frustrated in any plan to discipline elusive counterpoints. Most counterpoints seem eager to escape his jurisdiction!

The acoustical facts influencing open-air concerts vary with the same challenging diversity as the phenomena encountered indoors. It is a mistake to judge that all unenclosed performances can successfully be accomplished by the same adjustments of tempo, etc. Contrast, for instance, the probable acoustical differences of these settings and environments: flat terrains in park clearings; steps of buildings in front of high façades; platforms without sounding-board shells; platforms with quarter-circle shells; platforms hidden under the cowls of baldaquins; seating arrangements which require a conductor to scatter his chords and *fioriture* over audiences sitting below but in direct line with platforms; high ramping embankments on hillsides where people reach out fanlike to widespread tips; public-address loud-speakers altering quality and balance within hearing of the conductor or at such a distance that he gets no hint of the metamorphosis; homophony with the wind, polyphony across the wind, and complex rhythm against the wind; humidity and heat, or frigidity that makes little ice cubes of every quatrain of crotchets.

If a conductor consistently tries to solve the puzzles presented by such disparate conditions, his zeal will be rewarded by fairly acceptable performances; but if he is disposed to underrate the value of adjusting treatments to different symptoms, he is entitled to many a "lame and impotent conclusion."

When performers and audience are assembled at the same level on greenswards or flat terrains with no sounding-board devices, the conductor will find himself practically helpless to improve the situation. There are no means available for focusing tones. Readjustments of tempo and dynamics which aid in concentrating and giving direction to sounds indoors are valueless here. They are hardly less futile if the performers are grouped on a platform without sounding board or backstop. All intonations seem to vanish in the very process of making. I remember the embarrassing futility which attended my efforts in many awkward situations.

Fortunately, however, one is rarely invited to attempt a tour de force under such untoward conditions. We are in an era of summer park concerts, and seldom is the setting for them thoughtlessly unprepared. Electronic amplification, although still an uncertain influence on timbre, balance, and tonal definition, has lessened the conductor's burden, at least to the extent of promoting audibility. But there are so many occasions on which conductors must interpret music alfresco with inadequate or no aid from a public-address system that it seems profitable to examine the probably different needs of different settings.

The office of military and brass bands, playing through city streets or in stadiums, is not to make music as such but rather to contribute an enlivening force to gala events. Even sketchy march music promotes the pageantry of processions. Buildings abutting on the city streets quite generally form acoustical canyons as friendly to musical effects as the naves between Gothic walls. At a football game a bandmaster is a cheer leader intensifying the general *rah rah* with outbursts from trumpets, trombones, and tubas, inciting further excitement with piccolos, reeds, and cymbals. If drum majors toss bright-capped sticks in symmetrical circles and drummers beat urgently enough, all's well with music on parade! But in straightforward concert programs the bandmaster must take cognizance of the same hindrances as his colleagues of the chorus and orchestra.

As a general rule, if one may presume to suppose the prevalence of certain regular alfresco conditions, slower tempos are less ineffective than faster. Rapid successions of changing harmonies in the "undampered" outdoors create unpremeditated dissonances analogous to the overlapping chromaticisms of exotic progressions played on a piano with the sustaining pedal depressed. The slower the continuity of overlapping harmonies, the easier it is to prevent earaches in the audience.

Some conductors are deceived by the walls which stand up as back-stops behind a chorus. Frequently choruses must sing on the steps of public buildings, and the high façades before which the choristers are grouped usually promise more acoustical cooperation than they can organize. These serve admirably to bar the rearward escape of tones, but the tones drift upwards unhindered; in Dryden's words: "The trembling notes ascend the sky."

Much of the music soars out of hearing. Therefore, in such a *mise en scène,* the simpler the style of the music and the less agitated its delivery the more favorable are the chances for keeping its salient outlines in aural perspective. Quietly moving homophony, with frequently interpolated *fermata* rests, is most readily adapted to such a setting. A concert at the Greek Theatre, University of California (the arrangement was similar), convinced me, many years ago, that brisk tempos generally and lively polyphonies in particular require an overhead shell as well as an upright guard wall for adequate definition. I experienced little difficulty in project-ing chordal progressions and *adagio* contrapuntal figures even through the East Bay fog which enveloped that great Hellenic arena, but the *allegros* and florid counterpoints leaped off the terrace into the night without excusing themselves.

Quarter-circle shells are usually favorable to whatever acoustical coalescence may be achieved outdoors. Tones find themselves and identify their mates without much confusion in such protected areas. The sounding board in the Hollywood Bowl, California, is a con-clusive proof of the efficacy of a fortunately designed and constructed quarter shell. It fell to my lot in that modern habitat of the muses to undertake the perplexing task of balancing a chorus of five hundred voices whose timbres and intensities were admirably poised under the shell, with a complete symphony orchestra playing alto-gether in the open. The choral intonations were easily compounded, but flutes, fiddles, and horns were intent on losing themselves in the Hollywood hills, chagrined perhaps that the vocal *partitur* was more favored than the orchestration. In order to establish a modicum of affinity between the choral and instrumental units, it was necessary to retard the *con fuoco* movements upon which the programmed cantata depends for dramatic verve. The only resource at hand for impeding the flight of the orchestral timbres trying to slip lightly away on the zephyrs was the weight which slowness provides.

Semicircular baldaquins, domes, and allover canopies, unless spanned 'high above the performers, tend to depress and suppress resonance. Vibrations are "knocked down" by low ceilings. Whereas a conductor is concerned usually to curb the excessive buoyancy of open-air intonations, in these circumstances he must strive to increase it. The precipitate recoil of sounds from squat coverings robs them of *élan*, and, unless accelerated, *largos* and *adagios* are sure to be prosaic and listless.

Further speculation in these pages anent the relationship of fast and slow paces to the almost whimsical vagaries of extramural acoustics is unwarranted. Specialists in the physics of atmosphere might formulate modes of procedure to carry the day against the most hostile crosscurrents, but the recommendations of most reminiscent conductors have the value only of conjectural probabilities compiled from casual experiments.

My purpose in submitting the material in the last few pages to young conductors has been *to stress the necessity of appraising acoustical phenomena at the beginning of every performance, in auditoriums or in the open, lest the tempos well suited to the academic structure of a composition be defeatingly applied in the temporary circumstances.*

Psychology, phyletics, physiology, and physics merit due consideration as influences extrinsic to the aesthetic immanence of the music itself. They are perhaps sources of clues to desirable *readjustments* of tempo rather than to a first choice. The principal guide to a first choice is, certainly, the aesthetic intent of the composer as discernible from the structure of his composition.

Intelligent balancing of the data acquired by experimental analysis of compositions and extrinsic influences will usually prescribe a convincing manner of performance. Such preparation will not always avert inadequacies and errors, but it will effectively guarantee against bungling and complete mismanagement. The appointment of the proper tempos, modifications of tempos, and dynamic levels cannot dependably be made by casual choice. If a conductor's musicanship is meager, lacking orientation, or if the sense of the music is vague, he can only hope that luck will be kindly. One should soon recognize an insufficiency of musical understanding and set about remedying the deficiency. As to the ambiguities and conundrums of a score— well, the span of life is too brief to waste energy on tedious or inconsequential riddles!

The *melos* is not "the sole guide to the right tempo," but it contains the primary evidence of a composer's intentions. All modifications in favor of any of the four P's must be considered as tactics of the moment to assure opportuneness in varying conditions.

THE PSYCHOLOGY INVOLVED IN THE MODIFICATION OF TEMPOS

If it is futile and presumptuous to propose peremptory precepts for determining prevailing tempos, it is extravagantly arbitrary to establish definite rules for their modification. The choice of a prevailing pace is made on a ninety per cent *objective* basis—by a correlation of inherent data and the conditions surrounding a performance. But effectively artistic deviation from metronomic regularity is accomplished on a ninety per cent *subjective* basis—by the personal, aesthetic, and indefinable urges which stir the spiritual ego of the individual. One selects a general tempo by *logical* processes but is moved to delay or hurry a pace here and there by mysterious *psychological* directions. It is impossible to capture, clarify, and codify the sympathies, quests, and emotional excitations which importune *rallentando* now, *accelerando* then; *a battuta* here, *rubato* there; agogics in some measures, anticipated beats in others; *accelerando con crescendo* in these phrases, *senza crescendo* in those; *rallentando con* or *senza diminuendo*; *diminuendo con* or *senza rallentando*; protracted *lungas* or short *fermatas*. It would be even more unmindful of the subliminal forces which make artistry individual and intimate to dictate degrees of *rallentando* and *accelerando* or to attempt to specify the number of beats within which the robbing of *rubato* should be rectified.

Monotony is a dangerous feature in any art form (cf. the following pages). In sizable inventions it is a source of mental fatigue. The true artist is necessarily intent upon awakening intellectual and emotional faculties. Perhaps there is a thrill of a sort, for people who do not wish to be roused and enlivened, in the repetition of an unchanging pattern. Perhaps there is for all of us a certain gratification accruing from the reiteration of the same bold outlines of an idea. But I think that the imagination and the emotional susceptibilities of the majority require modifications in the minutiae of every repetition. Nature loves to present her details in infinite variety. In-coming and ebbing tides roll in and roll out from generation to generation with fixed regularity, but each comber encroaching upon the shore spends itself in its own way and recedes in an undertow of its own making, similar to but never the same as the refluence of any other billow. The personality of waves and the *rubato* of the sea are among the most satisfying phenomena of nature.

Season follows season with eternal timeliness, but never did two springs blossom with the same verdure. Never perfect twin-roses on a bush!

Monotony is monochrome. Whatever its actual color, it presently seems impotently wan or grimly gray to the average human. The reactions of the mind and emotions to sameness are chilling. Only apathetic persons hibernate in happy imperturbability. The more aesthetic and spiritual the temper of individuals, the keener their need for and the more varied their response to the nuances which differentiate each apperception of an idea from every other.

Thus, it may reasonably be argued, the true artist must find monotonous continuity dissatisfying, distressing, and defeating. This does not mean that he cannot appreciate simplicity. Rather, it implies that even simplicity has a thousand facets for him, each sparkling with a different glitter according to its turning toward the light.

The conductor who is alive to the subsurface subtleties of music is moved by sensibilities which abhor and are affronted by unvaried clock-like precisions. The consecutiveness of many measures meticulously timed to bring a composition through on a railroad schedule takes the meaning out of music for the listeners. They are deprived of the initiative even to guess what it's all about; the notes are like the drone of a memorized speech, the words of which seem suspiciously more important than the thoughts; the measures seesaw like tilting marionettes. Wagner insisted that the choice of the tempo proves whether or not a conductor understands a composition. I venture to go beyond his point in stating that, *by the modifications which he applies to a chosen tempo, the conductor reveals how profoundly he feels the spirit of the composition, to what degree the melodies and harmonies have stirred his aesthetic and spiritual comprehension, and, in general, how much the art of music means to him as a vehicle for expressing unphysical and immaterial values.*

If the same modifications habitually recur in the same places and in the same degree, one may conclude that the conductor has memorized his *rubato*. In this circumstance the changes of tempo, proposing reactions by rote, may be just as monotonous and mechanical as the click-click continuity of so many notes to a minute.

Modern composers indicate the broader variations of tempo in their manuscripts. But the extent of these variations is necessarily contingent upon the feeling of conductors. *Rallentando* means a hardly perceptible dallying to one, and a definite delaying to another. *Accelerando* may sometimes urge the development of a precipitate pace under another's baton, while under mine it may be a mere invigoration of movement. In the manuscripts of early music there are few suggestions as to tempo (cf. footnote, page 145). In much post-Renaissance music hints are too meager or too vague to be of much assistance. The *rallentando, accelerando* marks incorporated in published editions of medieval, early or late Renaissance, and much eighteenth-century music are the gratuitous interpolations of editors. Frequently these gratuitous modifications are admirably consistent with the idiom of a style and are safe guides for conductors. Sometimes, however, especially in editions of *a cappella* polyphony, both the tempo changes and the dynamic variations are obviously the conclusions of conjecture—foggy guessing about the interpretative proprieties of a partially understood school of composition. The markings included in editions of the manuscripts of the Dufay-Palestrina-Byrd-Sweelinck period *should not be followed indiscriminately unless the editor is a recognized archaist and a specialist in the actual performance of horizontal modal music.*

It is not in the quality of a conductor's response to the broad modifications of tempo as indicated by composers or editors that his artistic sensitiveness is most convincingly disclosed. His interpretative artistry reveals itself with greatest clarity, often independently of his conscious advertence, in the subtle elasticities which he imparts to phrases. The slight prolongation of a single chord, the gentle quickening of part of a clause, an esoteric *rallentando* at the beginning rather than at the end of a period, an *accelerando* in a cadence, the fluctuating appositions which make *rubato* so ingratiatingly mysterious—these are evidence that a conductor has sensed something in the music that notation and symbols cannot make patent. Furthermore, the fact that the varying circumstances of each performance of a piece—the tonal offerings of participants, the acoustics of the hall, the character and mood of the audience—impel him to a variable use of the prolongation, the quickening, and the appositions is striking confirmation of his true artistry.

The subtleties of music endow the art with its mystic, overwhelming, hypnotic, and irresistible power. The psychology of delay or postponement; the urgency of hurrying with an elusive inspiration which would fain slip away; the balancing of inexplicable yearnings, of peace and restiveness, of assurances and misgivings, of exclaiming and questioning, of laughing and sobbing, of bold impulse to the climax of great emotional portraiture; the awe experienced at some passing moment of beauty—these are the motivating reasons for modifying tempos and varying dynamic intensities. These are the influences directing escape from mere craftsmanship and the platitudinarianism which mechanical adherence to the monotony of an unrelieved *andante, allegro,* or *adagio* promises for the futility of music.

It would be superfluous to dilate further upon the necessity for fine shades of tempo changes if there were fewer conductors who are satisfied with the lukewarmness of precision procedure.

I do not mean to disparage the value and virtue of holding a group of singers or players steadily to a given tempo. On the contrary and unreservedly, indifference to such control must be condemned as slovenliness. Until a chorus or an orchestra has attained a reliable competence in performing with metronomic exactitude, it is unprepared to make convincing modifications of tempo. A fortiori, a conductor who does not instinctively sense the regular continuity of successive beats should shun *rubato* as an aggravation of unsteadiness. He must address himself sedulously to the task of acquiring a feeling for regularity.

It has been my custom for years to rehearse numbers which tend to provoke nervous irregularities of pace, with the metronome clicking out the beats, ignoring *rallentandos* and *accelerandos*. These can readily be introduced later. A chorus wabbling from faster to slower and louder to softer is at best an uncertain medium.

However, granted that a conductor and the performers can maintain a steady tempo, it is essential to the emotional needs of music to prevent monotony by employing modifications of pace. Other-

wise the music becomes platitudinous. Platitudes are solemn commonplaces oozing ennui, and in literature and music equally *one
platitude a mile is exactly one too many!* Unbroken tempos and
unvaried *mezzo-fortes* tend inevitably to superimpose upon the
most interesting compositions the dullness of trite and banal general-
ization.

Even in Gregorian chant, although the single notes (without the
lengthening dot) are presumed to have the same temporal value,
an occasional *mora vocis* (slight retard) is recommended.

It is true that rigorous purists find in an altogether unvaried
delivery of Gregorian chant an element of unemotional expression
which they fancy most fitting for religious utterance. Perhaps the
sometime insistence on this placidity has prejudiced many of our
contemporaries against the ancient plain song. Certainly there are
some musicologists who have been wondering if all the Nordics,
as well as cisalpine and transalpine Latins, were thoroughly satisfied with a par-temporal value for all Gregorian notes. It is easy
to turn one's mind toward a suspicion that the chanters from the
fourth to the twelfth centuries were moved by the same psychological impulses which are expressed in the more modern appositions
of shorter and longer, faster and slower.

In *a cappella* polyphony, the independent melodies, rhythms, and
dynamic undulations of the separate voice lines suggest that
rallentando and *accelerando* were applied, at points vertically feasible,
not only to stress the textual content but to enhance the aesthetic
effect of the music itself. It is improbable that the race waited for
the post-Renaissance period to discover the aesthetic values of
rubato.

Some practical suggestions should seep through the many foregoing reflections.

In *a cappella* polyphony, the implications of a text frequently
enjoin certain modifications of tempo, in spite of the fact that a prevailing sameness in musical structure does not suggest the nuances.
With some exceptions,[10] there are no purely musical reasons in the
majority of manuscripts for hastening or retarding a prevailing pace.
The sentences of the *Gloria in Excelsis Deo*, set to music by all the

---

[10] An interesting exception is Palestrina's change from binary to ternary
rhythm in an obvious attempt to emphasize a Christian dogma, "Filius
Patris." For nine (modern) bars the voices proceed with unmistakable awe.
("Gloria: Missa Ascendo ad Patrem.")

master polyphonists, vary in their mental and spiritual reaches. *Et in terra pax hominibus bonae voluntatis. Laudamus Te. Benedicimus Te. Adoramus Te.* ("And on earth peace to men of good will. We praise Thee. We bless Thee. We adore Thee.") These expressions prompt and are allusive to a more instant human understanding and elation than the presently ensuing *Domine Fili unigenite . . . , Domine Deus, Agnus dei, Filius Patris; Qui tollis peccata mundi miserere nobis.* ("O Lord Jesus Christ, the only begotten Son, Lord God, Lamb of God, Son of the Father; Thou who takest away the sins of the world, have mercy on us.")

The *Et in terra* shines on a radiant beam of joy inculcating the thought that *peace* may really someday, somehap, come to men. The *Domine Deus* contemplatively approaches the inscrutable mystery of the Incarnation.

Pax should dance merrily on clear clouds with the angels who proclaimed it. There should be no reluctance. The tempo should be enthusiastic, lightened and quickened by easy understanding. But the human mind, unaccustomed to fathoming transcendental ideas, needs time to *hear* aright the incomprehensible premise voiced in the *Domine, Deus, Filius Patris.*

Always, even in the running moments of a liturgical context, spiritually abstract allusions should be uttered more quietly, i.e., more thoughtfully than concepts which are charitably less bewildering.

The habitual choice of excessively slow tempos in religious music has already been disapproved as prejudicial to its essential value. The music of the Church must let hope and happiness and spiritual eagerness into souls as Her stained-glass windows let light and color into otherwise dark naves. Melody and harmony in the sanctuary must be transparent; they must allow their subsurface intimations to be perceived easily. But the heaviness of deadly slowness is opaque rather than transparent. Therefore the degree of *rallentando* which is suggested by the more profound and abstract textual sentences in polyphonic settings is slight, a prolongation just long enough to allow one to bow the head before a mystery. Protracted retarding, impetuous hastening, and sudden changes from *moderato* to *largo* or *allegro* are inconsistent with the properties which differentiate the Palestrinesque style from later music. These are rather among the interpretative resources upon which dramatic and time-pattern music depends, being necessary to the variable urgencies of personal sentiment and purely emotional expression. Sacred polyphony is characteristically non-dramatic and impersonal. The madrigal style is scarcely more emotive, for most of the madrigal texts are only quaint conceits and even when discoursing of longings, loves, and ladies, are more bubbling babble than deeply stirred feeling.

Thus, the modifications of tempo which may properly be applied in the polyphonic style, as a general rule, should be conservative and in keeping with the cool aesthetic reserve of horizontal music.

When all the voice lines proceed in synchronous rhythm, i.e., when the temporal value of a series of notes is substantially the same throughout all the parts, an impression of vertical music is created. There are moments in almost every polyphonic composition at which the harmonic effect developed by such vertical simultaneity is unmistakably homophonic. These episodes of homophonic analogy tend to invite more emotional response than the strictly contrapuntal phrases where of course the independent progressions traverse one another's rhythmical organization. The more homophonic the impression of related parts, the more elastic the durational freedom becomes for a sensitive conductor. Vertical chordings hint that they have time to wait for whatever treatment he wishes to administer, but the weaving process by which many voice lines are contrapuntally enmeshed discourages per se a motley *rubato*. The necessity of maintaining the three independences of polyphonic structure (cf. Chapter VII, Polyphony) disallows the *rallentando*, *accelerando* fluctuations of more modern music. A *rallentando* or *accelerando* employed to accentuate a figure in the alto line, for example, might trench upon the continuity of the equally self-determining tenor line, and thus by bringing alto and tenor into conflict instead of into reciprocal sympathy, violate the polyphonic schema.

At the oases, points of repose where all parts meet, rest, and make ready to wander off again on separate routes, a sense of relaxation is invariably suggested. Polyphonic specialists are wont to treat such cadences as the conductors of later styles treat the corresponding moments of modern music in the matter of tempo modification, if not so freely in the matter of dynamic nuance.

In modern lyric music, the slowings and the quickenings should be as in the verses of a poem well understood and well read, with here a halting and there a hurrying. As an adjective welcomes stressing, a chord invites holding; a happy arc of notes should smile the quicker, just as pleasant words should tell their tale apace.

Dramatic music requires the conductor to swing his sensibilities full-circle through the emotions involved. Perhaps mere craftsmen can direct performances of polyphonic and modern lyric music with passable if shallow rectitude, but no conductor is ready to conduct dramatic music until he realizes that the drama and the music have become an insistent force within him, a fretful potency clamoring for release, demanding expression. There must be a tugging tautness between the imagination of the conductor and the emotional pressure of the music itself. Without this tension, the first urgency of true drama is absent; *accelerandos* will be only faster sprints through several bars, *rallentandos* listless loiterings, *crescendos* just added decibels, *diminuendos* mere waning and weakening.

Only the compulsion of a conductor's increasing animation can force increased speed to real portrayal. Only the tenacity of an idea or the richness of a musical reaction can make him need the retard which will have artistic or dramatic effect. The emotional worth of modifications in tempo depends ultimately upon the fervors of conductors and performers. Prearranged degrees of retard or acceleration are usually mechanical and ineffective because they are prearranged. Living nuances of tempo bring themselves about, if the conductor is a sensitive artist, during the actual performance of music. Springing from the moment, they convey the feel of their spontaneity, the persuasion of passionate perception.

In the use of temporal and dynamic nuances, the intelligent remembrance of past performances is an important guide to a conductor. From such remembrance, approving or disapproving, facility in sensing the finer points of unfamiliar scores will develop as a natural corollary.

It must be noted that, while the effectiveness of *rallentando* and *accelerando* is in the ratio of the conductor's sensitiveness, the implied spontaneity requires approbation from the intellect. It is easy to be too spontaneous. The discipline of the mind must prevent caprice. Caprice is not art. Impulse alone is an unsafe cicerone. Thought and emotion must balance each other.

There are many traditional modifications of tempo in the general concert repertoire which can be traced to master conductors. These should not go unheeded, or at least unexamined. But the very fact that *master conductors* initiated the modifications suggest that these were dictated by the personal reactions of truly great musicians. A leader could not fairly be called a master conductor if he lacked the qualities of insight which have been discussed in the preceding pages. Sometimes these bequeathed alterations of tempo have failed to register the same subconscious reactions in succeeding conductors. Furthermore, there was often a sharply cut difference of opinion among the masters. It is easy for a young conductor to be confused as to the value of their various points of view. For instance, Wagner and Mendelssohn were at opposite poles in the matter of *rubato*. Mendelssohn regarded this as an impediment to rhythmical fluency, whereas Wagner, always delving and dramatic, considered the stealthiness of retards and quickenings essential to the emotional declaration of his own and others' music. I was surprised to find only a modicum of music in Mendelssohn's cantata, "Hear My Prayer," when I first heard it sung without *rubato*. The work is incomparably more telling when well-balanced modifications of tempo, especially in the 3/8 movement, reveal its eager intensity. Perhaps much of the alleged sterility and prosiness of the Mendelssohnian school may properly be debited against the stolidity which develops not altogether from the notes but as well from the monotonous baldness with which they are uttered.

It must be insisted, however, that the extravagances of capricious tempo changes are a more serious affront to music than the homeliness of monotony. Sudden spurts of speed which accomplish nothing but the destruction of the poetic movement, obviously urged only by whim, are as unforgivable as they are unmusicianly. Languishing *rallentandos con* or *senza diminuendo* whenever an opportunity presents itself for a chorus to make a "killing" with languorous chords are equally deplorable. Far better the tedium of unvaried sameness than the jerky surprises of meaningless and incompatible variety!

Two readings of the *fermata* in the Bach chorales are current, one favoring a protracted delay, the other a minimum prolongation. Many conductors seem to sense a point of repose in the *holds* of the chorales, and if the prevailing tempo is not sluggish, the extension of the time value by the *fermatas* is frequently effective. On the other hand, the fact that Bach did not always observe his own *lunga* signs when playing his chorales as solo organ pieces, indicates that perhaps he assigned them to sung chorales for a practical purpose, i.e., of permitting the singing congregation to catch up, every so

often, with the tempo set by the organist. The section of a congregation at the greatest distance from the organ pipes is prone to be
behind time after the first measure or two. A *fermata* at the end of
a phrase gives the loiterers a chance to make fresh efforts *a tempo*.
Usually an extra beat accomplishes this purpose of the *fermata*. A
conductor's choice seems to be indicated in the treatment of the
chorale *fermatas*. The more common usage among current conductors
is to approximate a *lunga pausa*. Sometimes the interruption of
rhythmical continuity is thus disturbed. For instance, in the twelve
bars of Bach's harmonization of "Mit Fried and Freud," there are six
fermatas, which if read as *lungas* obviously subtract poetic motion
from the hymn, substituting a broken series of prosaic *declarandos*.
A conductor must frequently remind himself that both versification
and music (even in free rhythm) require balanced contours, though
not necessarily the parities of time-pattern rhythm; these balanced
contours are inhibited by frequent stoppings and startings. The circle
of a melody is often composed of separable arcs, but these arcs must
comprise a periphery which is not excessively notched. Each long
fermata is a nick in the melodic outline. The Bach chorale too
commonly is presented with a cogwheel circumference, the *fermata*
indentations destroying easy mobility.

In the general repertoire of music the *fermata* has become a
plaguing nuisance. Many musicians have a weakness for the showy
places in a score. *Lungas* indicated by composers are frequently
insufficient to satisfy a subconscious exhibitionism which yearns to
display baubles, if they can be made to glitter melodramatically.
Thus, one finds conductors interpolating holds not intended by
composers. The effect is that of overpunctuation with exclamation
marks. It seems as if the maestro, urged by an unconscious self-
complacency, is inviting listeners to observe the extra nuggets which
he has mined from the score. Vocal soloists are more flagrant trans-
gressors of melodic propriety in this matter than conductors, but
some of the latter acquiesce so readily in the formers' ostentatious
distortions as to need reminding of their responsibility. Admittedly,
a conductor must often concede latitude and even license to vocal
stars, who otherwise might prejudice his standing with boards of
directors, etc., but as a rule he can impose his own interpretation
upon the soloists. Not infrequently, a singer or an instrumentalist
deliberately wrests control of the tempo from the conductor, to the
disadvantage of the ensemble effectiveness. The soloist too often is

interested more in the solo part and its opportunities than in its relationship to the concerted whole, but real artists can readily be convinced that a *lunga pausa* injected inopportunely into a melodic stream is disastrous to temporal fluency, and therefore to aesthetic worth. Operatic tenors are considered to be the most bombastic and unforgivable caricaturists in making the *hold* offensive. They are charged with an overpowering determination to hang on to a high C as long as the lungs will permit exhalation. But sopranos, mezzos, contraltos, baritones, and basses seem equally disposed to exhibit their vocal prowess at the expense of melodic continuity.

A conductor must know how soon to release a *fermata*. Many need to learn that *sooner is better than soon*, in spite of customs to the contrary.

Agogics, germane to *fermatas*, readily defeat artistic purpose when interspersed too frequently or sustained beyond a fraction of a beat or a full beat at most. The lengthening of the initial or first-beat notes in carols, folk songs, arias, whimseys, or ballads soon becomes annoyingly banal. They are like the *er* and *ah* of elocutionary affectation. Occasionally a slight delay on the starting note of a phrase is graceful and naïve, especially in folk songs and carols, but such delays readily degenerate into exaggerated trivialities. Conductors are often tempted by dissonant chords to increase their temporal value, hoping thereby to promote the satisfaction of ensuing resolutions. The agogic underlining of discords serves well to emphasize following consonances, but if applied with stylistic uniformity this nuance frequently magnifies a composer's purpose in using the dissonance. In the classical forms, the less harmonious chords were generally employed to savor a dominantly assonant movement and, like accidentals, fulfill the composer's intent without signal emphasis.

The *atempause* and the anticipated second beat in a Viennese waltz (*rubato* within a measure) are only slight qualifications of rhythmical regularity. They seem to parallel the graceful pedal movements of the dancers. Semi-occasionally one hears the *atempause* so overdone as to deprive the engaging waltz rhythm of its graceful charm. But the majority of conductors ignore the *atempause* altogether, thus denying to each measure the typical feature which differentiates the waltz from other three-four forms.

Animando, as a particularly definitive indication of increasing emotional expression, is occasionally prospered if the *crescendo* implied is postponed until the *accelerando* has had opportunity to enliven the movement. For example, in an *animando* of sixteen bars, my personal tendency is to begin the *crescendo* (graduated carefully *poco a poco*) at approximately the fourth bar. The developing speed of the *accelerando* has already begun to give a fillip to the clause; the delayed *crescendo* then corroborates the invigoration of the whole movement. It is a mistake to evoke all the resources of *animando* always at the start. This is a waste of assets. *Accelerando* and *crescendo* are usually coupled as inseparable units for *animando*. But if they are regarded as distinct forces, each can be invoked to contribute more specifically and progressively to the developing momentum. Increasing speed intimates growing eagerness. A notable increase of loudness, presaging at least a preparatory climax, suggests growing conviction and is often advisedly reserved for the concluding phrases of a dramatic sequence.

Therefore it is incumbent upon the young conductor to study the psychological relations of speed and quantity. The partly concurrent application of these forces, and the synchronous use of both throughout an entire clause, produce different effects. A student should scrutinize his scores with this fact in mind. Furthermore, in rehearsals, he should experiment with his group, trying one and another of the many possible ratios of tempo and quantity. For instance, animando by *acceleration* only is quietly effective, not only because it invigorates without overloading listening ears, but because it is rarely undertaken. Similarly, *rallentando* without *diminuendo*, or with slight *crescendo*, and *diminuendo a tempo* are unusual nuances rich in aesthetic value and "elegant as simplicity."

Grande pausa, like other dramatic expedients, if exaggerated or frequently employed, defeats genuine dramaturgy. Some conductors (they are few nowadays) have found delight in sudden cutoffs, and prolonged tacets after a climax. The nineteenth-century Italian school of conducting favored, at least in practice, these startling periods of silence. Trite melodrama was often the garish result. In opera, there is of course a real need for recurring long *fermata* rests, the fast-changing emotional moods, the importunities of theatrical "stage business," and the timing of entrances, exits, etc., that concur to require such pauses. In the general repertoire, however, the occasions on which a *grande pausa* promotes aesthetic effect are relatively few.

The considerations offered in the preceding pages regarding the modification of tempos, while avoiding an arbitrary series of peremptory suggestions, seem adequate to interest young conductors in the principles, musical, aesthetic, and psychological, involved in the relations of melody to tempo. Precepts which will always be academically sound and effective in practice cannot be formulated. Interpretation has a surface technique, it is true, and for this precepts are valuable guides. But the influence of tempo and the modifications of tempo on a musical presentation cannot be regulated by surface technique; these depend on the equation of the surface forms and the subsurface content. Logic and psychology and the exigencies of the moment will suggest to the true and studious musician the subtle nuances which are needed to make a performance convincing. Even Mendelssohn, bitterly opposed to interpolated modifications, was moved, at various performances, to select various prevailing tempos. Subsurface interpretation is not mathematical. Therefore it cannot be compressed into theorems; it is a matter for mind and mood, the imagination and emotions, and the stored-up memories of the subconscious.

Is it possible to develop the susceptibilities and sensibilities of which such interpretative musicianship is the manifestation?

Certainly, no technical processes can be successfully elaborated which will substitute for the psychological activity involved. Much has been written on the question of teaching aesthetic sensitiveness. Can one force spontaneity? Can a pedagogue persuade a pococurante pupil to personality?

The scope of a preceptor's influence is limited by the receptivity of the pupil. Probably the latter can usually be rendered more alert, by expert teaching, to the significance and application of principles. Craftsmanship, the control of technological skills, can be acquired; but it is most improbable that the intuitive realizations of the creative or re-creative artist can be earned by routine study or practice. These are definitely gifts from God.

I am convinced, however, from my wide association with men of many types that the gift of genuine artistry has been more abundantly and diffusively bestowed than its relatively scarce exercise would indicate. It remains a chrysalis in the majority, never developing into the imago. It is easy to pursue technique so avidly as eventually to become satisfied with it, to mistake the means for the end and thus to smother oneself with a false philosophy. It is easy so brilliantly to polish the surface as to mark as inconsequential the consistency of the fibers beneath. One must indeed become master of technical facilities, but one can avert, in the process, the snuffing-out of the poetic light which should be revealed through them. It is certain that one cannot *learn* personality, but it is likewise certain that the average person has much more subliminal quicksilver in his ego than circumstances have permitted him to divulge. Perhaps an inhibition from a childhood experience; a natural undefeated shyness; inadequate, misdirected, or sere pedagogy; lack of opportunity; unthinking acquiescence in the superficial manner of doing things, or any of many possible factors explains why potential artists grow into mere craftsmen. My experience with small boys and those of adolescent age long ago persuaded me that there is infinitely more *art* awaiting opportunity for expression in the natural endowment of our contemporary American youths than the smugness and shallowness of overt mechanical standards permit to mature.

The average musician is at heart much more of a musician than his performance attests. He hides behind the thoughtlessness of the age; he unconsciously appraises exhibitionism, which shows the sheen of the shining surface, as an economic necessity; he pays his rent with technique; he keeps his services in demand by submitting to current standards, and generally he is forced to make the dollar sign and the G clef look amazingly alike.

Given sufficient encouragement and effective pushes in the right direction, the average young musical craftsman may happily discover in his soul the urges and eagerness which have been hiding anesthetized in its fastnesses. He can be inspired to turn his craft into an art. When he is not frightening the big bad wolf away from his back door, he can find consummate joy in mining down below the surface of his musical understanding. At first he may be only surprised to discover such unsuspected richness of intuition, but presently he will be on fire to manifest and share it through the particular medium of his art.

The average young conductor on the podium today is not a bona fide artist. He is an artisan using the tools and resources of a musician. But he is a potential artist. It is necessary for music and for himself for him to believe this. *If only he can be persuaded to have a look at his real self, if only he can be converted from the heresy that music dwells in toto on clefs, in bas-relief designed of long and short notes, if only he can realize that the life and utter loveliness of music sing to his heart as well as to his ears, he will soon graduate into the ranks of those for whom music is an almost divinely blessed instrumentality.*

CHAPTER IV

DYNAMICS

The General Strategy for Dealing with Tonal Volume

A THOROUGH understanding of *quantity* in all its aspects is indispensable to true musicianship. Ignorance or misunderstanding of the implications of tonal volume is a hostile impediment to aesthetic interpretation. Confusion about suitable degrees of sonority inhibits artistic performance. Quantity is the principal custodian of quality, quality being the *sine qua non* of effective musical utterance. Quality is influenced by quantity because there are certain levels of dynamic expression where timbres necessarily lose character. Furthermore, rhythm depends altogether upon quantity levels for the appositions of stress and slack. Finally, lyric music cannot reveal its poetic fluency, dramatic music cannot convey its emotive content, and contrapuntal forms are deprived of their clarity, unless the modifying agencies of softness and loudness are deftly employed.

In this chapter, attention is directed to the general relationship of quantity to musical validity. The considerations presented here are the background for memoranda offered in ensuing chapters. The technique for dealing with *tension, dissonance, timbre, canon and fugue, ornamentation, high and low rilievos, arsis and thesis* is merely the tactical procedure which grows out of the inherent interdependences of melody and quantity. Student conductors must address themselves to these major relationships if their technique in particular styles is to be more than a superficial manner of conducting. This chapter essays to simplify an extensive and ostensibly complex subject in the following divisions:

Melos and dynamic force.

The choice of a prevailing dynamic panel for a composition or a single movement.

The degrees of *crescendo* and *diminuendo* appropriate to a piece as a whole and to particular phrases.

Subitos, impacts, and indirect attack.

Quantity in the treble, including *harmonics* in unison octaves.
Quantity in the bass and interior parts.
Approaches to preparatory and real climaxes.
Climax in general.
The fall-off from climaxes.

The application of *crescendo* and *diminuendo* in the *arsis-thesis* organization of polyphony is examined in Chapter VIII.

MELOS AND DYNAMIC FORCE

Notes in musical sequence, their quality, their temporal value, and their dynamic force are the elements of melody. When more than one melodic line is involved, the counterpoint of notes, the counterpoint of timbres, the counterpoint of rhythms, and the counterpoint of dynamics present for synthesis a complexity of forces. In this circumstance, the sum total of potential music is greater than the musical endowment of unaccompanied monody. It exceeds, too, by its merging of linear independences, straightforward homophony, which is, of course, one melody in the perspective of associated vertical harmony. The four counterpoints add cumulatively to the vitality of music. Artistic competition is in progress. Notes vie to outsparkle other notes; heterogeneous timbres, blended so as to appose rather than oppose one another, contend to make interesting rival contributions to an over-all uniformity; variously designed temporal patterns throughout the parts, arousing aesthetic curiosity, whet the appetite for combinations of complex rhythms; properly distributed diversities of tonal sonority make more discernible the sparkling of the notes, the sly cessions of one tone color to another, and the irenic coordination of mixed metric measurements.

In polyphony (cf. Chapter VII), the counterpoint of dynamics is the sentinel of the other contrapuntal crisscrossings and must be studied as an inseparable associate of these. Later schools of composition, however, being often meshes of interlaced styles (homophony with strict, free, desultory, or quasi-contrapuntal episodes) require that dynamic amplitude be analyzed as a separate and singly important interpretative resource. The structural features of pure polyphony in the score insist upon the dynamic fluctuations which *sua sponte* they disclose. Written into the curve lines of the separate parts, they are immediately perceivable to singers and conductors alike. But the efficacy of quantitative modulations in more modern music depends upon a conductor's personal perception of subsurface elements and his ingenuity in conveying his conclusions to the performers. The competency of a choral or orchestral unit to exemplify the nuances intrinsic to polyphonic scores and to fulfill a conductor's intentions in later music is taken charitably for granted. This is subject matter for *choral technique*.

Quantity is a qualification of sound which, measurable by logarithmic units (decibels), affects audibility, definition of tonal contours, and the pleasant or unpleasant reactions of listeners. Sounds can be so soft as to fail to reach the otic nerve, unless amplified by some device analogous to the loud-speaker. Conversely, they can be so strident or clamorous as to create confusion and bedlam in the middle ear. Melody is not recognizable if hushed below the threshold of perceptibility. Nor do the voices of the Muses please the ears of the average man in shrill, stentorian, or thunder-tongued uproar. There is a compass of soft and loud within which music functions agreeably for one social caste, but different minimums and maximums may impress other more or less cultured castes. It is probably true that, normally, the higher the degree of culture, the less tolerable is the noisy bombast of sustained loudness.

Acousticians have been zealously conducting research on the relationships of sound quantity to radio, the public-address system, and the cinema. They have discovered important facts about the definitiveness of radiofied sounds and the overloading of the mechanical ears of microphones. All conductors should be aware of the interesting data published frequently in journals of the acoustical engineering fraternity. *Susurrante* intonations are found to lack adequate address to the ear, being minus the energy required to stimulate hearing and to define vocal or instrumental lines unless fortified by so much loud-speaker reinforcement as to sacrifice timbre and its aesthetic communications. *Fortissimo* delivery, on the other hand, muddles the microphone, especially in high treble *rilievos*.

Much of what the acousticians have learned about broadcasting and recording musical performances must be deemed applicable to non-amplified music in churches, concert halls, and opera houses.

Obviously, sound physicists are concerned primarily with the acoustical bases and cognate phenomena of quantity. In this discussion cognizance is taken in every relevant instance of the acoustical derivations and pertinences of dynamic strength. But the function of quantity in making music musical extends beyond the scope of mechanical physics to the field of psycho-physiology. There are properties in tone quantity which stimulate different reactions, both conscious and subconscious, in different listeners. However, it is clear that soft sounds are generally conducive to the activity of the softer emotions, while loud sounds are plausibly related to agitation, determination, or heroics. Little interest has been manifested, within my range of information, about the preter-physical emotiveness of softness and loudness, and the intermediate degrees of quantity by which the one approaches the other. A bibliography on this topic is still to be prepared. The psychic effects of *subitos* and *poco a poco* furnish a broad field for research.

Physiologists know how the organ of Corti functions when its delicate filaments are activated. Possibly they understand why these remain as passive as possible to *pianissimo* stimulus, are agitated only to a medium degree by *mezzo-forte,* and shudder with shock when loud *subitos* or prolonged *molto fortissimos* suggest analogy to seismic tremors. Probably neurologists have a technical vocabulary for discoursing of the influence of the extreme panels of the diagram of dynamics on the nervous system and of the scarcely discernible effect of panel No. 3. Except for the monotony which develops from habitual use of No. 3, the reaction of listeners to this panel is generally neutral, for No. 3 is a safety zone where colorlessness, harmlessness, ineffectiveness, and all the other whitish qualities have found a stronghold of imperturbability. I am satirizing panel No. 3 because multitudes of musicians are pitiably nostalgic when coerced into performing elsewhere; they feel at home in No. 3 and want to be at home. Perhaps, too, there are some psychologists who have written clearly about the reasons for the singular effects of the dynamic panels on aesthetic sensibilities.

Nevertheless, the information which such specialists may have acquired has not been compressed into compact form. Most likely, the average conductor would regard such data as extraneous subject matter. He does not fret because knowledge about such items is not easily obtained. In fact, he doesn't fret about quantity at all. He is almost impervious to its importance. This is one of the outstanding causes of the mediocrity which is weakening contemporary musical performance. Quantity and force, properly understood and sagaciously used, promote the fine elements of quality; improperly understood and applied at random, they cooperate to steal from quality its artistic rights, and to violate therefore the fundamental purposes of music. Although the young conductor is harassed by many importunate needs, he must seek information from specialists and note pertinent material for collateral and leisurely study.

THE CHOICE OF A PREVAILING DYNAMIC PANEL

The happy choice of a prevailing dynamic level for a particular piece is often due to simple good luck. A conductor who is normally inadvertent to the aesthetics of quantity sometimes guesses correctly. True artistry, however, is not sired by chance or conjecture. It is the result of applying principles and agencies properly to performance. Valid formulae, if unapplied in practice, have only academic value.

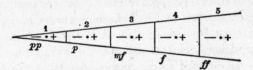

Fig. 26.—Diagram of Dynamic Panels.[1]

There are many books dealing with the theory of music. These tell of the safe fulcrum upon which music can move as an art. The qualities of individuality which add to aesthetic conducting must never contradict principles. Chronic guessing about quantity, and especially about the prevailing level of quantity for short compositions or single movements of a lengthy opus, is an irrefutable proof of inadequate musicianship.

Perspective is of constitutional importance in painting and music. The painter must establish a convincing field of view, the musician a convincing range of audition. Colors, tints, and shades are also determining influences on the truth of a picture. One need not be an expert appraiser of paintings to recoil from the falseness of violent daubs or immiscible miscellanies of offensive gaudiness. Similarly, dynamics affects the truth of a musical exposition, the tawdriness of noisy bombast smearing the fair contours of melody for the average listener and the music critic alike. Not infrequently painters and musicians fail to concentrate sufficiently on both perspective and

---

[1] Cf. Finn, *The Art of the Choral Conductor* (Boston: Birchard, 1939), pp. 200 *et seq.*

color. One who is careless of either is usually careless of both. Recently I watched a professional painter brushing his adieu on a canvas. He was finishing a picture which, he presumed, had captured that *something* that makes the shore line and the seascape at Carmel Bay, California, so overwhelmingly majestic, so eloquently aesthetic in its total of a thousand facets of the strange and familiar, so persuasive of spiritual aspirations, and so suggestive of the conflicts of spiritual experience. The painter seemed smugly satisfied with his portrayal. He possessed facile technique of a sort. He could draw adroitly and fill in with paint. He had a passable sense of dimensional largeness and smallness. But the *something* of Carmel Bay had eluded his perception with a pathetic altogetherness, leaving no clue on the canvas as to what or where it might be. In reality the *something* is the synthesis of many details which, being recorded in a painting, must merge in natural perspective and balance one another naturally. His perspective was wrong. The horizon on canvas, in spite of factual regularity far out from shore, danced to and fro, bringing the far and near capriciously close together and distorting proportions.

We have all listened to conductors attempting the portrayal of musical subjects with the same unconscious ignoring or evading of perspective and color. The fact that the painter at Carmel showed rocks, stretches of almost-sand, gulls, pelicans, and sandpipers and other minutiae did not redeem the futility of his effort. He missed the essence of the scene. Nor is the conductor who merely keeps flutes and fiddles, trebles and tenors twittering tunes in time less ineffectual. He can't hear the music for the notes.

Wagner, in his treatise *On Conducting*, argues for a proper perspective. Although he must have been acutely aware that this is predicated upon quantitative proportions as well as upon tempo, he practically ignores the influence of dynamics. His monograph is full of satire against destructive paces. He lashes many a contemporary conductor. He burns in effigy those whom he condemns for stupid inadvertence to tempo. But he spares the offenders against appropriate use of quantity. He snubs them, perhaps, by omitting to discuss the co-decisive effects of their derelictions. He makes one feeble complaint in this connection, viz., that the majority of performers in his day recognized only two dynamic panels, *piano* and *forte*. Perhaps elsewhere in his several prose comments on music he has accorded *Die Basis aller Dynamik* more consideration. These treatises are not available at this writing (1942).

The placing of melodies and harmonies in poorly proportioned perspective denaturalizes music. The loudness proper to a military march is unsuited to a liturgical motet. A prayer loses character in the gusto of a paean. The "Kyrie" and "Dies Irae" of Mozart's "Requiem" are both marked *forte* in some editions, but it is self-evident that the pleadings of the "Kyrie" and the ominous predictions of the "Dies Irae" should not be uttered with equal sonority. Just what does *forte* designate? It is far from clear, for relative, not absolute levels of volume are implied in the accepted nomenclature of dynamics. There is no acoustico-metronome by which practical conductors can even broadly pre-hear ratios of amplitude. There are a *minus* side and a *plus* side in each of the quantity panels. Obviously, if the "Kyrie" is to plead in a tone consistent with reverent and humble petitioning, it should be sung in the *piano* panel, reaching the *minus* side of *forte* only in the *stretto*; the "Dies Irae," however, is impressive and threatening only on the *plus* side. The nuances of the former should be toward the left side of the diagram, and those of the latter toward the right.

How, then, may one reasonably be guided by dynamic signs, and how proceed in the absence of these? Even if the signs are admittedly inexact suggestions, they indicate the quantitative proprieties within certain limits; but music of the polyphonic era furnishes no composers' directions and much music of later generations contained few composers' hints as to temporal or dynamic rendition.

Is there a logical method for reasoning about the composers' concepts?

Yes, there are bits of information in the compositions themselves which can at least head a conductor in the right direction.

In vocal music, the text quite generally supplies a reliable clue. Comparison of the mood of a text with concomitant musical features more often than not suggests the appropriate quantity level. Just as in the selection of a principal tempo, so in appointing a norm of amplitude, the conductor needs to search the implications as well as to know the definitions of the words. For example, the word *crucifixus* in a liturgical continuity may be consistently intoned *piano*, since it brings to mind an awesome belief of Christians. At other times, as in the reiterations of the word in Lotti's three great motets, *crucifixus* intimates more than awe. It sums up the cost of human infidelities and seeks to place responsibility for the death of Christ. The word in the Lotti settings also suggests the loud hammering of spikes and clamorous cries of cruelty. Therefore, these motets are effectively presented in a *mezzoforte* to *forte* perspective after the dramaturgical intention of the composer begins, near the start, to manifest itself. In the *Credo, crucifixus* is a tenet of faith and should be declared simply, which in terms of dynamics usually means *piano*. In the motets *crucifixus* is a robust denunciation.

The curve line[2] of melodies and the leanness or fullness of associated harmony and counterpoint give hints of the fitness of one or another quantity panel, not only in vocal music, but in solo and ensemble instrumental compositions of both *program* and *absolute* types.

The curve line of a melody is generally an indication of the dynamic energy with which it may fittingly be expressed. If it is simple, as in plain song, medieval and Palestrinesque styles, a gentle and never more than moderate sonority seems to be indicated. Frequently, too, a melody in prevailing conjunct motion is patently more lyrical rather than intense and is thus prospered by conservative volume. But curve lines spanning notably high and low *rilievos,* and arcs of melody that move in nervous disjunct motion are unmistakably signs that agitation is involved, that the emotive urgency is strong, and therefore that the restraint of lyric utterance will prove inhibitive.

The character of the harmony and counterpoint surrounding thematic material is a further clue to the dynamic requirements of a piece. Sketchy vertical harmonizations do not usually teem with dramatic purport. It would be surprising and droll to observe a listener convulsed with deep emotion by a two-part canzonet. Memories and associations stirred up by such a fragile *morceau* might account for emotional display, but the musical structure itself is not endowed with qualities to such end. Three-part vertical music is scarcely less shallow than two-voiced simplicities. Nor can four-part chordings produce much theatrical effect consistently through many measures, even when exotic harmonies are employed. The wide interstices separating, as a rule, the single parts of standard *S.A.T.B* compositions permit ready escape to elements which if pent up by six- or eight-part chords would strengthen the emotional character of a piece. Therefore, lean vertical harmony, suggesting the absence of dramatic excitation, invites congruously lean dynamic expression. A lengthy series of full chords, on the contrary, indicating that a

[2] This phase of the subject is isolated for special examination in Chapter V.

score is charged with emotional fervor, probably relies upon louder delivery for full effect.

When the harmony is thin but contrapuntal, the autonomous voice lines furnish energy to the whole which frail homophony cannot supply. Note against note and rhythm against rhythm reveal some measure of structural agitation. This may be construed as calling for exposition in a higher panel, perhaps No. 3 with nuances down to No. 2 and up to the minus side of No. 4. It has already been noted that the text which the music, vertical or horizontal, seeks to impress upon the emotional understanding is a safer guide to dynamic aptness than other considerations. Nevertheless, contrapuntal structure is itself indicative of greater resources in the music than homophony and, it seems fair to conclude, except in impersonal *a cappella* numbers, requires a more ample perspective.

Candidly, it must be admitted that absolute criteria may not reasonably be proposed for a fortunate choice of dynamic levels. If it is arbitrary and futile to dictate rules for tempo, it is stupid to write specifications for volume perspectives. Here, as elsewhere, the conductor must be analyst and logician, guided by as many clues as may be assembled, including those which are pertinent, by analogy, from the serial of the four P's.[3]

A precaution of great value to the average conductor is *to establish a dynamic perspective of slightly smaller dimensions than he favors temperamentally*. Almost invariably and unsuspectingly he will broaden its proportions as the performance proceeds. If one must err, let the error be toward the left side of the diagram. It is more readily reparable there. *Piano* is much more docile than *forte*.

The general tendency has long been to favor loudness. A premium seems to have been set on volume. Perhaps the din and shrillness of modern civilization have forced their way into music. The average chorus sings with poor quality and the average orchestra forfeits much of its timbre color mainly because quantity is deemed a virtue. Although good vocalism is conceded by all to be the primary criterion of singing, it has been almost universally sacrificed to modern standards of volume. Instruments are habitually urged beyond the dynamic limits of their inherent euphonies. Noisy impacts and trenchant delivery have turned slacks into stresses, metrical movements into garbled prose, and rhythm generally into uniform *marcato*. The

---

[3] *Slowness* and *loudness* are modally cognate, whereas *easily moving tempos* and *lighter dynamics* tend generally to promote corresponding effects.

doctrine of anacrusis is to many an unsuspected principle. The prevailing energy level of current music making is *mezzo-forte plus* with pseudo modulations toward *forte* and *fortissimo*.

In carelessly drafted tonal perspectives balance is threatened and often lost. Thus many voices and instruments fail to make their proper contribution to the ensemble. The potentially louder vocal and orchestral agencies are actually so loud as equivalently to silence those less resonantly endowed. The majority of choruses or orchestras fail to function with sufficient tonal tranquillity to create an atmosphere fit for aesthetic communication. Heavy voices assault chants and polyphonies in chancels; diapasons, gambas, cornopeans, and mixtures toil laboriously in organ lofts; choirs and instruments tote hullabaloo onto many concert stages; the technical virtuosity of great *a cappella* units and symphony orchestras is buried under masses of sound. The mesmerism of music is challenged on all sides by extravagant noise. Treble parts are super-shrill with acuteness while the stridor of competing voices or instruments foments harsh misconstruction in the bass, obscuring the definition of inner parts.

Blend of qualities and a flexible composition of participating forces are impossible when the chronic level of tonal strength is No. 3 plus. Long experience and observation have convinced me that a conductor's attitude about tonal amplitude is the determining factor in producing results commensurate with the resources of any vocal or instrumental group. Rigid, strained, and harsh intonation is the inevitable effect of rehearsing and performing all the year round at high quantity levels. Interpretatively, chronic expression in the upper panels robs the greatest music of suavity, suggestion, and suasion.

The quantity background of the average musical performance is injuriously loud. The latencies of music are its most potent forces. These are reluctant to appear in the midst of confusion.

Panels 1, 2, and 3—with *piano plus* as a normal background—should limit the scope of dynamics for the young conductor until mastery of quality and rhythm has inured him to economy of quantity. Apprenticeship at the left will train him to be selective at the right side of the diagram.

Mezzo-forte plus, forte, and *fortissimo* must be invited only purposefully to serve obvious dramatic needs.

Conductors who concentrate on quality rarely transgress the proprieties of quantity.

Degrees of Crescendo and Diminuendo

Having selected a prevailing volume level, the conductor must next estimate the degrees of louder and softer which will be appropriate for the simpler nuances. The relative extent of all variations in volume cannot be surveyed in advanced, since convincing dynamic modulations, just like nuances of tempo, frequently grow out of the promptings of the moment. It is advantageous, however, speculatively to set limits for the compass of variations: a *crescendo* in "Ave Maria" never to exceed a *minus forte*; a *diminuendo* in a Bach fugue never to reach *pianissimo*, etc. When attention is called to the item, few find difficulty in recognizing the incongruity of lowering a *plus forte* level to *pianissimo* whenever a slight decrease of quantity is indicated. Nor does normally good aesthetic judgment need to be reminded that every *crescendo* is not intended to be a push through to *fortissimo*. Nevertheless, the current casualties in the concert arena as well as in the chancel warrant the counsel to *predetermine tentative boundaries for all dynamic variations.*

Nuances of quantity and tempo are the garniture of musical expression, if deftly applied. They trim, twine around, and thus adorn the plainness of monotony. But if the garnishing is bizarre, the result is sure to be inartistic and even fantastic. The majority of experienced conductors seem possessed of good taste in this regard. Curiously, many are more discriminating in balancing the tints and shades to a prevailing quantity evenness than in choosing the mean level itself. But we are all familiar with the white-black-bird conductor who, with baton in beak, flies precipitately between *pianissimo* and *plus fortissimo* at every implausible opportunity.

Suppose, for example, that panel No. 3 has been selected as the quantity background. When indicated thus,

the *crescendo* and *diminuendo* would exceed aesthetic ratios if permitted to extend above *minus forte* and lower than *plus piano* respectively. A greater increase or decrease would upset proportion and poise. Thus, in this instance, *minus forte* and *plus piano* should be established in advance as the compass of the simple modulations.

Longer and more dramatic modifications, usually spanning many bars and marked thus,

should be graded differently, the *crescendo*, if from a No. 3 level, hinting at a *plus forte* or *fortissimo* apex, and the *diminuendo* from the same level suggesting attenuation to a *minus piano* or *pianissimo*. If the *diminuendo* is from the *plus forte* apex of the *crescendo*, it should obviously be discontinued at the No. 3 level, unless the composer has signified otherwise by adding *p* or *pp* to the symbol. Whenever modifications are indicated by conservative markings, the conductor must be on the alert lest the alterations in volume defeat artistic purpose.

I suggest, without being disagreeably opinionated, that the average conductor and the average soloist would be greater assets to their respective arts if they would reduce the prevailing robustness of their performances by twenty-five per cent and limit by fifty per cent the compass of their modifying vagaries.

I confess that for some years, fearing various and insidiously destructive aspects of quantity, I led a narrow and eremitical musical life in the quietness of panels No. 1 and 2, with an occasional bold adventure in No. 3. Blaming even well-behaved loudness (there probably is this kind of loudness) for every choral dereliction, I unwittingly used the old whipping-boy scheme, not indeed chastising small choristers, but vigorously flogging the *idea of quantity* rather than disciplining other specific causes of defects, as Pope Clement VIII is alleged to have flogged d'Ossat and Perron (later cardinals) for the transgressions of King Henry IV of France. Life in the *pianissimo* hermitage having become too monotonous and some control of dynamic strength having accrued, I began eventually to appreciate the importance of the upper panels in the aesthetic scheme. I have no regrets for the "days in the desert," for I learned then what later decades in the dramatic *fortes* has confirmed, viz.: *that loudness is not only fiercely hostile to choral technique*, but that in interpretative musicianship *it is the principal and ubiquitous peril to artistry*.

Shades of expression imparting meaning, feeling, and color to phrases are contrived normally by simple modifications of tonal volume. Extensive changes are more frequently than not incongruous. Far-reaching *crescendos* and vanishing *diminuendos* intimate marked degrees of varying intensity; but these intensities are usually clearly indicated in the score. *Subitos*, loud and soft, ordinarily connote sudden perception of and reaction to an acute emotional excitation. Certainly the broad resources of dynamic emphasis are needed to convey the dramatic content of a long *poco a poco* or the histrionism of *sforzando* and *subito pianissimo*, but regularly recurring short *crescendos* and *diminuendos* involve only slight movement to the right or left of a prevailing quantity locale.

The force of emotional appeal may be strengthened or weakened by nuance. If shades of difference in degrees of loudness are replaced by notable *alterations*, the element of surprise makes its appearance. Surprise is a theatrical resource invoked artistically only for a specific and dramatic purpose. Wide fluctuations in the quantity of normally proceeding lyric music impair its validity in the ratio of the inopportune agitation or violence.

It is important for conductors to conserve psychological and aesthetic values by restricting frequently recurring shadings to inconsiderable proportions.

Elegance of style is enhanced or impaired by one's habitual attitude toward volume in the coloring of short phrases.

"Style is the dress for thoughts," wrote Chesterfield to his son. Broadly, good style is the synthesis of clarity, circumstantial fitness, imagery, and elegance. The characteristic to be noted here is elegance. This is a grace which, unessential to lucidity or to temporary aptness (probably it is more closely allied with imagery), adds refinement to literary and musical expression. In music, clarity accrues from the underlining of melodies in the transparency of a concerted whole, aptness from opportune adjustments to the variable influences assembled in the serial of the four P's. The elegance with which a conductor conveys a composer's thoughts and his own apperception of them develops from cultivated (sometimes intuitive) appreciation of the less patent reciprocities of contiguous nuances. Both literature and musical performance fall short of greatness if clarity and circumstantial suitability are not complemented by the glow and afterglow of unaffected elegance. All mediums of art need that extra quantum of magnetic address which elegance imparts. Elegance, the refinement of essential details, must not be interpreted narrowly, for sometimes it is manifest in the persuading of boldness to a more convincing boldness or ugliness to a more ugly ugliness.

The word *elegance* being used in its specific relation to the niceties of dynamic fitness, it is found condemning inapt levels of prevailing quantity and all avid ill-proportioned processions to and recessions from established levels. Masefield doesn't find much music in "Bugles that whinnied, flageolets that crooned, and strings that whined and grunted" nor Dryden much peace when "The trumpet's loud clangor excites us to arms." Shakespeare fancied that music "will sing the savageness out of a bear," but much of the vociferation which counterfeits vocalism can only provoke madness in bears and hectic flurry in normal human beings.

In 1742, Johann Stamitz, a Bohemian, initiated a new scope for dynamic fluctuations. Perhaps, considering the era, they would more exactly be termed vagaries. He experimented with the Mannheim Orchestra. "True," writes Alfred Einstein, "musicians had long before understood how to vitalize their melody by dynamic means for the sake of expressiveness and animation in performance. But with the Mannheimers a wealth of tone-gradations between extremes of *fortissimo* and *pianissimo* and abrupt dynamic contrasts formed an essential effect of their art, which they exploited to the point of abuse and deliberate disregard of the natural accent of music. This was the 'Mannheim mannerism' against which Leopold Mozart once warned his son."[4]

The disapproval which Leopold Mozart and many colleagues hurled at the "Mannheim mannerism" failed to stem its progressive acceptability. Although Haydn, both Mozarts, and Gluck did not favor the new scale of dynamic intensities, Beethoven and a host of contemporaries saluted it as a happy displacement of musty medievalism. Drama was beginning to show music a new course to follow. The Stamitz concept of dynamic effectiveness antedated the style of composition to which it could be appropriately applied. The expression needs of earlier music and of the idioms of his time are quite evidently well served by the moderation and restraint which the "Mannerheim mannerism" was developed to supplant. The influence of Stamitz waned, after a few generations, for Wagner complained that German orchestras played consistently in only two panels, *piano* and *forte*; but the great man of Bayreuth restored it, and

[4] Alfred Einstein, *A Short History of Music* (New York: Knopf, 1938), p. 153.

it flourishes today, here and there like a brilliant flower, but rather more generally like a destructive tare.

The rendition of a considerable repertory of nineteenth- and twentieth-century music, notably in operatic and purely orchestral forms, is improved by the great reaches of theatrical dynamics, but a more considerable repertory is commonly frustrated by indiscriminate use of the Stamitz-Wagner *crescendo, diminuendo*, and *subito*. Violent alternations of loud and soft, tilting to heights and depths, mock the simplicity of pattern melodies. The smoothness of lyric music is disturbed by sudden fanfare or under-breath murmurings.

Generally, in this epoch, the misapplication of dynamics is music's greatest liability, which earnest conductors must collaborate speedily to liquidate.

Often, phrases of several bars are set into the fabric of a complete movement as a commentary on or reflection about preceding periods. Such an interpolation may require its own special quantity level. If it is an inconsequential interlude, the level may be lowered or raised only moderately. If, on the contrary, it seems to connote great depth of feeling, quantity should be adjusted accordingly, less to pensive interludes, more to exclamatory, elating, or hortatory parentheses. It pleases me personally to hear episodes of fugues, isolated from the main activities of subject and countersubject, making their diverting comments with less sonority.

Repetitions in unmarked music often profit, without offense to the composer, by delivery in a panel below the original, after the approved manner of madrigal singing.

Copying and invariably applying another's characteristic mode of nuance has all the weaknesses and inadequacies of rote tracing, being a left-handed effort to duplicate the effect of an original. The original came from the inside, out; the copy starts and remains on the outside. Copies are almost always only imitations of surface features. *Crescendos* and *diminuendos* built on another's processes, reflecting no inner urges of the conductor of the moment, are lamentably sterile. One must *sense* what was in the mind of the originator to produce a living replica. In readings of symphonies, performances of oratorios, and shadings of arias the deadening influence of the appetite for copying is apparent. Signor X developed a mighty climax, beginning *piano* at measure 112, culminating with great power at measure 128. Signor M follows the same procedure and develops at measure 128 not a climax but only an empty *fortissimo*!

Even in the Responses of the Liturgy the ineffectualness of mere copying is evident. In addition to a uniform banality of harmony which organists of Catholic and Anglo-Episcopalian churches have inherited from some secret source, the supposedly dynamic finesse accorded to some liturgical sentences is enervating. Sometime, somewhere, perhaps at Canterbury or perhaps at St. Paul's, London, a choirmaster softened to a whisper, very effectively, the Response at Evensong: "And take not Thy Holy Spirit from us." Similarly, the short doxology at the end of Psalms and Canticles in the Catholic Liturgy, Gloria Patri ("Glory be to the Father and to the Son and to the Holy Ghost"), was sung *pianissimo* in contrast to *forte* verses of the Psalms, and adjudged to be reverent in some particular church (probably not a monastic church). But the almost invariable susurration of the Episcopalian response and the Catholic Gloria Patri give evidence of superficial copying of an old exemplar and teem with unreality. A variety of dynamics in answering the versicles of the various Liturgies enhances the contribution of music to ritual, but rigidly to follow a plan of dynamics spontaneously adopted by one or more eminent choirmasters is to drown in a shallow stream. Sentimentality, at best a mawkish nursing of emotional weakness, always on the verge of tears and often near the swooning point, is a flaccid imitation of religious ardor.

How frequently are the short classics of secular music ridiculed by out-of-place *crescendos* and *diminuendos*! Ben Jonson's "Drink to me only with thine eyes," caricatured by vocal pantomime at the last word of the stanza, "But thou thereon didst only BREATHE!" And the lonely lamenting in "The Last Rose of Summer" converted into heroic *declamando* by the deeply dyed *forte* at "All thy lovely companions are FADED AND GONE"!

From this point on, frequent references are made to Chorus No. IV of the "German Requiem" of Brahms, the reduced score of which follows. I recommend this number as the keenest choral-orchestral composition in the whole repertory of music for sharpening one's wits about dynamics. It is a code easily decoded. Few musicians who have come to know this number as it must have lived in Brahms' own aesthetico-spiritual consciousness will be found making disastrous blunders with the dynamics of any composition.

The quantity level of the composition as a whole having properly been established at *piano*, the ratios of *crescendo* and *diminuendo* should be consistently small because (1) the music is unfolding a

Chorus No. IV The German Requiem

JOHANNES BRAHMS

Fig. 27.

FIG. 27 (*cont.*).

Fig. 27 (*cont.*).

Fig. 27 (cont.).

Fig. 27 (*cont.*).

Fig. 27 (cont.).

Fig. 27 (*cont.*).

FIG. 27 (cont.).

Fig. 27 (cont.).

pensive text; (2) the climax is delayed to the concluding section; (3) there are four apexes, preliminary to the climax, which must be prepared by slightly increasing degrees of volume. (Cf. the section on Climax, pages 143 ff., for examination of the progressive movement of this number.)

In the matter of slender ratios of change in volume, measures 7-12, 18-24, 47-48, 55-58 are suggested as meriting careful study. The extending of any of these and similar *crescendos* beyond *minus forte* would invoke so much loudness as to deprive the number of its meditative character, the *thought* not being sufficiently evolved to thrive in sonority. The curve line (see Index) of the melody also indicates, by its simplicity, that the increase in volume should be sparing. The short undulatory *crescendos* and *diminuendos* of this and similar lyrico-dramatic compositions are the important resources for developing a piece to its most telling moment. The rise and fall on the single notes in measures 158, 162, 164 is a key to the efficacy of the undulation which Brahms evidently wished for the composition. The mystic loveliness of these single-note inflections depends altogether on the gentleness of the dynamic undulation. Since the alternation of louder and softer upon which the nuance depends is usually either ignored or magnified, I habitually direct attention toward it, for it epitomizes the dynamic trend of the number as a whole.

These single-note nuances and the measures designated in the preceding paragraph are sufficient to inculcate a complete philosophy and schema for minor dynamics, generally. A student will find there the theory of undulation—gentle, wavy motion—implied and the values of its application underlined.

SUBITOS, IMPACTS, AND INDIRECT ATTACK

Subito changes of quantity and the influence of impacts generally require examination here. *Crescendo* and *diminuendo* imply gradual movement from one panel to another. *Poco a poco* modification is disturbing neither to the tenor of a composition nor to the equanimity of an audience, for such unruffled expression establishes natural equations with the reactions of listeners. But the aesthetic equilibrium of people can be readily disturbed by much *sforzando* or *subito pianissimo*. These are, in some measure, startling reagents. Unexpectedness is a quality of experience which promotes satisfaction in some persons but hinders it in others. Furthermore, *subitos* in music may be either encumbrances or helpful expedients, depending upon the method of treatment employed. *Sforzando* in the *plus fortissimo* panel is disastrous to the poetic motion of music when it resembles an explosive blast; it is probably effective in dramatic music as a manifestation of power or a challenge to disagree. In this role, a sudden excess of quantity seems to threaten and browbeat. It can be an all-out dictatorial command to attention.

Sforzando, however, is not always cast in the dramatic role by composers. Conductors often misinterpret its function. A good composer indicates *sfz* only when he wishes to reinforce an idea or to interpolate an associated idea in italics, and by peremptorily emphasizing a note, a chord, or even a measure or two, to stress the relevancy of the interpolation. *Sforzando*, well applied, may be a valuable oratorical means of driving home a principal point.

The sign *sfz* does not always mean a jerky jump to *fortissimo*. The increase of volume should be eased by the same standards of measurement that are reliable in regulating *crescendo* and *diminuendo*. A too lengthy leap is an antic of the exhibitionist, a jump for a jump's sake. The altitude of notes and the timbre of the voices or instruments intoning them help to reveal the degree of sudden stress which they can appropriately sustain. If a single note is in high treble *rilievo* and the intoning timbre pungent, *sfz* should be sounded *minus forte,* for in this panel the carrying power accruing from the pitch vibrations and the piquant overtones of an energetic *klangfarbe* (tone color) address the ear with about the same force as a lower note of a gentler timbre at *fortissimo*. In a *sforzando* chord or series of chords, the proper degree of unprepared loudness, for the sake of artistic congruity, should be related also to the consonance or dissonance of the chord. In the ordinary procedures of music dissonance profits by relatively quiet delivery.

If a chord is a first inversion, the quantity may be greater than when the harmony is poised on the root, for the third, used as bass, seems to explain the increased energy by its odd permeation of the superstructure. The keynote, save in modernistic music, imparts a taken-for-granted feeling and is less expectant of increased animation. A chord on the second inversion, being cousin to a discord, presents the paradox of weakness when strengthened by many decibels.

If *sforzando* chords, knitted closely in harmonic texture, extend to a high treble *rilievo* or if they are crowded into a bass-clef area, they should not be released at *fortissimo*. Great energy is concentrated in a web of harmony at an acute pitch, and meager reinforcement by quantity is adequate to *sforzando* purposes. Full pressure overemphasizes the chords, and the *sforzando* is sure to be intolerably harsh. For example, the progression in Fig. 28 is so self-assertive that a better-than-average conductor would not permit it to exceed *mezzo-*

FIG. 28.

forte. Acuteness of pitch clarifies and intensifies sound so poignantly that the addition of much quantitative power tends to ostracize such a progression from aesthetic association. The same chordal progression written as in Fig. 29 requires restraint for the opposite reason,

FIG. 29.

viz., the slower vibrations of low notes tends to obscure the definition of their respective pitches and to lessen the lucidity normally necessary to music. *Fortissimo* renders opaque bass-clef chords so dense as to reduce them to the acoustical status of noisy thuds. Therefore, in this instance, especially if thick timbres predominate, the conductor must be as conservative as in the instance of acute *rilievo*. *Mezzoforte* for the fractionary second of impact with each chord, followed by immediate recession to *plus piano*, seems to be the safest recommendation, at least theoretically. But in practice the conductor must experiment, weighing the tonal properties of voices and instruments and their particular peculiarities in low areas.

In the *rilievo* lying between Figs. 28 and 29, a *plus forte* or even *fortissimo* may be needed to produce the intended *sforzando*.

Subconscious curiosity is perhaps the first reaction of listeners to *subito pianissimo,* curiosity as to the *why* of the sudden surcease of *forte* affirmations. It is natural to be inquisitive, emotionally if not intellectually, about a swift plunge from a high to a low plane. Curiosity is attended in this circumstance by relief from the tenseness of listening to loudness. In the instant of wondering about the unexpected quiet, the narcotic of *pianissimo,* speedily effective, is a soothing and therefore welcome agent. If presently, however, another mighty *sforzando* ruthlessly arouses, the relaxed nerve centers are again and more violently assaulted. Too many round trips between *fortissimo* and *pianissimo,* disturbing the equipoise of the aesthetic nerves, can create bad habits of expectant listening. People may readily lose sensitiveness to the normal undulations of music and become addicts to alternately exciting and sedative drugs. Some spellbinders are pleased with the illusion that wibble-wobble shouting and whispering are graces of musical oratory. But who among aesthetes has not fidgeted with squirming restlessness trying to guess when a rabble-rouser would next elevate his voice, like Stentor above the battle cries of the Trojan war, and when, suddenly spent, with a mute on vocal cords and resonance chambers closed off, he would resume almost inaudible labial pantomime?

Certainly, there are innumerable moments in great music when both the close apposition of *subitos* to a prevailing level and the bolder effects of *sforzando* and *subito pianissimo* are indispensable to authentic interpretation. Nevertheless, all *subito* contrasts are hazards. It is good policy to be concerned about them. Casual trifling with unnecessary risks hints of poor judgment. Exuberance unchaperoned by circumspection prods conductors to extremes. *Fortissimo sforzando* in outlying *rilievos* is a greater disfigurement than *subito pianissimo.* Refined musicianship proscribes both. We shall serve our art the better if "out of this nettle, danger, we pluck this flower, safety."

High-pressure *sforzando* is one of the glaring defects of current musical performance. Many conductors thoughtlessly disregard the need of relating *sforzando* to the dynamic plane of preceding notes. A *crashing collision* would be a succinct description of the catastrophe, hardly to be averted, of dashing full force, head on into every measure marked *sfz.* The carelessness which permits such collision is to be debited against a chronic inadvertence to the difference between *attack* and *impact.*

In music's nomenclature attack does not connote *assault.* It means simply a clear-cut addressing of notes at the beginning of a beat or subbeat. A musician learns such attack to be an imperative need in the early days of his schooling. Anxiety to meet this need may so dominate his mind as to exclude consideration of various modes of attack. There are three of these modes. The first, the normal mode, is the delivery of all notes without sluggishness and *without dynamic modification*, unless some modification is marked in the score or is demanded by rhythmical stress and slack or by opportune accentuation of syllables. The second mode is attack by impact, i.e., by encountering initial and other notes of phrases eagerly, whether or not unction is implied in the context. The third mode is the *indirect* attack, accomplished by *gliding* into notes which, if addressed brusquely, would contravene the intended smoothness of a period. This method includes a graceful gradation of less quantity, at the moment of address, into slightly increased quantity as the note continues. The process involved is analogous to the *poco crescendo* (without the ensuing *diminuendo*) attack so potentially effective at measures 158, 162, 164 in the "Requiem" of Brahms (cf. page 119).

Many conductors exemplify the first mode consistently. The majority evidently prefer the second mode in spite of consequent solecisms. Few, as far as the evidence is dependable, have discovered the worth of the third mode.

It seems self-evident that none of the modes is always appropriate. The first mode, direct attack without dynamic modification, is normally indicated, and a conductor may reasonably congratulate himself for following this orthodox and righteous practice. But orthodoxy and righteousness can be too inclusive or, if you will, unnecessarily exclusive. I have in mind the severe absolutism which characteristically disparages the poetry of music and cries it down as dangerous whimsicality. It is rather harassing to observe the rigid and embarrassed efforts of an ultra-orthodox conductor as he vainly tries to unfold the naïve untruthfulness of carol yarns, the metaphors of madrigals, and the extravagances of satirical conceits. Personally, I think that a conductor who adheres to the prosaic first mode, often missing the allusions of music, is therefore unsuccessful in revealing its poetic movement.

Attack by impact is effective only when the score calls for it, many improprieties making appearance whenever this second mode of address is due to *laissez-faire* nonchalance.

The third mode is ingratiating and surreptitiously effective. The soft intonation of a long note, followed by development to greater quantity, provides opportunity for such a note to sing its secret thoughts. A conductor must be a discriminating judge of the latent inherences of music to decide the timeliness of this mode of attack. An excellent illustration of the indefinable enhancement which accrues from *gliding into long notes* is found in the sequence of dotted half notes, measures 1-5, and of the still more diffuse prolongations of measures 14 *et. seq.* in the excerpt from Mozart's "Requiem" (page 176). Here the wistful hopefulness, hidden in the words *Recordare Jesu Pie* ("Remember O Kind Jesus") and challenged only furtively by dissonance, is expressed far more devoutly by delicate address at *pianissimo* and a surge to *plus piano* than by a forthright attack at *piano* (which of course is generally *mezzo-forte*). For the gentle rise symbolizes the growing confidence which develops naturally if each sustained note of the prayer *begins humbly*. In his "Requiem," Brahms did not fail to make excellent use of the gliding attack. The long notes in measures 26, 34, and 36 caress the word *lovely* and emphasize the beauty it idealizes by the hardly perceptible stress which this mode of address employs.

Habitual impact with new phrases or the higher notes of a phrase in progress frequently robs a number of its preconceived trend. Direct hitting gives an impression of pounding acquired from an "unlettered Muse." Carefree swinging of choruses and orchestras into always vigorous startings and restartings, entrances and reentrances, at a higher dynamic level than the mood of the moment dictates is one of the inexplicable licenses of many professional conductors. One would be tolerant of such inadvertence in an amateur, but in a professional exponent of the art—a presupposed expert, a tutor of students—inadvertence is neglect and abuse.

The common practice of beginning each successive phrase with a fillip is a childish misapplication of dynamics. It implies lack of discrimination. Sopranos, ending a phrase *diminuendo*, start off again louder. Why? Because they are making a fresh start. Altos, tenors, and basses use booms after punctuation. Why? Why not? Impacts are clearer than commas! Strings, up-bowing delicately, challenge serenity with ensuing down-bows. Why? Often, just because a little something is being finished, going up, and another equally little something is beginning coming down. Horns, essaying a mystic effect, frustrate the aim at every few bars. Why? Because each breath the players take hankers—like new money—for immediate spending.

Musico-psychiatry might offer explanations of such a procedure, but none that would be aesthetically valid.

Habitual collision attacks, even if not over noisy, reveal a chronic condition of *forte* tic for which the conductor should know the therapy. If he is wanting in interest or unequipped to prescribe for the twitchings, the disfiguring commotions will continue and multiply.

If the spasms of *forte* tic were only semi-occasional, they still would be a menace to natural expression. But they are not rare occurrences. They have become regular irregularities of utterance, causing wry grimaces at starting points, pulling stress away from the right words and pushing it onto the wrong, distorting the syllabic structure of language, and diverting phrases, clauses, and whole musical sentences from a semblance of sense. Texts in every category, liturgical, extra-liturgical, and secular, whether poetry or prose, are robbed of elegance by the unwitting thievery of undisciplined impacts. If the vocalists were reciting the texts, they would presumably apply stress naturally to the proper syllables. It is strange that, upon the elevation of recitation to a higher plane of communication—singing —the affliction of *forte* tic begins almost invariably to caricature the rhythm of correct utterance.

This indifference to the effect of undue impact on the basic poetic motion of music is obviously another aspect of the prevalent imperviousness to the requirements of rhythm in general. Harum-scarum bobsledding about, knocking into every snowbank on the course, doesn't give one a good slide. A good slider *glides*, avoiding collisions and consequent upsets. Collisions and upsets have been so long damaging the rhythmical structure of all music, Gregorian, polyphonic, and modern, that the period of its hospitalization may be lengthy. It should not be postponed.

Except when there is a clear reason for adding energy, each succeeding phrase should be intoned with slightly less quantity than that used at the end of the immediately preceding phrase. This is a good prescription, for it provides a conductor with an effective prophylactic against the tic. Many years ago I was fortunate in seizing upon this principle of pedagogy as applicable to the art of conducting: *Never think to secure desired results by indicating what must not be done. Show singers and players precisely what to do.* For example, if I sense that my performers will succumb to tic and stress a note or chord too vigorously, I don't ask them to avoid excessive impact; I say with conviction, "Please mark that note or passage *piano*. Be sure to render it softer than the final note of the preceding phrase."

This simple means of using a positive instead of a negative method in the practice room has proved its worth through many years. By thinking the initial note of a new phrase softer than necessary, the performers will probably deliver it with adequate propriety. There is psychological force behind this sort of pedagogy. I found it extraordinarily helpful in drilling choruses to make real *crescendos* and in inculcating facility in rhythmical accentuation.

The reader might reasonably demur here and, citing the data concerning the accentual needs of rhythm, ask how one may accomplish contradictory ends simultaneously, the opposing ends in this instance being the accentuation of a downbeat and the lightening of a slack syllable when both fall on the same note. How treat the seemingly anomalous association of musical accents with syllabic anacrusis, and vice versa? Such queries are pertinent and demand direct answers.

A conflict between the rhythmical rights of music and text seems to be revealed in such circumstances. Theoretically, the conflict is real; in practice, the strategy of *splitting the difference* can mollify theory so pleasantly that the disagreement may be only a sham battle waged on paper. But if a plan of legitimate compromise is not employed (too rarely is it employed!), the contest will be a blow-for-blow struggle, "a very pretty quarrel as it stands," but a fray very ugly for art. Focus attention upon text or music singly, and concession to the other seems impossible. But place the two media in nice juxtaposition to the unified aesthetic purpose of vocal music and the impasse can be neatly avoided.

There are no absolute rights inherent in language or music. Double negatives are required by some languages to pronounce a negation; in English they make an affirmative. Even the widely accepted conclusions of the physics of sound, over the centuries, have been applied with qualification. Periodicity of tone vibrations always determines pitch, but periodicity in relation to rhythm can be either free or strict, e.g., Gregorian chant or time patterns. Certain vertical arrangements of notes have made beautiful harmonies for one era, but have produced a grievous out-of-tuneness for another.

Organum was delightful in the twelfth century, but its consecutive fifths and octaves affronted later taste. Medieval disapproval of the

tritone and unprepared dissonance ceded to a postponed appreciation of both. Semitones and microtones have been challenging tradition but will not forever be excluded from the order of consonances.

In all the arts, propriety of expression has been determined by the
current understandings of an epoch. Frustration and futility are forecast whenever two art forms are combined with no provisions for
reciprocal concessions, e.g., architecture and sculpture, language and
drama, language and music. Neither music nor language can make
satisfactory contribution to the compound art form, vocal music, if
either is fixed into hardwood formulae by mathematical nails. If
the bard enjoys exemptions by his ancient writ of poetic license, are
not the musician and the singer entitled to corresponding dispensa-
tions?

One may posit as a reasonable basis for an entente between musical
and syllabic interests, that dramatic music will often require the
cession by the text of its accentual rights, and that lyric music will
generally subordinate its rhythmical patterns to syllabification.

We are treating of emphasis here. Dramatic music is pre-eminently
the emphasizing of concepts, pictures, and epics with any or all of the
resources which comprise its histrionic and consequent emotive suasion. Conceived as a theatrical agency, it must be performed accordingly. Its essential content must be defined. The composer presumes
that, in performance, his portrayals, appeals, urgings, and full-circle
swings through the gamut of emotional sensibilities will be duly
interpreted. Otherwise, his melodies, harmonies, and figures will
have lost meaning and acquired a poverty-pale flaccidity. This means,
succinctly, that degrees of volume must not be tempered just because
an unaccented syllable is involved. If music is supplying the dramati-
zation, the text obviously must yield to the music. Language long ago
ceded priority rights to a lesser need, i.e., the caesural pause. Witness
the distortion of pronunciation involved in the scansion of the first
line of Virgil's Aeneid: *Arma virumque canò‖Troiae qui primus ab
oris.* In prose and in simpler poetic forms the word is *càno.* This verse,
in dactylic hexameter with an arsic movement to the pause, seeks
its apex on an unaccented syllable.[5]

If there is a place for dramaturgical effects in vocal music, the

[5] Although poetry was not scanned on an accentual basis in Virgil's era,
the quantitative basis produced the same effect at the caesural pause. At any
rate, a forced mispronunciation of *cano* is a good example of the point
under consideration.

deference of the text to the dynamic requirements of the music must be taken for granted. How absurd to deny drama to melody because the associated syllabification is sometimes impugned! Drama is urgent, proceeding steadily with emotional variations to histrionic climax. Therefore, dramatic music utilizes all available resources, sometimes borrowing with grace, often seizing ruthlessly.

The line of demarcation between dramatic and lyric music cannot be finely drawn. Moreover, in compositions dominantly of either type frequent episodes in the style of the other are interspersed. Furthermore, if the traits of these two genera of music could always be identified and listed accurately, such cataloguing would be of scanty import, for *conductors must, by the urgency of spontaneous artistry, reveal their personal reactions to music, provided that*

1. *they know intimately the structural characteristics of the composition to be performed, and*
2. *they do not neutralize an obvious intention or contravene a specific direction of the score.*

Lyric vocal music, being a more refined because a more restrained medium than dramatic music, exacts greater delicacy in adjusting opposing claims to accentual preferment. Lyric vocal music may be defined, broadly, as a *contabile* embellishment of words, the investiture with melody of texts which otherwise would be simply inflected. Thus, lyric music generally needs fitting to the words. Greater care on the part of composers to preserve the lyricism of their works by indicating the relation of unaccented syllables to accented notes, and vice versa, might influence conductors to cultivate appreciation of this widely ignored aspect of musical exercise. As a rule, composers fail to include in their scores the accentual signs which would be helpful to this end. Conductors are left on their own to discern and regulate the precedence of musical or syllabic stress.

In a high percentage of instances, *downbeats* associated with slack syllables are permitted to distort the contours of words to unseemly disfigurement. The average soloist is unconcerned if the rhythmical continuity of a verbal phrase is disrupted. Many conductors pay no heed to careless and obviously unnecessary affronts.

I beg to call attention again to the almost universal disregard of *quantity* as a basic influence on aesthetic performance.

Nowadays we all have daily opportunities to study the ruinous effects of misapplied quantity. For example: I recently listened to a mechanically excellent recording of a celebrated "Requiem" as sung by a celebrated chorus in concert with a celebrated orchestra under the baton of a celebrated conductor. The experience was discomfiting. It was discouraging too, because the four-ply "celebrated" heralded a peerless performance. I was forced to ask myself quite dismally: "Are we making no progress toward an understanding of the rudiments of poetic motion which is an indispensable property of lyric music? Are we doomed to remain forever unacquainted with the comeliness of beautiful language uttered becomingly with seemly melody? Why do conductors permit the hardly interrupted sequences of thumps and impacts and destructive derangements which make of every beat and every syllable, in whatever dynamic panel, an inconsonant and inconsistent attribute?"

The recording of the "Introit" and "Kyrie" revealed an ensemble unconsciousness of the difference between dramatic and lyric expression. The "Introit" is a calm wishing prayer that the dead may rest in sweet peace, and the "Kyrie" an entreaty to God to forgive the derelictions of us who live. Forthright drama in such music is affectation and bombast. But the recording metamorphosed the prayers into operatic and turgid declamation. The text is pure Latin and Greek prose. The final syllables of the words used are never accented save in the unescapable fervor of impetuously dramatic exclamation. Without musical or psychological reason every final syllable was proclaimed as though it were a high-strung Wagnerian monosyllable. In lieu of *Rĕquiem aetĕrnam dŏna ēis Dŏmine, et lŭx perpĕtua lŭceat ēis*, and *Kȳrie, Chrĭste Elēison*, I heard the text garbled melodramatically into *Requiĕm aeternăm donă eis Dominĕ, et lux perpetuă lucĕat eis*, and *Kyriĕ, Christĕ Eleison.*[6] If this were the performance of an amateur group I would forego reference to it. But the concurrence of a *celebrated* chorus, orchestra, and conductor in the production warrants both reference and critical censure. The participants were reasonably assumed to be setting forth a standard of high excellence. They failed in an essential of interpretation that should be exemplified even in the performance of less renowned forces.

The suggestion that zealous students listen carefully to the olios of dynamics that turn radio and phonographic *exemplary* renditions

[6] It would be more accurate to report that *each* syllable was stressed and the final syllables brought more vigorously *en dehors.*

into minstrel shows of rhythmical oddities is one of the most salutary hints in these pages.

To revert to the technique by which a real conflict between musical and textual accentuation may be avoided: it should be remembered that the first fractionary second of attack establishes its character, promoting the interests of words or notes or discommoding them. If one glides into a downbeat, a slack syllable is not disturbed, for this procedure creates the impression of consonance between syllable and note. The swelling of the note after its indirect, quiet address is too late to dislocate the rhythm of the word but not too late to give the downbeat eventual recognition. Such gliding attack preserves textual rectitude while "covering for" the musical accents with its little artifice. Frequently, I admit, the artifice is useless, especially when at the end of a phrase a slack syllable falls on a concluding downbeat. In this oft recurring circumstance the musical accent should be disregarded altogether, just as in dramatic music the syllabic slack must often be ignored. The gliding procedure obviously must be reversed when, in lyric music, a syllable needing stress coincides with a weak musical beat; i.e., the note must be slightly stressed at the moment of address and softened immediately thereafter. A good example of this relationship is found in common-time hymns where, in the final measure, an accented syllable is assigned to the third and fourth beats.

The fact invoked near the beginning of the preceding paragraph is important enough to bear repetition: *the first fractionary second of attack establishes its primary influence.* From this fact, an eager student conductor can make practical conclusions which will nicely compose the prima facie contradictions encountered in the outstanding majority of lyric compositions.[7]

When the feasibility of effecting a satisfactory entente between the text and music, at a *forte* level, seems improbable, the conductor will ease an uneasy situation by adroitly lowering the level. Amplitude of quantity is not always necessary to produce the slight *marcato* of accentuation. Chiaroscuro (*q.v.*) is usually adequate for lyric purpose. Chiaroscuro here implies an inconsiderable intensification rather than well-defined increase of quantity. Many understand intensity and quantity amplitude to be synonyms in musical terminology. But these words do not convey identical meanings. It is

[7] Cf. *anacrusis,* p. 20, and *a precept* about unaccented notes, p. 23.

true that intensity and amplitude are intimately associated. But they are separate agencies. Intensity indicates a mental or emotional reaction. Amplitude of sonority may be only a manifestation of a taste for dynamic pressure; unless evoked moderately, and in fair ratio to the exigencies of the moment, it has no aesthetic or even dramatic value; it is principally a physical force. Intensity arranges its chiaroscuro through concentration upon ideas and emotional activities. The editor of the *Liber Usualis* expresses the thought succinctly: "*The ictus* [rhythmic step] *is more in the mind than in the voice.*"[8]

There is no conjecture involved in suggesting that the most intense communications between humans have been exchanged at the faintest *pianissimo*. One may advert here to the "sweet nothings" which, it is chronicled, whispering swains and damsels have been pouring into one another's ears since the sun (or moon) first shone in Eden, and to the *forte declarandos* which Eros causes wildly to resound in hearts, from scarcely audible murmurings. But such illustration is insufficiently formal or academic to engage professional attention!

The technical point to be noted is that intensity derives not only from emotional agitation but as well from the clarity—including the suitable routine for conveying it—with which any idea is understood. Perception of the metrical appositions of text and music usually directs the right degree of stress or slack to the right syllable and the right note. *If accent and anacrusis are thought through thoroughly, physical expression will, most of the time, automatically adjust itself conformably* (cf. page 20).

Rinforzando is only akin to *sforzando* but is often treated as a *subito* by conductors. The term *rinforzando* is not found in many modern scores. When used, it is a signal not for sudden increase of decibel strength, but only for adequate underlining of a single vocal or instrumental line. This device of interpretation is incorporated in the various recommendations, distributed through this volume, for conducting contrapuntal figures and notably the thematic interrelations of canon and fugue. The term *rinforzando* is purposely omitted throughout these pages lest students conclude that if the word is not printed in the score, the procedure would be inopportune. For the same reason, in simplifying the *rinforzando* require-

---

[8] *Liber Usualis* (English ed.; New York: J. Fisher, 1938), p. xxix.

ments of *a cappella* polyphony in an ensuing chapter, the term is waived. *Rinforzando* is as essential to contrapuntal definition, however as *anacrusis* to rhythm and chiaroscuro to musico-verbal fluency.

In concluding the consideration of *subitos*, impacts in general, and the three modes of attack, I offer no apology for reiterating my theme song, viz., *the measure of a conductor's real musicianship may safely be estimated by his tints and shades of quantity color.*

QUANTITY IN THE TREBLE, BASS, AND INNER PARTS; HARMONICS IN UNISON OCTAVES

In these subdivisions, the influence on ensemble effects of quantity as applied to high, middle, and low contrapuntal or chordal lines is epitomized. Much is written in later pages concerning the relations of rilievos and timbres to the symmetry of concerted music (cf. Chapters V and VI). It seems advantageous to preview here the major integrants of these relations, presenting them as aspects of *quantity as quantity*.

Having successfully solved the enigmas which so often cloud the assignment of appropriate dynamic levels, the calculation of suitable degrees of *crescendo* and *diminuendo*, and the setting in proper perspective of the minutiae discussed in the preceding section, a conductor may nevertheless be defeated in his efforts to control quantity. He must never forget that he is coping with an elusive agency. The puzzles already glimpsed do not comprise the sum total of challenging conundrums. While all misapplications of quantity tend to deprive music of its essential grace, the most grievous are those forced upon the aesthetic consciousness from the aeries of treble heights. They are signals to the Muses to hie to the caverns on Mt. Olympus and hide from lightning on the loose. Excessive treble force ignores acoustical equities, screaming its scorn for the amenities of art. It is arrogant, derisive, and blatantly decisive against the naturally demanded accordances of balance. All this because the rapid vibrations of acute pitches generate more shrill and piercing tones than the slower vibrations of lower notes. Therefore the conductor must direct his most anxious attention to the quantity of the treble line.

Historically, the centrifugal force which threw out all the sparks that now scintillate as harmony and counterpoint was the *cantus firmus*, a melody in the tenor or alto (high tenor) line. The bass was not of primary significance, the *cantus firmus* practically controlling its contours. And the soprano notes were but shimmering light play, an aureole of reflected brightness. It is reasonable to conclude, then, that the great masters of polyphony and the choral instructors of the Dufay-to-Sweelinck epoch must have subordinated the quantity expression of treble and bass to that of the primarily important *cantus firmus*. Certainly they would not have caricatured the cause by distorting the *effect*. They were too scholastic to make such a blunder. If the treble grew out of the tenor-alto zone, the former owed deference to the latter. One may be logically certain that Renaissance music did not suffer affront by treble explosions. Gregorianists (it is not reasonable to suppose that boy sopranos were allowed to outsing the adults in monastic chanting), and polyphonists until the second half of the sixteenth century, used the treble line most conservatively. Probably they were subconsciously fearful lest acute pitches would draw attention away from the substance of the music.

One rarely discovers a soprano part extending beyond

in the classic polyphony. Even that moderately high note is obtrusive if thrust forward importunately. Its brightness is only an emanation from the light glowing in the axis parts, and the conductor must forbid it an unbecoming brilliance.

I remember a review of a performance of the "Ascendo ad Patrem" (Palestrina) which I conducted at the Metropolitan Opera House in New York. W. J. Henderson, able and famed critic of the New York *Sun*, took me to task for allowing too much prominence to the top line whenever it reached the high note of its compass. The G above the treble staff appears frequently in this elaborate polyphonic number. There is a closely concentrated power in the alto and two tenor lines. Obviously it is from these lines that the efficacy of the composition derives. The chorus singing the work was distinguished for the disembodied and volatile buoyancy of its treble quality. At that performance the sopranos gently *brushed* the top G's. Factually, the physiological functions of their larynges could not have been activated with less pressure on the vocal cords. Nevertheless, Mr. Henderson complained about excessive quantity! Naturally I was puzzled at first that so great a critic could have been so grievously confused. Presently, however, I realized that he was preaching a fundamental doctrine of polyphony bearing upon the quantitative relationship of the component parts. Possibly he felt that the soprano line should have been even less audible than it was, that at the top of their *tessitura* the choristers should have hidden behind the hedgerows of heaven and projected a sort of pale, cold shimmer as from a semi-clouded moon. His point of view was correct: *too much treble destroys polyphonic authenticity.* He probably had expected me to employ a technique which, it is alleged, was common to the usage of the past, viz., at such hazardous spots in a treble continuity to reduce the number of singing sopranos. Personally, I had long held such technique to be evasive and perhaps disingenuous. But nowadays, balancing the academic and the practical with better judgment and realizing that the full beauty of music depends upon astute tactics for expression, I would in similar circumstances appoint a small group of the lightest sopranos to the top-of-the-*tessitura* phrases.

It is interesting to note that the greatest choral epoch frowned upon the dominance of high pitch. But music has long since outgrown control by a *cantus firmus.* And it has escaped entirely from the Guidonian restriction of the treble and bass compasses.[9] A *laudator temporis acti* might argue that the substance of effective music is still to be found within the approximate limits of the hexachords. And he would be right. Not, indeed, because his sympathy is hoary with age and therefore convincing to antiquarians, but because, *de facto,* the greatest beauty of tones and timbres abides in that area. The added high and low notes of modern usage have extended the dramatic usefulness of voices. The *alt* and *altissimo* octaves have increased the potential brilliance, and *basse ottave* the solidity of instrumentation. Brilliance on high and extra strength in the bass, however, are still more suited to special than to normal musical effects. These special effects are predisposed to promote the theatrical in the best sense of the word. High-pressure dramatism in high *rilievos* suggests "whirlwinds of tempestuous fire" rather than "the hidden soul of harmony." Many pyrotechnical flashings of coloraturas are not so much music as glottis acrobatism which delights the boxoffice.

Although the probable practice of polyphonists (subordinating the sopranos to tenors and altos) cannot fairly be adduced as adequate

---

[9] Guido provided one distinctly bass scale, two treble scales, and *four* positions for the tenor-alto needs. In three of these positions either alto or tenor can function without difficulty.

reason for keeping modern treble parts in the background, the acoustico-aesthetic fact from which this practice stemmed has not been contradicted by time.

There is never too much of anything in a true product. Its ratios are balanced by principles or facts. Excessive background or foreground denies perspective to a picture. Too bright a sky darkens the subject of an attempted portrayal. One cannot descry the theme for the dazzling. Shrill pungency and acute loudness obscure essential music, depriving it not only of luster but, too often, of even pale perceptibility.

Sometimes the treatment of treble notes as harmonics of the fundamentals appearing in lower parts is gratifying. In unison octaves the higher part is equivalently the reinforced first overtone of the lower part. In full chordal spans there are generally octave duplications of several notes. The commonplace orchestral or double-chorus chord in Fig. 30 includes six mounting allusions to the

Fig. 30.

fundamentals B flat, F, D. There are four soundings of the tonic, three of the dominant, and two of the mediant. Are all these intonations entitled to equality of volume? Are the three repetitions of the tonic of the same dynamic importance as the fundamental B flat? Or should each superimposed B flat, following the diminishing-audibility schema of harmonics, be softer in the ratio of its distance from the fundamental? If the chord were analyzed and written as an acoustical paradigm, it would be marked as in Fig. 31 Certainly,

Fig. 31.

groupings of notes are not intended to be read and sounded according to a scale of vanishing overtones. Therefore this marking of the

second and third sections of the complete chord is not proposed as
a basis for the distribution of tonal energy when all the notes are
played by an orchestra or sung by a many-voiced choir. It is offered
merely as a suggestive example of how physics would construct the
chord in dynamic ratios, if only the first B flat, F, and D were
intoned. In vigorous chordal music and signally independent contrapuntal figures, literal cognizance of textbook acoustical ratios
cannot be taken, but the quantitative interrelations of overtones and
fundamentals could well be accepted as a theoretical norm by which
broadly to regulate the higher to the lower parts. If a conductor is
physics-minded, he will rarely project a high treble line out and
beyond the extreme limits of acoustical fitness, and never beyond
those of artistic propriety.

Orchestral conductors are familiar with the sense of *remoteness*
inculcated by the *played* harmonics of violins, violas, and cellos.

This notation ≡ symbol is usually an indication that the com-

poser wishes to subtract weighty elements from even the lightest
fundamental tone and permit its octave to *float* with a sort of oblique,
transcendental intimation. The played string harmonic is the loveliest nuance, and the most immaterial resource available to the
technique of any art form. Although ineffective, because of its
disembodiment, in normal, physically embodied music, the harmonic
mystically enhances every episode that fain would establish a spiritual
atmosphere.

It is not impossible to intone some octave harmonics vocally. But
the process often involves abnormal use of the vocal cords—the
technique of *falsetto* and quasi-Tyrolese yodeling—and thus, by a
suggestion of affectation, tends to jeopardize the simplicity of the
effect sought. I am directing attention here to the possibility of
achieving the natural aura which emanates from soprano octave
tones when these are softened over alto fundamentals, tenor over
bass, and *alt* octaves over the whole substructure. To inhibit such
astral tonality is to deny to music the incorporeal freedom which is
one of its most distinctive attributes. Music is like the clouds, sometimes seemingly dense, dark, and solid, sometimes fleecy and flimsy,
but always volatile enough to roam the empyrean unhindered. Shelley
wrote of his "Cloud": "I pass through the pores of the ocean and
shores."

Good *magadizing,* i.e., intoning in octaves *with quantity tapering toward the top,* is one of the most effective and artistically convincing natural expedients of choral song. Examine the phrase in Fig. 32, to be sung by a standard S.A.T.B. chorus. If such a phrase were part of a sturdy declamation, the disembodiment of the sopranos' and altos' tones and the slight underlining of the tenor and bass tones

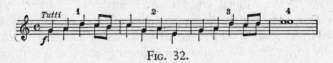

FIG. 32.

would be inopportune, since *declamando* usually connotes only energy and forthrightness. A direct pronouncement depends more on clarity and force than on nuance. But if this unison-octave phrase were an excerpt from a non-declarative, pensive, wishful, or wistful period, the substance of the melody would be improved and thus more advantageously set forth by the lower voices at *minus-forte,* the treble-clef notes being delivered at *piano.* The quality of remoteness, to which I referred in a preceding paragraph, is imparted to the more acute voices if thus intoned.

Volatileness is an invaluable property of high-pitched tones. In order adequately to reveal the dignity of fundamentals, the edginess of sharp octaves must be dulled. If a chorus magadizes thus, not only is the melody itself made agreeably manifest, but its nimbus as well. The nimbus to a unison-octave chorus is as the halo to a saint.

FIG. 33.

If the alto singers are likely to contribute a weighty or strident tone in such a phrase, they should be directed to sing in the tenor compass, as in measures 3 and 4 of the arrangement in Fig. 33. If they remain on the treble line, they should be kept at *pianissimo.* The ensuing markings, carefully accommodated to the voices, should *infuse* the foregoing lukewarm melody.

Such simulation of the effect of harmonics cannot be altogether ineffective (except in *declamando*), because it conforms to the ratios of audibility inherent to the sounds themselves. Even an imperfect gradation of quantity, in this fashion, relieves the clumsy plainness of diatonic unison octaves.[10] Nature is not averse to a little artistic touching-up of bald spots. Conductors who have not yet applied the *harmonics* treatment will be surprised at the ease with which effectiveness can be supplied to otherwise dull or vapid phrases.

Another gratifying use of the harmonics technique, although not directly pertinent to quantity, is suggested here. Sometimes the treble line lies too low for lucid definition whether at the top of a unison octave or of a chordal or contrapuntal arrangement. The deficiency is considerable, if the part is sung by boys or light female lyrics whose timbres are too fluty for efficacy in such circumstances.[11]

When the personnel of the chorus is too limited to allow the borrowing suggested in the footnote, the sustaining of the soprano part an octave higher at *pianissimo* is a most helpful expedient. For many years I have resorted to this means of clarifying and animating what would otherwise be a vague and inert choral line. Generally I assign a few flexible voices to the octave. These voices *vocalize* the harmonics of the low line on *vee* as far as F on the fifth line, and on *voo* if above the staff. The practice is indicated as most effective when the treble line is written in this compass 𝄞 . The soft vocalizing at the octave raises the melody into a lambent radiance, while not discernibly wresting the soprano part from its appointed site. There are always a few sopranos in my groups who are nicknamed "Harmonics" and who are ready, at a signal, to send their vocalizations floating into the higher spaces to augment the overtones of the fundamentals below.

The same procedure is effective in many T.T.B.B. settings. The top-tenor line, vocalized by a few sopranos at the octave, is invested with mystic quality just as a low soprano line in S.A.T.B. is thus

[10] *Chromatic* progressions, as the adjective implies, are never so altogether colorless.

[11] If there is an insufficient number of string or reed sopranos to define the low *rilievo*, and the other resources of a chorus permit, the choirmaster can remedy the inadequacy by supplementing the soprano timbre with mezzo-sopranos (not contraltos!), contraltinos, English altos (never by the more hollow countertenors), or by light string or reed tenors.

supplemented. A couple of boy sopranos can *over-tone* a men's chorus, if the men's "voices are good, and the same well-sorted and ordered" (Byrd), with a sort of Caribbean-sunset timbre. I have often observed the heavy lead melt away from a Palestrina "Lamentation," a motet of Annimuccia or Vittoria, and even from a modern chorus for adult male voices, under the gently solvent influence of vocalized octaves. A chorus of men's voices, effective and satisfying as it so often is, soon has evoked its totality of timbre resources and thereafter begins to weary listeners with its sameness.[12] A legitimate and facile means of increasing this totality is to draw upon the reserve of beauty which harmonics make available for approved purposes. Even exploratory experiments should reveal to a conductor the value of this special technique.

It would be absurd to recommend the *harmonics' scheme* as a plan for regularly trying to improve choral scores. Well-written scores rarely profit by the redaction of interpreters. But when, as in circumstances considered in the preceding paragraphs, the device tends to improve the *physical production* of the composers' concepts, there seems to be no valid argument against its employment.

The principal value of appraising treble lines as harmonics, as often as may be feasible, is evinced in the general management of quantity in the treble. One cannot afford to forget that the physical activities, in high rilievos, of soprano instruments, human and mechanical, are regulated with greater difficulty than those of the lower agencies.

Class the expedient of the overtones technique among the more highly refined (and, therefore, to many, the most negligible) nuances of choral singing, if you will; but you are merely opinionated if you try to gainsay the dictum of physics, viz., that harmonics give quality to fundamentals and that what happens musically in the heights influences the status of everything below. If there is too little sunshine the fruit cannot grow; too much, and even the leaves and stalks wither away.

Composers for string instruments prescribe the playing of harmonics usually to suggest the *remote* and *metaphysical*. Conductors of choral music should, correspondingly, signal for occasional har-

---

[12] Like complaint may be lodged against lengthy programmes of *S.S.A.A.* settings. The expedient for relieving monotony in such programmes is to include *accompanied* numbers which permit stressing of *low* instrumental tones.

monic effects when the genre of the composition is unmistakably spiritual, and whenever the quantity of a soprano line might otherwise escape control.

As an interesting experiment, I recommend that conductors try two readings of the Brahms' excerpt (page 119), measures 165 to the choral finish; first, the usual reading, which allows equal quantity to all voices in those engrossing moments of double magadizing; and the *harmonics* reading, which, in this double episode, quietly shows the sopranos as *sheening* the tenors, and altos *octaving* the basses. It is difficult to comprehend a conductor's choice of the first reading after listening to the mystic intimations (inherent to the primary purpose of the composition) revealed in the second.

Finally, in this connection, it is necessary to note again that music, like all true art, is a synthesis of spiritual and physical forces. Conductors who have not grasped this basic truth will profit little by debating the worth of worthlessness of any nuance of tempo or dynamics.

Once this conviction has become the hinge of his musicianship, a conductor spontaneously seeks to adjust his interpretations to some inexorable dictates. His *sounding* technique will be promoted by his aim to serve the spiritual content of music. He ceases to be a gourmet of tidbits. He soon begins to understand *quality* as including more than *klangfarbe*, a mere timbre pigment whence to extract a variety of hues to enliven otherwise lackluster sounds. Quality, leading him beyond acoustical chromaticism, commences to demand more of innuendo and greater refinement than the science of tonal physics requires. It is something like this: many thoughts and aspirations cannot make themselves understood through correct or clever phraseology alone; a subtle inflection, a smile or a frown, a sparkling or a pensive eye is needed to convey their implications. Quality in music is that property which unerringly appeals to a man's instinct to catch the supersensible significance of what he sees or hears or otherwise experiences. There must be more than mere timbre in a sung prayer; the spirit urging the prayer must hover about. Acoustical facts, no matter how astutely invoked, cannot alone reveal the urgencies of hope or dread, of love or hate, of commendation or obloquy, of intrepidity or timidity, of victory or defeat.

The pipe organ, to illustrate, is necessarily the least *emotionally* effective of the concerted instruments of music; it has a wealth of timbres, but little *quality* in the sense in which this word is used here. It necessarily falls short of this property, being altogether mechanical save for the management of key controls. The intimate psychic reactions of the manager of the controls are not communicable to the wires, magnets, wind chests, or pipes which comprise its sounding processes.

Only in the measure of their adaptability to the promptings of an idea or emotion may timbres be said exactly to possess quality. Such adaptability is predicated not only upon the physical attributes of tone colors, but upon the pliancy with which human sensitiveness can infuse them.

No conductor, therefore, can evoke from a chorus or an orchestra the plenitude of its endowment who has not described this difference between timbre and superphysical quality. The difference is not a finely spun academic distinction. It is real and vital, timbre being related to and limited by physical facts, while quality reaches out to limitless metaphysical semblances. The student may demur at the terseness of these statements. But, consistently, he should also demur at the inexorableness of mathematical principles and the rigidity of all basic natural laws. Faultfinding with the law of gravity does not suspend its compulsion. Nor does the reluctance of a conductor to be concerned about the spiritual (I don't mean *theological*) connotations of music make it possible for music to attain its natural ends without them. True music depends almost abjectly upon the willingness and the ability of performers and conductors to correlate its psycho-physical properties.

In no phase of the conductor's art is this fact so abundantly demonstrated as in the relationship of quantity to musical efficacy.

If quality is the emotive agency of music, it follows conclusively that the influence which can affect it most vitally must be the most thoroughly comprehended. Quantity is this paramount influence. Some may incline to the opinion that pitch more actively modifies quality than varying degrees of loudness. Very high and very low pitches unquestionably alter the timbres from which quality derives. But we are not concerned with the *altissimo* or *profundissimo* areas of vocal or instrumental intonation. We are interested in the aesthetic impressions achievable within the compass most convincing to average listeners, and within which the most effective music has been written, viz.

In this area quantity is certainly the determining factor of quality, it being assumed of course that defects and inadequacies of vocalism or instrumental execution are deemed unworthy of listing as influences. Continued excessive softness can blanch out all hints of penetrability from timbres, and continued excessive loudness emblazons and exploits them beyond their aesthetic resources. Since a timbre can maintain its distinctive traits only within the quantitative limits set by its physical organic structure, the spiritual texture of quality, *a fortiori,* can survive only by a most delicate *finessing* of quantity.

Thus it is incumbent upon the aspiring young conductor to delve deeply into the abstract interrelations of musical quality and quantity, and to experiment in his rehearsal room with every practical expedient which intent study suggests as a reliable custodian of them in performance.

If he fails to address himself to these important undertakings, his music will probably be never more than clever but futile tooting.

Climax; The Approaches to Preparatory and Real Climaxes and the Fall-off

The implications of climax in music and the interpretative treatment of approaches to and recessions from climactic effects offer an interesting field of inquiry.

If *climax* were generally understood in its first dictionary sense (i.e., a series of ideas or expressions arranged in ascending scale), there would be no need of considering the approaches, because there would be none to consider. But an irregular use of the word has gained such vogue as to constitute, in current vocabulary, its regular definition. Today climax means the culmination or apex of the development of a series of ideas and lower apexes. Therefore this meaning of the term and its etymological suggestion of a *process of climbing to the eminence* may be studied concisely, cheek by jowl.

In practically all the arts, the climax is the outstanding particular

toward which the totality of minutiae has been progressing or contributing.[13] True artists are intent upon conveying a concept or
suggesting an experience. They have an end in view. They don't
design or fabricate, chisel or mold, draw or paint, or set melodies
in harmony and counterpoint purposelessly or at random. The
climactic detail of artistic creations (of sufficient dimensions to show
such a detail) is that in which something from all the other details
seems to be compounded for emphatic effect. It is easy to understand
how the items contributing to the principal particular and this itself
became confused in one term. Often, unfortunately, the means and
the end, in every phase of human thought and activity, are jumbled
together indiscriminately. The revelation of an idea is the *end* of the
artist; the ascending scale of the less striking through the more to
the most striking items is only the *means*.

Climax, in music, is the moment which themes, rhythms and
harmonies, tempos and dynamics have been awaiting from the start.
All of these in conjunction prepare the convincing instant. Without
preparation the culminating point would be ineffective. There
would be no unavoidable impression of *finality* imparted. *There
would not be a climax*; its counterfeit would have no title to
emphasis.

One may posit at once, therefore, that in this as in so many other
connections the conductor must try to perceive the *end* of the composer and to sense the relative importance of the minutiae which
are his *means* of achieving the end.

All well-wrought details are both separable and inseparable from

[13] Cf. pp. 153, 154. Many artistic creations are conceived as idealizations or
concentrations upon abstract ideas. Such as these are not prospered by the
outranking of one detail by another. In such creations the minutiae do not
converge upon any physical particular, the *ensemble* itself constituting the
indivisible unit of efficacy. For instance, the most spiritualizing communications, in statuary and painting, about Christ and the Madonna avoid
anthropomorphic emphasis of eyes, hands, mouth, or any other anatomical
feature; while the less spiritualizing draw attention to some detail which,
often with clinical accentuation, exaggerates a merely humanistic idea.

There are some effective presentations of abstractions in music; not
many. Mahler's Symphonies are a good example of at least attempted effectiveness. Some musicologists find meaning of a sort in such music. But,
generally, music must excite emotions for its effect. Of course there is no
real climax in a short hymn tune (unless one fancies to find one in the
highest notes), but in the broader forms of music a *physical* tuning to a
mental concept is generally accomplished by setting forth in progressive
sequence the elements which are sure to impress palpably. Such procedure
connotes convergence upon a climax.

their associations. Here we have another pretty paradox, but only a tissue-paper issue. A spire, well designed and executed, is a tapering column whether as the outstanding architectural function of a church or as a pyramid or cone "set up on its own." If just an isolated obelisk, it may be a symbol of something, or it may just be gracefully meaningless. To capture general attention, a structure must declare its *raison d'être* to the speediest glance. Placed atop a church, a spire is a climax recognizable immediately as an emergence from foundations, naves, etc.; but if aloof, it is often like the lonely obelisk—of passing inconsequence. But the issue is thin, because normally structures do explain themselves. Steeples are not strewn casually in parks, nor are musical climaxes isolated from their contexts. (Of course, we know of the pyramids in Egypt and of many lonely monuments in symphonies . . . !)

Unquestionably there are some textbook architects whose creative sensitiveness seems indigoed by excessive thinking in blueprints. Such men are not more fired by spires than by walls, by belvederes than by floor spaces, by symbolism than by differentials. They enjoy a hearty happiness if their classroom measurements are applauded by engineers and contractors. But they don't animate their formulae. Their dull crayons are too heavy to be the wands of magic. Probably this is why some church buildings are so indefinite—just four walls and a roof with an apologetic hump!

There have been, too, a few "standard" composers whose highest vision compressed their music under nothing more pyramidal than a mansard covering.[14]

But among choral and orchestral conductors we find a considerable number of prim formalists who are just as textbookish as their architectural cousins. They are intent upon pointing out designs carved on hard surfaces. They study the steel matrix of each score and are coldly joyful in tracing with very heavy batons the severely engraved intaglios of notation. Naturally, such conductors do not rise with feeling to greater awareness of a composer's thoughts and impulses as the music nears its most declarative moment. They rarely proceed spontaneously *pari passu* with a composer's fancy to its peak of gaiety or descend with him to the nadir of its melancholy.

[14] Early chants, medieval and the stricter styles of Renaissance polyphony were *properly* thus enclosed. Trenchant effects were antipathetic to their approved character. Climax as an important element of appeal, except moderately to emphasize a textual particular, did not reveal itself assuredly until the Monteverdi school became solidly established.

Surely enough and too surely are their phrases and periods neatly apposed! Their procedure is mathematically holy, but with that "holier than thou" holiness which anesthetizes the imagination, the faculty that understands music more keenly than the intellect.

Therefore, the prim conductors are not qualified to convey to their performers a psychic sense of movement toward or arrival at any clearly perceived emotional objective. Symphonies and oratorios which proceed in futile dullness under such leaders reveal astonishing resources of climactic energy under conductors who have cultivated the psychic sense. Of course a climax of a sort is sure to creep in somewhere, even though the pendulum on the podium is willing if not determined to exclude it. But it is a climax only of a sort. The allocation of notes and measures provides a *theoretical* climax. The composer's purposes cannot be altogether frustrated: "In all well-written music, the aesthetic concepts of the composer will discover themselves to listeners, if given fair chance, without much importuning from the conductor. Admittedly, however, the conductor must know how to accord the music its fair chance." (Cf. page 8.) Thus, if the notes are sounded as written, their progress to a summit is usually discernible, but with scarcely more effectualness than a descriptive program note would suggest. The climax does not need *creation* by the conductor; it is there on the clefs waiting *in potentia*, but it must be "given fair chance" if it is to impress and stir *in actu*. Fair chance is unwittingly withheld by conductors who perceive only the academic expansion of periods. Fair chance for true climax is accorded only when its emotional surge has been felt by the maestro. The spire needs the church to explain its final *epi*, but the moment of musical preeminence rising from foundations, nave, etc., needs more, i.e., the vitality which only the conductor himself can impart.

At the opposite pole of ineffectualness one finds musicians and their architectural kinsfolk who are keen to force attention to every semblance of climax. These ardent devotees of the spectacular defeat their purpose by converting the simplest rises in a period to the status rightfully belonging only to the preeminent feature. When every slight *animando* of a score is exaggerated, preeminence is impossible. Unregulated quantity is hoist with its own petard. The full resources of dramatic emphasis being preempted by preparatory phrases, there is nothing left for a true climax. The graduated scale of dynamic growth almost invariably required for effective climax is displaced by a series of almost equally underlined progressions, and the development of a supreme episode, particular, or moment is prevented from the start.

Master building presupposes the conviction that the sense of all minutiae be epitomized and stressed in the preeminence of a *single* consummation.

Once the underlying concept of the composer has been ascertained, the conductor must note the locus of the last term in the ascending scale of periods. Architecture, being a direct medium to the eye and intellect and only indirectly addressing the imagination, shows its spires unmistakably; but music, appealing through the ear directly to the imagination and emotions and only indirectly to the intellect, is subtle and confusing. Some analysis of the details is frequently necessary before one may be certain as to the locale of the climax. Having assured himself of the exact position of the topmost peak, the conductor must next mark the serial rank of the lesser associated crests and finally survey all the approaches to and recessions from these points. Only after such reconnaissance can he reasonably expect to adapt all the integrants to a convincing and conclusive presentation.

Chorus No. IV of Brahms' "Requiem" has been proposed as a thesaurus rich in illustrations of the quantitative ratios of music. This composition has become for me a cyclopedic volume of applied truths of dynamics—one of the "volumes that I prize above my dukedom." The reader is referred to it here (cf. page 111 *et seq.*) in connection with the following items, some of which have already been considered in the abstract:

1. The principal *idea* of a composition.
2. The culminating feature in the expression of the idea.
3. The relation of preparatory or quasi-climaxes to the real climax.
4. The approaches to quasi and real climaxes
5. The *fall-off* from climax.

What is the motivating impulse—the pervading thought—of this number?

Throughout the "Requiem" Brahms envisages the endless happiness in Heaven after the grave has locked men against the failures and sorrows of life on earth. He is balancing two certainties—death of the body and joyful immortality of the soul. In the other six numbers of the "Requiem" both certainties are propounded with climactic emphasis. But close scrutiny of each number as a complete musical entity made up of separate units will show that the greater emphasis belongs to the main idea of the oratorio. In Chorus No. IV, however, the *singleness* of the concept which Brahms unfolds is immediately evident. He is here concerned only with the contemplation of the beauty of the Lord's abode, to which a Divine invitation offers hospitality to all men of good will. Having quickly dismissed the misgivings which harass all mortals when thinking of death, Brahms devotes himself to an uninterrupted proclamation of "How Lovely is Thy Dwelling Place, O Lord of Hosts!"

The culminating particular in the unfolding of this thought is readily recognized (measures 165-174), if the conductor does not allow himself to be distracted by the interpolation of the fugal movement, measures 124-154, which is not a summation of the pervading idea, but a candidly parenthetical "Te Deum." Although sufficient arcs of melody are distributed throughout the voice lines to impart a horizontal character to the choral movements, the principal melody is usually in the soprano part.

Observing the curve line of the choral *face melody* (cf. curve line and face melody in the Index) from its entrance at measure 5, we soon see that the music is proceeding in a series of circular segments. Each of these is, as it were, a crescent of increasing light. If all of the many successive crescents were of equal importance, the salient points of each would deserve parity of stress. In such circumstance, the movements of all the segments would be without an objective. *Climax is the common apex toward which all periods and figures must direct their course.* Therefore each crescent, approaching and retiring from its own salient, must be considered as contributory in some particular to the energy which, cumulatively, will produce the supreme final result of component melodies, harmonies, and choral-orchestral colors. *If quality as well as timbre has been preserved in each crescent by careful allotment of quantity, the climax is assured eloquent effectiveness.* Many conductors, nevertheless, permit each crescent to diffuse too much brightness, thus weakening in advance the refulgence of the high light of the composition.

Here is a brief survey of the sequence of segments. It is offered as a logical and practical plan for ascertaining the *progressive* activity of this music—and of all similar music—toward a true climax. I find it conformable with the musical content, and convenient, to separate for examination the seven crescents through which the choral lines develop to the eighth, the climax. The segments or crescents are tabulated alphabetically.

Measures 5-24 (A) outline the design of the curve line to be followed throughout. This outline reveals a rise to and a decline from salient points. In this crescent there are two salients, the soprano G in 10 and E flat in 20. The upward progression anteceding these notes will tend to project them too forcibly. They must be denied any save the slight prominence which will accrue to them naturally as the highest notes in the crescent. Whenever I hear the conductor of a choir which has been well enough trained to fulfill his intentions, underlining equally the progressions to and these salients themselves, I immediately conclude that he is not aware of the trend of the composition, and that there will be neither psychological nor musical climax, the ensuing segments probably to be only duplicates or revisions without notable supplement. The average conductor permits crescent A to promote itself to the disadvantage of the number as a whole. The first task of the astute conductor, in this matter, is to restrain it within the narrow limits of its *introductory* function.

Measures 25-44 (B), although not carrying the soprano line as high as (A), diffuse more light on the picture which is beginning to evolve, by the use of imitation. This device of composition, when employed directly through many measures, gives an unmistakable impression of forward movement. In other compositions such succinct copying of one part by the others often leads to a more immediate climax. Here the imitation contributes only moderately to the organization of the whole. Its purpose is frustrated, therefore, if the conductor allows the successive entrances to be made with impacts *or the whole period to be delivered at a higher dynamic level than crescent A*. The development of the musical picture has not yet reached the point where *crescendo* (except to the minimum degree implied in indirect attack; cf. pages 120 *et seq.*) will be promotive.

Measures 47-63 (C) attest the gradually gathering momentum. The imitation here is more animating than in (B) because of the long *crescendo*, 49-57, which proceeds over the most extended vocal curvature of the composition, from the bass D to the high A flat in the soprano line. This combination of *crescendo* and curvature can readily induce a conductor to attach too much importance to the crescent and therefore to evoke excessive quantity in its execution. The temptation to urge all forces to their utmost at 55, 56, 57 is difficult to resist. It must be resisted, however, for the culmination of this period is too short lived to be the climax of such a number. Furthermore, there are more than a hundred measures to follow. Brahms could never dally so long with post-climax allusions. The conductor needs to be vigilant lest too much energy wrest the *crescendo* from its serviceable place by an almost traditional exaggeration.

The soprano A flat in 57 should be restrained to *mezzo-forte*, since the high pitch of the note and its position as the final point of the *crescendo*, at greater dynamic strength, would concur to give the episode undue prominence. If the high A flat is to be sung at *mezzo-forte* and the long preceding *crescendo* is to be a genuine *poco a poco* growth, it is obvious that the starting point of the *crescendo*, measure 49, must be intoned at *minus piano*, with the accompaniment at *pianissimo*.

Measures 66-85 (*D*), having been infused with the animation of the rise, 49-57, importune the music to greater energy but not to its fullness. Here again the salient of the crescent is not sufficiently sustained to be accorded the eminence it usually arrogates. Nevertheless, progress toward the supreme moment is intensified until, at measure 85, it is evident that Brahms is going to look over his shoulder to review the progress already made, lest even with all this preparation he approach the peak of Parnassus too soon.

At measure 86, the wood winds return to their original theme. Curiously Brahms assigns the countermelody to the French horn rather than to the cello. Perhaps this is a subtle hint that he is rearranging his forces for the culmination.

Measures 90-109 (*E*) are not merely a repetition of measures 5-14, but a mnemonic as well of the original promise of the composition. The recollection of a first glance at, a first encounter with, or an understanding of something worth remembering often expands and enriches the implications of an original experience, especially if new intimations are thus communicated.

At any rate, the conductor has opportunity, during this repetition, to underline arcs of melody in inner parts which perhaps he had allowed to be subordinate to the soprano progression. This crescent shows no signs of a proximate climax. The short ensuing choral episode, 112-114, indeed, seems to hold back the flutes and oboes which at 109 give evidence of eagerness for the finish.

Measures 116-124 (*F*) dally almost sluggishly until surprised by the interpolation of the contrapuntal exclamations, 124-154. It might be well argued that this interruption in *fugato* style could have been omitted with advantage to a more direct climax. Perhaps, however, postponement of the culmination makes its eventual appearance more dramatic. Obviously *the sonorousness of this interpolated period must be most sedulously restrained*. Presently, after the short crescent, 155-165 (*G*), the plenitude of tempered quantitative power is to be invoked for the true climax.

It has been necessary to prepare the moment of climax *remotely*; it is of paramount necessity now to exercise the greatest care in the *proximate* approach. A climax in music is like the crisis of a drama or story. One must not be over-agitated too close to it. A popular novelist put the idea into the mouth of his leading character: "I started at the wrong point—too near the crisis. Everything depends upon the lull before the crisis. And it must be a genuine lull. You must almost forget that there's a storm coming."[15]

In the eleven measures of crescent *G* there is a genuine lull, one of the most effective conjuring-up type of abeyances in music, during which the metaphysical loveliness of Heaven is imagined rather than perceived in reality; as it were, an impression of supernal beauty, silhouetted by clairvoyant melody.

Measures 165-174 (*H*) urge all factors to the high pinnacle of expression. Here is the awaited climax. The cathedral spire is at long last set up in its proper place over the broad plinth of foundations, nave, transepts, etc. In the vocabulary pertinent to the other metaphor—*crescents of increasing light*—the soprano-tenor ascent,[16] 165-170, clarifies the adumbration essayed by the flute, 109-114. The alto-bass concurrence changes the impression of crescent (*G*) into indisputable actuality, its contrary and oblique motion intensifying the sustained notes of sopranos and tenors to their maximum communicability.

It is quite clear that there are four apexes in the remote movement toward the climax. These may influence some conductors so sensibly as to coax premature *plus fortes* and *fortissimos*.

The true climax must never be anticipated.

---

[15] Charles Morgan, *Sparkenbroke* (New York: Macmillan, 1936), p. 273.
[16] Cf. page 141 for the harmonics treatment of the double magadizing here exemplified. At measure 168 it is my custom, abandoning the harmonics technique, to send all voices *allargando* and with *poco a poco crescendo* to a *minus fortissimo* at 170. (It must be remembered that the average singer and player will distort tone timbre and exaggerate disastrously, if not restricted to the left side of the *fortissimo* panel.)

As far as the ultimate climax of this composition is involved, these apexes are references only, allusions to the final musical objective. These preliminary high spots should be allowed only passing recognition if the mistakes of untimeliness and exaggeration are to be avoided. Serially, these apexes appear in the following order:

1. Measures 54-57;
2.   "   71-73;
3.   "   81-83;
4.   "   102-106.

Among these, apex 1 is the most serious threat to the growth of the number to its intended stature. The zeal of the composer manifests itself eagerly here for the first time, and the long curvature, *crescendo*, and implied *animando* concur appreciably to stress the importance of the period. Although encountered early, this apex is second only in significance to the climax. Such an anticipatory semblance of the culmination is always a hazard, for it tends to draw upon the resources reserved for later use.

Apex 2, in crescent *D*, develops more quickly and *misteriosamente*. (Cf. the dynamic symbols *fp* used.) The sense of *animando* is more acute and insistence is more clearly defined. It is less significant, however, because it is practically a reorganization of the factors leading to apex 1.

Apex 3 is another rise to eminence in crescent *D*. Although carrying the soprano line higher, it is worthy of note mainly for its further stressing of apexes 1 and 2.

Apex 4, in crescent *E*, elevates the choral protocol (5-24), hinting that completeness will soon be complete, i.e., when the episode, 112-114, crescent *F*, and the fugal insertion, 124-154, have finished their interruptions.

Academically, compositions may approve themselves without the punctuation of such secondary apexes or salient points. Practically, such punctuation is indispensable to the emotive efficacy of all compositions of the dimensions of this Brahms number, especially if the climax is placed with literal finality in the concluding period. The functional purpose of the apexes is to awaken, further, and sustain expectancy to the climax.

Apex 1 views the length and inclines of the structure with a full swing of the searchlight, the others bringing details into nearer focus and increasingly clearer visibility. *But all the apexes are dis-*

suaded from their purposes if dynamic ratios are neglected or ill regulated. These apexes are only auxiliaries and the plan of the composer is thwarted when they affect the importance of principals.

A conductor who accords to any secondary agency the prerogatives of primacy is, in effect, redesigning and rewriting another man's music. Thus are the great classics too frequently recomposed; not, indeed, by alterations in the printed score, but by tantamount changes superinduced while notation is materializing in intonation. *Subito* inhibits development. Growth is denied; there never was an acorn, it was always the oak. Sturdy and mature, it has had, *da capo,* only the alternatives of decaying or petrifying as the measures are ticked off *al fine.*

There are men and women to whom delay is always repugnant. They seem unable to *wait* for anything. They fret inordinately over routine processes. Frenetic conductors are members of this neurotic family. They can't build; a structure must pop up whole and complete out of a thaumaturge's bag of tricks, or they will have none of it. Psychologically they start at the finish which is not a good beginning. Certainly it is necessary to preview the end before commencing, but a serial arrangement of things to be done and steps to be taken must be prepared and conformed to, if the end is actually to be attained. During my boyhood the paterfamilias nudged me frequently with an old French adage: *Quand vous commencez, commencez au commencement* ("When you begin, begin at the beginning"). Probably he had often caught me evading a chore by starting (and finishing) at the end of a job which he would be most likely to observe. (I used to shovel the snow off only those paths which he used.) This was good nudging. The admonition has priceless value for all who seek substantial results.

Precipitate employment of resources intended for the finish impoverishes this by inflating the beginning. Similarly, the resources provided for use en route must be duly apportioned.

The four apexes antecedent to the climax in the composition under examination, and all such risings in music as are obviously intended to prepare a climax, must not be permitted to encroach upon the dynamic force of the supreme moment.[17]

[17] The culmination is not necessarily the *loudest* particular in all compositions. In certain types, such as the serenade, lullaby, berceuse, elegy, etc., the most important moment is frequently the *softest,* albeit the most intense or pensive. The dynamic movement in such numbers is obviously in inverse ratio to the progress of the majority of compositions.

In some musical forms e.g., military marches, waltzes, etc., there is no genuine climax (cf. footnote, page 144). The troops march with the same tread throughout the parade, and the waltzers beguile the moments with the same gliding grace at one end of the *salon* as at the other. Sometimes more profound music cannot afford to concentrate on any single item as of outranking importance, e.g., settings of the *Credo*, in which all the tenets of belief must be accorded the same degree of faith. There are, in modern settings of the *Credo*, dramatic moments—apexes—in separable movements, but a conductor will make a structural as well as a theological blunder if he attempts to establish any of these separable divisions as the climax of the whole. The *Incarnatus est, crucifixus*, and *passus et sepultus est* are sung *piano* appropriately to the reverential mood intended to be evoked (a reverential *piano* at these words is not a *hushing*; cf. page 110), and the *Et resurrexit* more jubilantly because of the hope the phrase connotes, but histrionic effects must be tempered to a parity of religious belief. Neither Bach nor Beethoven believed one symbol of the creed more faithfully than another. The conductor who is ever on the alert to discover and properly reveal the dramatic content of a composition may make more mistakes of interpretation in a Credo (but only in this relevancy) than inferior colleagues who, always stressing, rarely bring an idea or a period into prominence.

Climaxes in lyric styles are usually less gripping than in dramatic presentations. But lyric or dramatic, music normally depends upon the gradual maturing of a melodic embryo to the full stature of its inherent potentialities.

As the efficacy of a whole composition requires the graduation of all constituent parts to its climactic feature, so each single segment derives its import from the inclination of a phrase toward an apex. Climax is inevitably cheated of eminence by magnifying antecedent high spots. Similarly, the potential influence of a crescent is forfeited whenever a conductor permits the measures preceding its apex to assume, by intensity or tonal amplitude, excessive importance. Therefore the intensity and volume of such measures need careful adjustment.

A master interpreter, sensitive to the psychological as well as the technical inclusions of a score, is not heedless of the approaches to the minor apexes. He consistently treats these with the same care that distinguishes his attention to the other cardinal points of dynamics, viz., *anacrusis* (cf. pages 20, 46), *quantity levels* (cf. page

99), *the relativity of* crescendo *and* diminuendo (cf. page 105), *the mode of attack* (cf. pages 124 *et seq.*), *quantity vs. quality* (cf. pages 141 *et seq.*, and Index).

Crescent *A* has been designated as the choral protocol of the Brahms number, its rises and falls indicating the curve line followed throughout. It has no apex in the sense in which I have used the word in the serial on page 151. Necessarily it proceeds to a *logic accent*, for in the simplest musical and verbal sentences there is one pithiest expression. But the logic accent is included in the undulation of ordinary utterance and is not enriched by notable emphasis.

The culmination of crescent *B* is not included in the serial of apexes because it is the beginning of the unfoldment of the idea suggested in *A*. However, since these measures, 25-44, might satisfactorily be used as a short Responsary in a Protestant service, it is not irrelevant to note that the elevation at 40 will be effective if prepared by a *minus* to *plus piano* delivery of the tenor and bass parts, and approached, *tutti*, at *piano* to *minus mezzo-forte* from 35 to 40. As part of the whole composition, this period is usually a destructive episode because the tenor seems to arrogate to themselves the prerogative of announcing the sum total of what Brahms evidently expected to be proclaimed by the ensemble at 39-41.

The approach to apex 1, crescent *C*, affords unexcelled opportunity for restrained but telling animation. The whole period is a dynamic manifestation of the spiritual yearnings of men, the music corroborating the text with spontaneous acknowledgment. But the music is to comment further on the text. Therefore the music must not spend itself utterly at this juncture. This means, for practical purposes, that the conductor should lead his forces from a *pianissimo* at 49 *poco a poco* to *forte* at 57, the sopranos being restrained here to *mezzo-forte*. Attack by impact (cf. pp. 120 *et seq.*) at the various entrances in this crescent is certain to rob the apex, 54-57, of its influence.

Crescent *C* is suggested to the student as one of the most enlightening periods of all music in the extremely difficult matter of adjusting the excitation of a single period to its own apex, and the correlation of such an obviously stirring episode with the totality of the composition.

At apexes 2 and 3 we find the high points of crescent *D*. The soprano fifths, 67-68, 69-70, develop the material to apex 2 quickly. Such long leaps appear here for the first time in the treble line, producing an impression of excitement which singers are wont habitually to disclose at *fortissimo*. Clearly, *fortissimo* is still inopportune. The climax is even now on a distant horizon. Moreover, this particular apex is too speedily reached and abandoned to merit real climactic treatment. The staccato f/p of all accompanying strings, save the viola, imparts a furtiveness to the choral movement which, when the mysteriousness is dispelled by the light at 71-73, will insist upon revealing too much if the treble fifths are delivered louder than *plus piano*. The volume of the soprano part, 71-73, should not exceed *mezzo-forte*.

An equivalent repetition begins almost immediately, leading to a second culmination in crescent *D*. Using the same thematic strands dyed to a brighter hue, Brahms proceeds more cautiously to apex 3 than in his approach to apex 2. The same tendency will present itself here, i.e., to rise to so great a height as to overshadow the climax. To prevent this, one must hold the trebles to *mezzo-forte* at the apex, 81-83, while allowing the other parts to sing *forte*. The measures preceding the apex must be consistently delivered at lower dynamic levels.

Apex 4 gathers in a penultimate concentration all the impetus acquired in the earlier periods. This apex could properly lead to the great climax, after a necessary lull, but Brahms chose to stop to praise God before rising to the zenith of the vision. At apex 4 it is my custom to maintain the sopranos in panel 3 while the other choral lines proceed to panel 4. In the approach, 90-96, more volume is suitable than at 5-11 in the protocol. The increase in decibels, however, must be niggardly because this crescent is the last preliminary development of characteristic material. At this point I bring the tenor line to the surface, and the unexpected dominance of a concomitant melody over the treble figure is sufficient to furnish the progressive vigor to the crescent.

In practically all time-pattern music, musical figures are *going somewhere*. They are attracted by a beam. They may not drift around and be blown happily into port by the gentle zephyrs that serve music in free rhythm. The latter is like prose, unrestricted by the exigencies of versification. The former is poetry, indeed; and once the form and meter have been established, progressive motion must continue to a high point, and often beyond the high point, through a cadence to its predetermined point of repose.

If all the crescents in this composition have been bound together in graduated ascent (not merely *lined up* like a series of episodes), and if, finally, the contrapuntal interpolation is delivered properly as if in parentheses,[18] the ensuing lull being a genuine calm, the great excerpt of the Brahms "Requiem" may be judged prepared for its climax. If, unfortunately, the intensity and volume have not been graduated, or if general defects in the application of dynamics have been notable, the true climax of this subtle music cannot be attained. The conceptual purpose of the composer will have been frustrated; the melodies, harmonies, and orchestral graces will have been squandered.

Brahms' curve line (*q.v.*) is akin to the regular archings of Gregorian chant and polyphony. It spans greater distance, however, and is more abrupt in descent than in ascent. Witness the fall-off from the salients of crescents *A* and *B*, from the four apexes, and from the climax itself. Each apex, with the exception of apex 2, is approached gradually, but the recession is always immediate. The music twins with the text.

Although the fall-off from each height is accomplished more quickly than the ascent, these Brahms cadences, and all similar cadences, accomplish their musical and psychological purposes more congruously by *diminuendo* than by *subito piano* or *pianissimo*. *Subitos* tend to challenge the rights of the apex whence they so speedily snatch the music. In the average musical score, a *subito pianissimo* is effective after the *forte* of an apex only when the *forte* is a sign that a dramaturgical culmination is, in a manner of speaking, overwhelmed by its own force. The *subito pianissimo* is a sort of echo of this surprise. For example, contrast these Brahms recessions with the fall-off in Arkhangelsky's "The Day of Judgment," in which, after the mighty dissonant climax, complete emotional exhaustion is registered by a *pianissimo* gasp an octave below. A well-executed *diminuendo*, after an apex has been reached, is the normal acknowledgment of the higher estate of the peak. Ascent and descent are thus two natural slopes, the one this side of the hill being negotiated more slowly than the downward incline on the other side. There are more precipitous drops in other numbers of the "Requiem," but there are none so sheer as to prevent safe control in descending. Light and shade construe a color. Approach to and retirement from an apex explain a musical period.

This brief survey of the crescents and apexes which provide the progressive movement to the climax of Brahms' "How Lovely is Thy

[18] Cf. *canon* and *fugue*, pages 209 *et seq.*, for general technique of fugal conducting.

Dwelling Place, O Lord of Hosts," has been offered as a general plan for measuring the dynamic dimensions of other modern compositions. It is of no import that other conductors may disagree with specific items of the analysis. My concern has been not with an academic dissection of periods and phrases, but with the allocation of sections of the number to its conceptual purpose. I wrote on page 156 that "in practically all time-pattern music, musical figures are *going somewhere.*" Where are they *going?* Does a conductor know? If he doesn't, the itinerary will be a silly adventure. The composer had the right to embark upon an adventure, but once he wrote down his course on paper and handed it to conductors to follow, the element of adventure was finished. There is evidence to show that, occasionally, some of the great composers were lost for a while, emerging into the clear only by good luck. Therefore they could not map their wanderings. But the average well-written piece of music is excellent cartography, and a conductor will find there plenty of hints as to the surest route to the destination set by the composer. The conductor must know how to take the curves, when to shift gears, when to accelerate, when to retard in gear or by the brake, and when to coast along to a stop. He must know where he is going and how to get there. A piece of music needs study as a road map does.

The chart which I have submitted of the Brahms ascents, descents, and curves (with their dynamic implications) may induce young conductors to cultivate the habit of analyzing the volume requirements of all the music which they undertake to interpret.

Of course, I am aware that modernistic tendencies in performance as well as in composition are replacing many old-fashioned purposes and proprieties. Certainly all modern music is not stridor, but, beginning with the Wagnerian era, volume of sound has been winning increasing approbation even among academic musicians. Quantity has been, perhaps inadvertently, set up as a criterion of excellence. Contemporary composers have reacted to the loudness prevailing in performances by writing much music which depends avowedly upon *fortissimo* for its effectiveness.

I admit that it is easy to be one-sided—on either side—in this matter of quantity ratios, but it seems psychologically saner and aesthetically more sensitive to incline to a bias for the softer side. The "Mannheim mannerism" (cf. page 108) showed a trend in dynamics quite different from the current proneness to over-all loudness. The Stamitz plan was freely to run through the dynamic panels from one extreme to another. Today's mannerism—the *forte* background —is sufficiently frenetic to be branded an extravagant eccentricity. Musicianship seems to be disorganized. Mild-mannered listeners are urged to repent of the heresies of nuance, balanced dynamics, prepared climaxes, and the other silly nonsense of an effete and moribund culture! The current undisciplined volume is alienating organic properties of music from their logical connections.

Perhaps *music* is not the right word for much that is being purveyed in auditoriums. Probably the sweeps and surges, the heaping of din upon clamor—Ossa upon Pelion—should be designated by a new nomenclature. Certainly *music* is too gentle and sensitive a term to embrace tremendous outbursts and distorting expansions in its inclusions. An exchange of roars between Titan ashore and Neptune "under the 'whelming tide" would be too tumultuous a vociferation to be included in the definition of *conversation*. The bases of communication crumble in continued loudness.

While awaiting a better name from the pen of some colleague, I am enjoying the irony of the compound *megasonica* (great noise) in connection with the clattering clashes of modern performances.

If the zealots of contemporary volume were content to serve up the modernistic ragouts *fortissimo*, the defenders of the aesthetic in music might leave well enough alone. But too many of them force Beethoven, Mozart, and Bach into the noisy panels. The classics cannot survive in "the immense and contemptuous surges." To a conductor seriously infected in the widening epidemic of *megasonica*, such things as *apexes*, *fall-offs*, *poco a poco*, etc., are just items in "the silly nonsense of an effete and moribund culture." The invalid may convalesce if he retires to an environment of peace and quiet. He should look at no lurid pictures. Stravinsky's *Le Sacre du Printemps* should be turned to the wall and the etchings of Pergolesi with some eighteenth-century water colors displayed.

It would not be factually honest to belittle the contributions of the present era to the emancipation of music from certain platitudinous restrictions. Greater freedom in harmony, counterpoint, and form has lured composers to new fields. But it is evident that there has been little progress in the interpretation of music. It is true that both chorophony and symphony are beginning to interest musicians in their more admirable endowment on the purely physical side. The art of interpretation, meanwhile, is sadly neglected, superficial techniques, and the din of choral and orchestral paroxysms depriving music of elegance, seemliness, and even acoustical orthodoxy. If music has been trying to step forward on its right foot, its advance is impeded by a recalcitrant left.

Music, distinguished from megasonica, *depends upon degrees, shades, and gradations of quantity as well as upon structural excellences for validity as an art form.*

If this be heresy and "silly nonsense," St. Ambrose, St. Gregory, Hucbald, Josquin des Pres, and Palestrina were the heresiarchs and Simple Simons of their eras, and Bach, Handel, etc., the later propagandists of error.

In concluding the survey of these aspects of the relationship between music and dynamics, I repeat a sentence written near the beginning of the chapter: *Ignorance or misunderstanding of the implications of tonal volume is a hostile impediment to aesthetic interpretation.*

CHAPTER V

DYNAMICS (Continued)

The Curve Line, Tessitura and Rilievo

IN THE preceding chapter the general relationship of tonal volume to aesthetic communicability has been surveyed. Some conclusions were drawn from the consideration of the major aspects of this relationship. These conclusions may reasonably be posited as the bases for a successful strategy in dealing with quantity ratios. It is profitable now to examine the structural features of compositions as indices of the tactical, here-and-now appropriateness of volume levels. In this chapter the curve line of principal melodies and the *tessitura* of periods and phrases are discussed. Ensuing chapters are devoted to the consideration of timbres, tension, and counterpoint as influences on dynamic propriety. The special stylistic properties of *a cappella* polyphony and the rapport of *face* melodies with concomitant melodies in vertical harmony are canvassed in the chapters on polyphony and homophony. *A cappella* polyphony, both sacred and secular, depends altogether for acceptability to modern ears on the due allocation of quantity variations throughout the horizontally moving lines. Hymn tunes, part songs, glees, and vertical music generally require careful analysis of the concomitant melodies latent in the harmony in order that the constituents of the homophonic organization may be aptly and artistically correlated.

The design of a principal melody is often a clear clue to its character. A prevailing pattern of intervallic appositions is the curve line of a composition. Broadly, curve lines vary significantly in the regularity or irregularity of ascents and descents; in the manner of approach to and retirement from peaks; in the characteristic type of motion, conjunct or disjunct; in the span from lowest to highest notes.

Tessitura is the general locale or *lie* of the total of arcs contributing to a design. *Rilievo* is the term applied in these pages to the lie of particular periods, phrases, or even measures which by their individuality establish a temporary *tessitura*, thus indicating the need of quantitative modifications. Pitch and volume being intimately related in an aesthetico-acoustical affinity, both *tessitura* and *rilievo* need study as important guides to an effective economy of dynamics.

The sensitive and well-schooled conductor finds in the compass and genre of melodic intervals a *verbum sapienti* which he is quick to heed. Frequently the curve line indicates to him the category of a composition—non-emotive, impersonal, lyrico-romantic, lyrico-dramatic, or intensely dramatic. If the notes of a principal melody are compressed within an inconsiderable compass, the curve line is obviously slight; and unless special emotional intensity is suggested by a text or the markings of the composer, one should conclude that a minimum of dramatic intent is implied, and further, that only a modicum of volume and volume shading is congruous. Similarly, if the melodic flexures of a more ample curve line are slight, the design indicates a lyric gentleness which is impugned and affronted by loudness and extensive variations of quantity, unless, of course, such simply constructed passages are segments of a definitely dramatic period. Melodies written in a prevailing conjunct motion, intimating little of emotional agitation, are disparaged by histrionic dynamics.

Fig. 34 is an example of a melody with a simple curve line.

FIG. 34.

The chord (in the geometrical sense) which may be drawn between the termini of each small arc is short. In each instance except the last, the chordal line marks a fourth; the grace-note effect which extends the compass of the last arc to a sixth can be eliminated without altering the substance of the melody. The span of the combined arcs is a seventh (a meager compass for voice or instrument), and the melody proceeds in conjunct motion, save in the second arc where minor thirds modestly intrude. There is no associated text to prove a mood; no program note indicates that the melody is an excerpt from a dramatic sequence; there are no markings for a dynamic level.

What, then, is the appropriate quantity level for these eight measures, even if developed consistently to a thirty-two-bar episode, performed as a brief entity? And what degree of *crescendo* and *diminuendo* is aesthetically implied in the third and fourth arcs?

Certainly, a higher level than the *minus* side of panel No. 3 (cf. page 99) would insinuate greater depth than is usually intimated by so simple a design. The nuance, to avoid unseemly extravagance, should be accomplished between the *minus* and *plus* sides of the same panel. In the absence of textural implications and markings which would add to the definitive intent of such a melody, the segments of the circlet of notes, contiguous and without abrupt demarcation, suggest only equanimity and calmness. There is no hint of latent agitation. The intervals, being closely ordered, offer no room for dramatic gesticulation. Therefore, the reticent melody should be performed without ostentation, i.e., quietly.

I remember having been puzzled, while an adolescent student, by the failure of the liturgical chants to impress me with their alleged aptitude for spiritual expression. They had come down the centuries the approved media of religious utterance. Perhaps I debited an ever-increasing dissatisfaction with the historical psalm tones to my youthful insensibility to esoteric or formally academic values. But later I learned the real reason for my earlier apathy to the chants when I heard them sung in the proper dynamic panel and shaded with well-proportioned nuances by the then-exiled monks of Solesmes at Quarr Abbey in the Isle of Wight. It was the correspondence of curve line and dynamics that put the melodies right at the Abbey, and the lack of this correspondence that had robbed them of effectiveness in the churches where they were shouted. Immediately after the enlightening experience (it was a real adventure) at the Abbey, I began seriously to examine the curve lines of compositions as criteria by which to estimate appropriate quantity ratios. I found indifference to curve lines as revealed by unsuitable ratios a major cause of distorted interpretations. In what a multitude of Catholic churches the Sixth Gregorian Psalm-tone, and in what a multitude of Episcopal churches the Anglican single chant (a major third over-all in both instances) have been vociferated with the abandon suited only to a frenetic *stretto*, accompanied the while by sonorous open (*very open*) diapasons! And the impersonal *cantus firmi* of the polyphonists, how ruthlessly have they been wrenched from the tranquillity of their purpose! And what of the easy-running *fioriture* of the eighteenth-century ornamentalists? How disastrously thick and ponderous the *fortissimos* have made them, suggesting the travesty of making lace with inch-thick ropes!

In another book I used a phrase from Browning in referring to lyric voices "gone wrong" through overexpansion by incompetent teachers; here I invoke the phrase to satirize the conductor who, vainly undertaking to convert tiny arcs into great vaulted arches, "blows out his brains upon the flute."

The following interpolation regarding freedom in interpreting Gregorian chant is not irrelevant. Structurally, it is obvious, Gregorian chant is non-dramatic. The *cantus firmus* of *a cappella* polyphony, being usually a design within a Gregorian octave, imparts a quasi-impersonal character to the contrapuntal style of the Renaissance.

The melodic fluctuations of plain song are confined, with an occasional exception to the general rule, within the compass of the final note and its octave in authentic (odd-numbered) modes, and within the stretch from the fourth below to the fifth above the final in plagal (even-numbered) modes. Frequently, melodies in the latter modes are imperfect, i.e., they fail to descend to the notes lying below the final. Thus many plagal chants present a contracted curve line which further restricts the meager-enough rhetorical resources of perfect melodies. Chant melodies tend to pivot around the dominant notes of the modes in which they are arranged. The compactness of Gregorian forbids expansive expression as antipathetic to its nature. The Reverend Alec Robertson, A.R.A.M., Chaplain of Westminster Cathedral, in an interesting treatise, *The Interpretation of Plainchant*,[1] pleads for more interpretative latitude than is generally conceded in the singing of the chant. He finds the average rendition of the great old melodies of the Church to be insufferably unconvincing. Where there should be the vivifying life of religious communication, there is too often inertia. Many chant choirs seem to have swallowed puritanic narcotics. They sing drowsily. After an antiphon or two they are asleep, continuing to mutter a jumble of *puncta* and compound neumes. Soon a congregation becomes somnolent itself and is lullabied to lethargy. Music is permitted association with the Sacred Liturgy to *invigorate* worshipers; enervating intonations contravene the ends of public worship. My discontent with the chant stemmed to the *noisy* delivery which was characteristic of Italian, German, and North American performance. But Father Robertson decries the "ladylike, namby-pamby, pernickety imitations of French monastic singing—a thing beautiful in itself." These imitations have gained vogue

---

[1] Published by the Oxford University Press, Humphrey Milford, London.

in England and have been imparted to some American liturgical sarcophagi. Certainly nobody who really understands the spiritual and psychological reactions (these are closely allied) of worshipers to all the accessories of ritual can reasonably deny that his aim is in the right direction. His target is realism in chant. The degree of realism achievable may be said, analogously, to be the distance a Gregorian arrow can travel. But the bowshot of the neumes is short. If the bow is bent with excessive strength, it will break. Short-distance archery is indicated.

The resources of general music interpretation may be applied to Gregorian melody only within the strict limits of its nature. The rhythmical stress of chant is not the measured, bar-line, time-pattern recurrent accentuation of modern music. The metrical underlining appropriate to the music of Bach, Beethoven, or Brahms might and probably would be unseemly caricature in chant. Its simple curve line bespeaks a smooth undulating rise and fall of sound. Like the ripples of "Sweet Afton" (cf. page 18), its melodies must be bidden to "flow gently." *Sforzando, subito pianissimo,* long *crescendos* through the dynamic panels to *fortissimo, diminuendos* from vigorous apexes to vanishing points, *accelerandos* and *rallentandos* (which startle tempos out of pace), *fermatas* and the *grande pausa* are interpretative expedients apt only for the broader forms of music.

It is unreasonable to expect the same results from child and man. Gregorian chant has the fragility of the child. Broad dynamic changes or histrionic *rubato* would be exploitation of its delicacy. Music was a long time growing up from its Ambrosian infancy and Gregorian childhood through polyphonic adolescence to its present stature and ruggedness. It did not jump from the cradle to the modern concert platform. Even the intricacies of sixteenth-century counterpoint failed to increase substantially the histrionic content. The contours of Palestrina as well as of the Gregorianists must be spared mauling.

It is unnecessary to cite many examples to prove that a gentle curve line generally indicates the propriety of gentle dynamics. Frequently, in compact conjunct motion, varying degrees of intensity are intimated, but ratios of intensity are not necessarily influenced by ratios of volume (cf. page 131).

Although the seventeenth and eighteenth centuries witnessed the divorce of melody from many traditions, melody remained lyric or lyrico-dramatic by reason of the still prevalent taste for conjunct progressions. Perhaps the ornamentations and *fioriture* of those centuries were a compromise with traditional taste. Disjunct long-leap melodies were soliciting vogue and it is quite likely that Bach, Handel, Haydn, and Mozart employed the *fioriture* to maintain a semblance of conjunct motion in the changing style (cf. chapter VI).

As a rule, prevailing conjunct motion, the span approximately of an octave, and general adherence to a key tonality, which includes conservative use of chromaticism, concur to advise restraint in the application of tonal quantity. The student conductor is urged to verify this conclusion by playing on the piano several melodies thus designed at different dynamic levels and with greater and less degrees of modification. A careful student will find that simple curve-line melodies, minus qualifying textural association and composers' instructions, are invariably distorted by notable volume and extensive fluctuations. The *forte* panels suggest excitement; the gentle curve line suggests composure.

Therefore, it should be jointly inferred from the same premises that the greater the span of the curve line, the more disjunct the design, the sheerer and more excursive the melodic reaches, and the more striking the chromaticism (due either to aberrations from key tonality or to the mixture of many timbres), the clearer the intimation of latent vigor. Extensive and irregular segments are the pattern— the musico-geometry—for music impelled by eagerness. The dramatic intent of music that is prospered by *forte* delivery and marked degrees of *crescendo* and *diminuendo* is usually manifested by the text and dynamic markings or by the title of the composition. In modern music one rarely has only the curve line of a movement by which to appraise the character of a piece. Histrionic and massive music is usually identified by a caption or by its place in the general context. The *fortissimo* and *pianissimo* of great emotional activity reveal their opportuneness unmistakably. The clamor of a triumphal march prescribes itself. Usually, however, there is a correspondence between the emotional intent and the design of the melodies through which the vagaries of reaction and excitation are to be expressed.

The great volume of the musical repertory is comprised of compositions whose principal melodies follow a moderate curve line. Between the extremes of utter simplicity and stark theatricalism are the lyric odes which are the best agencies of natural music. It is in the accommodation of tonal strength to this vast library that the acumen of true musicianship is revealed.

There are two inclusive reasons why the *forte* and *fortissimo* panels should be used with hypercritical discrimination in setting forth moderate music. First, because a moderate curve line usually indicates only moderate fervor, and second, because high dynamic pressure throughout the average piece is lavish expenditure of power, preventing rise to climactic features. In normal human relations, loud declamation prejudices communication. Sympathetic understanding is not engendered by shouting. Niggardliness and noise make an attractive affinity. Obviously, a high prevailing quantity level excludes the possibility of dynamic development which is a rich resource of interpretation.

The left side of the diagram of dynamic panels is the safe side for the greater number of compositions, vocal and instrumental. Crescendos *to great loudness and* subito fortes, *with their opposites, should be rated as expedients for securing signal emphasis.*

Effective presentation of moderate melodies requires the treatment known to painters as *chiaroscuro*. This is defined in Chambers' *Encyclopedia* as "the art of representing light in shadow and shadow in light, so that the parts represented in shadow shall still have the clearness and warmth of those in light, and those in light the depth and softness of those in shadow."

Chiaroscuro means simply the establishing of recurrent contrasts without violence; in painting, without discordant irrelation of colors; in literature, without mismatched ideas; in music, without disproportionate dynamics; generally, without such degrees of modification as would startle or distract. Such degrees are intrusions upon the aesthetic homogeneity of all artistic portraiture save the depiction of passion, heroics, crisis, or catastrophe. The excitation properly associated with the exposition of major emotional states and experiences is altogether uncongenial with the temper of the majority of motets, anthems, and part songs which the average conductor interprets. In the usual repertory, the opportuneness of passionate utterance is rare. Chiaroscuro prescribes a moderate volume background and nuances that are only the "shadow of a shade." Mildness as opposed to bluster. Quiet restraint in the rise and fall of dynamic power. Chiaroscuro anathematizes exaggeration because vulgar, extravagance because falsifying, the lurid because horrid.

Just enough *forte* for clarity and vitality; just enough *piano* for grace and proportion.

The curve line is a guide to appropriate degrees of sonority because it helps to disclose the dramatic intent of a melody. The lie of melodic phrases advises of relative dynamic warrants by its acoustical connotation. The subject of *tessitura* has been introduced in connection with the dynamic treatment of the treble, middle, and low lines of chorus and orchestra (cf. page 133). Additional data are presented here in answer to the following questions:

1. Is a melody or phrase in high *tessitura* to be treated dynamically as a melody in a lower area?

2. Do changes in the *tessitura* of accompanying parts involve corresponding changes in quantity ratios?

Singers and conductors are wont to overlook the inferences to be drawn from the lie of a composition or any of its integral units. *Tessitura* is defined by the lexicographers as *the area in the range of a voice part in which most of its tones occur*. Vocalists often appraise a song by its *tessitura*—high, middle, or low—adverting to the comfort or discomfort and the greater or less opportunity for vocal display involved in its performance. They rarely consider the dynamic implications of the lie of phrases, *forte* always being a mandate for the same degree of laryngeal pressure, at the top, middle, or bottom of the compass. It is difficult to associate true artistry in any era with chronic unawareness of the interrelations of pitch and volume. In this era of phonograph and radio, facts about pitch vibrations and quantity are common knowledge. Performers and conductors, therefore, may not ingenuously plead ignorance.

Acousticians and radio engineers have promulgated two basic tenets about broadcasting which have not escaped the attention of active musicians: *high notes in the* forte *panels disturb the microphone*, and *low notes and* pianissimo *are, equivalently, an aphonic combination*. Master technicians of the physics of sound are convinced that piquant pitches and mordant timbres are so pungent in themselves that more than a modicum of volume may distort them to graceless stridency; also, conversely, that low pitches because of slow periodicity, and dull timbres in the ratio of their murkiness need the definition and reinforcement that increased volume can supply.

If shrill, high treble *fortes* are taboo and the less lively pitches and tone colors are intensified by increments of quantity in the best broadcasting and recording studios, it must be evident that a general principle underlying the proper relation of pungency and volume is revealed. The special needs of the studios have emphasized the necessity of recognizing the principle. Its validity is clear in the exacting conditions of radio and cinema. Is it negligible as a guide to dynamics in concert auditoriums? Probably the failure to apply the principle in the auditoriums is less detrimental to aesthetic effect than in the studios, but it is evident that the synthesis of pitch, timbre, and volume should, under all circumstances, be the best possible balance of energizing factors.

A large percentage of the potential effectiveness of music is sacrificed by conductors who have not realized that the more acute pitches and timbres should be moderated and the less acute proportionately invigorated.

If the *tessitura* of solo numbers has an acoustical import, should not the lie of choral and orchestral compositions suggest the dynamic equities? The obvious answer is that it is practically impossible to judge the prevailing tonal level of single choral or orchestral lines in any lengthy movement, because the site of the constituent melodies is temporary and ever shifting. Therefore the term *tessitura* is not sufficiently comprehensive. The accepted understanding of the word is applicable to songs, ballads, and short arias. I find it necessary to extend the concept to include *sectional tessituras*. Most often, a short tune of sixteen bars can be appraised as maintaining a certain *tessitura*, but occasionally one encounters a melody of this length which moves in two distinct loci.

FIG. 35.

The sixteen-bar melody in Fig. 35 lies in a medium *tessitura* for soprano or tenor. The moderately high notes in measures 9-12 are momentary digressions from the main musical idea. But substitute

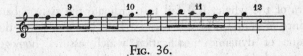

FIG. 36.

the sequence in Fig. 36 for the notes in measures 9-12, and immediately a four-bar phrase at a different altitude presents itself. It is in a high *sectional tessitura* dissociated from the other twelve bars of the melody.

The several *sectional tessituras* to be found in almost any modern composition of sizable dimensions require each a "fair field and no favor." Each demands adroit management. The acoustic pressure varies on different musical strata. Music cannot function with aesthetic effect if the same energy volume is applied at all levels *Do re mi fa sol* may spell one idea at a low level and another at a notably higher level, just as the Hellenic use of aspirated or unaspirated vowels, the ensuing letters being identical, imparts different meanings to words.

Frequently changing levels will be designated hereafter not by the clumsy and confusing term *sectional tessituras*, but by a term which I borrow from the art of sculpture, *rilievo*. This word, properly qualified, denotes the degree of sharpness with which subject matter is presented. When applied to music, it can by easy analogy signify the altitude at which melodic phrases are assembled. *Tessitura* may therefore return to its familiar page in the dictionary, and *rilievo* enter the vocabulary of musicians with this specific connotation.

The sequence, 9-12 in the first framing of the melody given above, is not isolated from the medium *tessitura* of the whole, but the substituted bars of the second setting clearly introduce a different *rilievo*.

One may not establish positively any specific number of measures or any precise degree of aloofness as unmistakable proof of a new *rilievo*. The personal sensitiveness of conductors to changes in the melodic locale determines the reactions of individuals. If, however, one is apt to ignore the facts of acoustics or the principles of continuity, his reactions are unreliable.

Personally, I am sensitive to the change of atmosphere which is produced when a melody migrates from an established locus to a lie an octave above the tonic or a fourth below, and sojourns there for four bars. Thus, in the substituted measures 9-12, I am immediately aware of a high *rilievo* and am impelled to correlate it with the *tessitura* of the whole. If I fail to coordinate the sixteen bars in a semblance of continuity, it is because I neglect to employ the easy technique of dynamic modification which assures homogeneity. When a melody sojourns as in the substitution shown in Fig. 37 for the original measures, 9-12, the necessity for equalization is likewise insistent.

Fig. 37.

Few choral conductors heed the interpretative orders issued through shifting *rilievos.*

The original melody in Fig. 35 is marked *mezzo-forte.* The only adjustments which even a rigorous acoustician would prescribe here are slight decreases in volume at the high notes, E, F, G, (9-11).

The *rilievo* in Fig. 36 sets forth four measures at a notably more penetrating pitch. If these measures are sung *mezzo-forte,* the combination of high pitch and volume will produce the effect of a *plus forte.* Therefore, in order to maintain the general *mezzo-forte* level designated for the melody, the new *rilievo* should be sung *piano.* One glance at measures 9-12 in Fig. 36 should persuade a good conductor of the need of this softening. The *rilievo* substituted in Fig. 37, on the contrary, requires reinforcement to remain in a *mezzo-forte* relationship to the whole, and therefore should be performed at *minus forte.*

The examination of *tessitura* and *rilievo* in connection with dynamics will be generously repaid by new concepts of erstwhile unsatisfactory figures. Suggestions for the solution of enigmatic movements may accrue, troublesome parts may more speedily find their places in the mosaic, moods and dramatic intimations may be more readily discerned.

A sudden change of *rilievo* without a compensating modification of volume is certain to impair the balance which is essential to the unity of any artistic product. An equation of dynamic ratios on the basis of correlated high, middle, and low pitches is an ideal which every conductor should aim to attain. The equalizing of diverse elements and tonal disparities can be accomplished only by counterbalancing the influences of pitch, timbre, and volume.

Quantity ratios in the accompanying harmony (polyphony has idiomatic needs) should be devised on the basis of their service to the principal melody.

At this point and hereafter in this volume, the third major responsibility of the conductor—*the correlation of the melody with all associated integrants both manifest and implied* (cf. page 9)— claims attention. Shifting *rilievos* in the harmony necessarily affect the cogency of the melody. Careless management is usually mis-management, and indifferent distribution of *fortes* and *pianos* throughout the figures and choral structure of simultaneous lines tends to misrepresent the melody.

It is profitable frequently to remind oneself that, at least in the traditional forms of music, melody is the primary substance and harmony only a variable accidental. The dynamic motion of a principal should never be disturbed by the vagaries of an accessory. Melody cannot endure overloading; it can carry just so many decibels of associated sounds. Characteristically, and therefore most frequently, it is fragile (although the reinforcement added by Wagnerian brasses and the clamor of modernism have increased its vigor) and disintegrates readily. Freedom from undue encumbrance is assured to melody by minimizing the momentum with which harmony often seems to impinge on its fair contours.

If a high degree of tension against a melody seems imminent, the conductor's first office is to identify the source of the impending disturbance. This may be, perhaps, the interpolation of exotic accidentals in the harmony, a sequence of deterring dissonances, a bold shuffle of accompanying timbres,[2] or merely the change of the harmony from one *rilievo* to another. Such shifting occurs in the following circumstances:

1. When melody and harmony proceed generally in the same direction, by similar motion. The sudden migration of an extreme accompanying line to a notably higher or lower site either hinders or helps the melody. If the shift is to a higher plane, the tension is naturally greater, since the vibrations of the accompanying line increase in frequency, thus making the latter dangerous. If the change is to a lower area, the line, instead of offering a challenge, enhances the freedom of the melody. Sometimes the shift is to so low an area as to give the unpleasant impression of deserting the melody altogether.

Such shifts in similar motion occur usually when the harmony is suddenly reduced from four or more parts to three or two. Frequently the basses join the tenors in unison; sometimes instrumental figures are transposed up or down an octave. Similar motion, drawing meagerly upon the resources of harmony, does not present troublesome situations frequently, although *basso-continuo*, by reason of its recurring high and low areas, needs ingenious management.

[2] Cf. accidentals, dissonance, timbre in the index.

Since the practical scheme for preventing excessive tension, while harmonies gad about in their sundry fashions, is substantially the same for all, it is given in connection with the considerations presented on pages 181 *et seq.*

2. When oblique procedure against sustained notes intensifies or diminishes contrapuntal pressure. Whether the sustained notes are functioning as a definite *canto fermo* (cf. measures 1-5 and 14-18 in the excerpt from Mozart's "Requiem" in Fig. 40) or in the role of harmonics to a keynote, as in the example in Fig. 38, they are susceptible to the magnetism of slanting movements. If a figure is gradually climbing to an apex near the sustained tone, it should be restrained, lest the purpose of the prolonged note be frustrated. On the contrary, a descending figure, obviously effecting a contrapuntal fall-away, is frequently in need of a slight *crescendo*. Certainly the bass line in Fig. 38 requires one reading in the first four and another in the second four bars.

Fig. 38.

The insistent rise of the bass (1-4) to the environs over which D keeps lonely sentinel readily converts itself into an impetuous assault, contravening the intention of the composer unless checked by the conductor. With an energetic ascent through a compass of an octave and a fourth, the bass begins at once to place the treble D in jeopardy, and in measures 3-4 would fain defy the frightened note to remain in perspective.

Harmony and counterpoint are declared allies of melody. Presumably the conductor is a diplomat especially commissioned to effect the fulfillment of their pact. Curiously, many ambassadors of the art permit violations to occur, either unobserved or unprotested. Perhaps they are afflicted with fact blindness. Possibly they are so distracted by a multitude of duties on the podium that they pay scant attention to the more surreptitious cabals subtly developing under their batons. Probably, however, and most likely, they take for granted that melody and harmony must, by a natural law, cooperate in amity, and where a severance of these amicable relations is in reality responsible for disagreeable results they honestly, if naïvely, place the blame on poor singing, poor playing, or poor acoustics!

Melody sometimes struggles vainly for its life (never, of course, while Monsieur Fracas and his "famous swing orchestra" are in charge), and too frequently it is embraced to death by the pythons of noisy harmony. When huge choruses and orchestras together loosen their forces in charivari, concert halls become the shambles of music.

3. When the harmony is in contrary motion to the melody. If the *rilievos* of the melody and harmony are far apart, little difficulty is experienced in achieving a correct balance of ideas. But if encroachment is indicated, even if only at the start of a phrase, authentic interpretation demands that the conductor be on guard. Fig. 39 is an excerpt from a simple hymn tune which is easily distorted by mismanagement of the bass and tenor attack in the passage shown. The preceding phrase finds the bass on A flat, first space. The leap of the

Fig. 39.

bass to its octave, for measure 1, can surprise the serenity established in the earlier bars of the hymn. There is no reason here for surprise. New though short *rilievos* are about to begin for all parts. After mounting to unexpectedly high notes, the tenors and basses are assigned a descending arc in thirds in contrast with the ascending arc of sopranos and altos. The bass (more important here than the tenor on account of two leaps in the same direction) has already vaulted an octave to A flat, measure 1, and immediately jumps an additional fourth. There is a hint of a menacing approach to the soprano. Add the tenors, and instantly a possible usurpation may be sensed. The tenor and bass seem about to infringe the rights of soprano and alto. Furthermore, the middle register *rilievo* of the latter voices is unsettled by the high tritone (bass D flat—alto G) and dissonance (tenor F—alto G) *if the* D flat *and the* F *are addressed vigorously*. Either the tritone or the dissonance in this juxtaposition can interrupt the lyric continuity proper to any part song. High untempered descants, so often used to embellish simple hymns, frequently rob them of fluency. The descending thirds of tenors and basses should be underlined rather than the coruscation of the soprano and alto thirds in measures 2-3. But the D flat and the F must be met by *indirect attack* (cf. page 124) and the dynamic prerogatives taken over quietly.

Clear-cut changes of melodic *rilievo*, convolutions of harmony in similar, oblique, or contrary motion or in a mixture of these styles, and excursions of counterpoint to upper octaves, constantly introduce new conditions. A *status quo* of eight bars may be definitely altered in ensuing measures. Necessarily, then, a conductor has no choice but to cultivate a perspicacity, tantamount to intuition, for discerning the new conditions and appraising them aright. His application of the resources of interpretation to each variation will be fortuitous if his diagnosis of warning symptoms is casual.

The excerpts from the "Requiem" of Mozart and the "German Requiem" of Brahms in Figs. 40 and 41 offer material, relevant and informative, for profitable examination.

In the introductory measures of the Mozart number a plan of contrary motion is fixed as the design for the composition. High and low lines, descent and ascent, consonances and dissonances in the form of passing notes or tied suspensions are adroitly woven into a fine fabric. But the filaments are so delicate, as they often are in involved inventions, that a conductor exhibiting the lacework may unwittingly allow them to become inextricably knotted, and the display is only a snarled disarray. Mozart offers an ingeniously graphic pattern which the conductor must reproduce in sound with equal ingenuity in intertwining the dynamics. Mozart evidently purposed to awaken a sense of quiet strife by the changing *rilievos*, the crisscrossings, and the offsets which abound throughout this number. Such contrapuntal tension is music's most successful medium for describing confusing and wistful experiences. The text, a stanza from the "Dies Irae" written probably by Thomas of Celano in the thirteenth century, in this instance helps the student to that conclusion. The soul is impelled, first in one direction and presently in another, to mediate upon two seemingly irreconcilable attributes of God, His justice and His mercy. The soul is represented as consciously aware that its infidelities caused the Passion and Death of Christ, and subconsciously hopeful that Christ will be forgiving for that very fact. Mozart, finding in the contrapuntal reciprocities of music a subtle

FIG. 40.

Fig. 40 (*cont.*).

FIG. 41.

means of expressing some awareness of the Great Mystery of the Atonement, has successfully conveyed the conviction of guilt, a prescience of forgiveness, and the resulting wonderment of the soul, through the *philosophical* correspondence of the resources employed. The conductor, then, is held to the obligation of revealing the compositive parts in logical interrelation by balancing the contrapuntal volumes. Therefore no single element can be emphasized too energetically without weakening the import of the others. The mystical transcendence of the two thoughts, justice and mercy, may be found in the rising dissonance of the treble, measures 1-6, and the hope of reconciling them is intimated by the cello figure. All movement starts at the unison F. The cello begins with confidence, but not boldly. Hope will be justified gradually. Even if dissociated from all "program" connotation, the dissonances and contrapuntal figure must not be permitted to conceal the general melodic progression, F G A Bb C, 2-5. *Acoustics demands that all potentially deranging sounds be delicately interwoven.* The art of chiaroscuro (cf. Index) should be invoked here, else the disembodied spirituality of Mozart's concept will be replaced by a harsh and cacophonous medley of meaningless noises. The upward leaps of the cello, 3-4, and its procession from A, 5, to B flat, 6, where it is party to a double dissonance, tend to invite undue attention. These progressions are obviously a challenge to the treble line and must be restrained within the economy of the whole. The ascending movement of the cello in medium *rilievo*, 7-12, suggests the need of greater amplitude, and the high interlacing of the treble parts in these measures requires notable decrease in quantity.

A detailed analysis or synthesis of all the components of this number is superfluous. My aim is to impress upon conductors the persistent need of first separating single elements, studying their individual characteristics, and then only combining them in a texture of relative quantities. All pieces of music from the simplest unisonous melody to the most complex inventions of elaborate symphony require academic scrutiny of the apposition of *rilievos* if their aesthetic content is to be disclosed. Mixtures of high with low *rilievos*, ascending with descending motion, dissonant with consonant harmony must be put through a fine sieve to be readied for artistic interpenetration.

A preeminent virtue of good contrapuntal writing lies in the thorough sifting to which a composer has submitted his material.

The outstanding defect of contrapuntal performance is the presenta
tion of ingredients as though they had not been sorted. Counterpoin
on paper may show the lovely mezzotints of a master picture; the same
counterpoint in the concert halls is frequently reorganized into a
rude motley of incongruities.

The excerpt from the "German Requiem" is offered as another
example of the intricate but delicate counterpoint which habitually
evades the grasp of incurious conductors.

Perhaps some conductors wear both opaque lenses and thick
ear muffs, for, ostensibly looking and listening, they permit melodies
to be assailed from above and below, melodic arcs to be flattened out
or bent into crooked angles, menial passing notes to don the vest
ments of *canto fermo*, and internecine warfare between parts to
lay waste rich fields.

I have set down these measures of Brahms not because they contain
items for further study, but because they corroborate the conclusions
which the serious student has probably deduced from the Mozart
juxtapositions.

The only dynamic instruction for the twelve measures of the
Brahms excerpt is *forte*. Does this indication mean that the same
quantity of tone is to be invoked throughout, regardless of the dull
ness or acuteness of the *rilievos*? Obviously, no. The composer is pro
posing the general effect of *forte*. To achieve this, adjustments are
necessary. In the opening measures, the strings are low; the sopranos
enter at a pitch considerably more than an octave higher. The
orchestral figure should proceed probably at *plus forte* and the
voices attack at *mezzo-forte*, if a quantitative equation is to be estab
lished. At measure 4, the relationship changes, requiring a corre
sponding shift of the dynamic proportions. *Plus mezzo-forte* will
perhaps suffice to inspirit the vocal line, and *minus mezzo-forte* will
be ample stint for the high strings, the cellos, and string basses con
tinuing at *plus forte*, etc.

As an experiment it is profitable to conduct the Mozart and
Brahms excerpts in two ways.

1. Disregard the dynamic equations implied by acoustics; a chaos
of incongruities results. Dissonances nose impudently into a pro
gram of consonances; oblique passages, with high-pressure sirens,
noisily wrangle their way through sustained notes; high strings
screech in aeries; fragments of contrary motion fly off at tangents.
Like mutinous chessmen each malapert establishes an eccentric

route, the bishop moving like a knight, the knight like a bishop, the pawn like a queen, the castle offering no sanctuary, and the king's crown being knocked off more quickly than in the "scholar's checkmate." The *aesthetic* circuits of contrapuntal dynamics demand protection which the art of music can furnish only through fine adjustments of quantity ratios.

2. Apply these ratios, and observe how orderly and satisfying the blending of properties becomes. A rational idea is presented. Reasonable contrasts evolve from seeming incongruities, because dissonances now are made integral to consonant phrases; the detours of oblique figures are carefully indicated; only murmurs come from the aeries; movements in opposite directions are defined with symmetry; and the chessmen adhere to the rules of fair play!

Acoustic and dynamic equations are readily sensed. For practical purposes, a profound understanding of their mathematical relations is unnecessary. A conductor can easily work out for himself a scheme for correlating the energy induced by tonal vibrations and dynamic amplitude. Except in the music of the *a cappella* polyphonic style in which the acoustic and dynamic variations are, relatively to modern music, slight, and where the equations evolve principally from the relation of arsis and thesis (cf. Index), the conductor may be guided by the following considerations:

1. In high *rilievos*, acute voices and instruments (sopranos, mezzo-sopranos, piccolos, oboes, violins, treble brass) are insistently telling, by reason of rapid tonal vibrations and piquant overtones; therefore conservative use of quantity is prescribed.

2. Ascending passages, especially through treble octaves, need tempering for the same reason.

3. Descending figures in oblique or contrary motion, tonal vibrations decreasing, usually need dynamic reinforcement.

4. Chordal contrapuntal activity, as in measures 6 *et seq.* (Brahms) is endowed with such concentrated intensity as to require considerable reduction of quantity, except in very low areas.

5. Sudden leaps, especially in extreme parts (treble and bass) or when the jumping voices or instruments are reedy or notably sonorous tend always to arrogate attention; the change of acoustical atmosphere effected here is balanced by moderate indirect attacks (cf. page 120); i.e., if such a leap is to a note marked *mezzo-forte*, the latter should be addressed *piano* at the moment of impact, broadening immediately

thereafter. Otherwise the leap will be tantamount to a *sforzando*, and the balance of the ensemble imperiled.

6. Notes brought into dissonance with preexisting notes in all *rilievos*, particularly in the heights and when a more acute is superimposed on a less acute timbre (oboe on clarinet, violin on viola, trumpet on horn), must be introduced in a lower dynamic panel. Otherwise, the gracefulness of the dissonant figure is forfeited. Except when a prepared dissonance is employed for a startling dynamic effect, the amplitude of the preparatory note should be greater than that of the ensuing encumbrance.

7. In epitome: High and ascending phrases are maintained in equable proportion to the ensemble by lesser quantity; medium, descending, and low figures, when contrasted with the more acute, are prospered by judicious amplification.

Pitch and timbre are the agencies by which various degrees of penetrability qualify sounds. Quantity, in this connection, may be said to be a secondary agency. It is evident that an orderly disposition of vigor throughout a composition must be predicated on the opportuneness of greater or less service by the secondary agency. Volume is a reservoir of energy from which the conductor discriminately should draw to supplement the inadequacy of pitch or timbre in certain juxtapositions.

Here follow considerations about the attributes of some common timbres in their relation to quantity ratios. Since there is a tonal affinity between chorus and orchestra, I avail myself of the simple nomenclature of orchestral instrumentation to designate the timbres.

The simple *klangfarbe*[3] (Helmholtz) or *clang tint*[3] (Tyndall) of a flute exerts only a modicum of influence upon a concerted texture, its only easily discernible overtone being the octave. But the pungency of the double-reed quality of the oboe is so assertive as often to demand modification if ensemble balance and proportions are to be maintained.

In the example in Fig. 42 the silvery tones of the flute merely mingle quietly with the fifteenth of the dominant G played by the cellos. The timbre of the instrument is so placid as to suggest nothing more than a slight reinforcement of the harmonic. The clang tint of the oboe, however, gives the few notes such independence and insistence as to challenge the effectiveness of the strings.

[3] Sound color.

FIG. 42.

Therefore, with the strings at *mezzo-forte* the flute may also play safely at *mezzo-forte*, but the oboe should be restricted to *piano*. If both flute and oboe are to play, the *mezzo-forte* of the strings will be adequate only if the flute is reduced to *piano* and the oboe to *pianissimo*.

If French horns were assigned to B in Fig. 42 instead of strings, the penetrating pressure of the characteristic horn timbre (especially in the *rilievo* of first and third horns) would probably require *forte* from the oboe at A. With trumpets and trombones furnishing the B background at *mezzo-forte*, the flute would necessarily rise to *fortissimo* and the oboe to *forte*.

If B were to be distributed among violins, cellos, and basses, and A assigned to violas as an obligato line, the *mezzo-forte* at B would require a *plus forte* from the reticent violas at A.

Trumpets playing A over strings at B would disrupt balance if louder than *plus piano*. Trumpets playing in duet (the first at A and the second on the second line of B) would require more volume from the second than from the first.

If oboes, English horn, and bassoons were carrying B and clarinets A, the latter, being less pungent, would need some reinforcement —not much since the higher pitch of A tends to balance naturally.

Similarly, strings, woods, and brasses playing B at *mezzo-forte* would indicate a carefully adjusted increase of volume for first violins playing A.

These hypothetical appositions of instrumentation and the suggestions for corresponding quantity ratios in Fig. 42 clarify the tenet that timbre is an agency that cannot safely be overlooked in judging of dynamic proprieties.

To bring these orchestral relationships to bear upon the organization of the chorus, one needs only to substitute *coloratura* for *flute*, *light lyric* for *violin, broad lyric* for *oboe, mezzo-soprano* for *trumpet* etc.

The *klangfarbe* of the various voices and instruments unquestion-ably affects the dynamic needs of a melody in contrapuntal surround-ings. So, too, in vertical harmony the timbres of component parts are clues to appropriate stints of volume. Furthermore, the even continuity of a melody itself is frequently harassed by changing clang tints. The need of quantitative adjustments, in this connection, is greater in choral than in orchestral music. Here is the reason: The timbres of mechanical instruments are fixed by the features of their con-struction. Usually composers, knowing their individual characteristics, write accordingly. Except in some instances, the timbres of instru-ments are homogenous throughout their respective compasses. Com-posers, however, cannot safely rely upon fixed timbres in vocal units.

The skillful composer for orchestra provides the conductor with scores in which problems of timbre relations are rare. The latter, of course, must always be interested in the acoustical connotations of the instrumental network. But the orchestra of voices, the chorus, inde-pendently of the skill of the composer, is constantly presenting difficulties to the director.

In the average chorus, the irregularity of vocal colors is the relentless nemesis of melody. In the orchestra, erratic combinations are unusual; in the chorus, indeterminate timbres provide a queue of dilemmas. Many singers seem to prefer whimsey to order and often a beautifully written choral line surrenders an inherent elegance to vocal caprice. Homogeneity between registers and blended clang tints are virtues rarely exemplified in concerted singing. A flute is always a flute from the moment it leaves the artisan's hands. It will function according to canons of sound, mechanically assured to the instrument. But when is a soprano a soprano? Conductors, as a rule, are uncertain as to the sequence of timbres which the treble singers of a group will contrive in different registers under varying circumstances. Boys trained after the fashion of English cathedral choristers, and female coloraturas are practically the only stable vocalists. They ejaculate their utterances according to an invariable though ineffective norm. More fluty than flutes in the flesh, they are unchangingly the same—hollow and vapid. Choirmasters who know the limitations of these strange tonal properties may learn how and when to invoke the resources of dynamics to make them uniform if artificial carriers of melody. Other voices, however, frequently wander restlessly through registers, changing appearance like nervous chameleons. Unwittingly they juggle the colors of registers that have not been blended, necessarily rendering melody fitful and uncertain.

The eight bars in Fig. 43, if played by a unit of violins, are guaranteed a string timbre throughout, but the average soprano chorus will break the passage into four distinct and unrelated color sections, thus robbing the melody of a determinate personality.

Fig. 43.

At *A* the clang tint may be of the string-clarinet hue; at *B* it often borrows guttural darkness from the contralto or resolves into a colorless huskiness; resuming at *C* the original timbre, with the noticeable twang of the oboe, the tendency is to address the four difficult notes at *D* with such uncertainty as to render prediction of likely tint gratuitous; at *E* a taut discordant piquancy (as of a squeaky recorder) is often added—a sound "out of tune, and off the hinges."

Melody cannot successfully struggle through several totally dissimilar qualities unless the conductor is a master of the compensating devices mentioned on page 181.

Not only in the soprano section, but throughout the entire choral entity, voices must be equalized according to criteria which assure the steadiness of orchestral instruments. Each instrument, if well constructed, preserves a general uniformity of utterance throughout its compass (there are some exceptions, notably the clarinet); each voice must be so placed and regulated as to achieve a kinship between its low, medium, and high registers. A human voice is a double reed pipe, and physics as well as aesthetics demands that it perform with the true *klangfarbe* of double reeds at all pitches.

A conductor in refining dynamic features encounters puzzling data. The task of initiating and maintaining characteristic and blended timbres in each choral line is not the least of which he must acquit himself. An alternation or sequence of heterogeneous timbres in any single choral part can despoil even a simple hymn tune. Disintegrated voices habitually cause the dismemberment of melodic structure. They propose a subject in one patois and vainly attempt to develop it in a confusion of dialects. A fugue well sung is mixture enough; but when, in single parts, the subjects or answers, countersubjects or embellishments are articulated with changing argots, a jargon of idioms results—a polyglot conversation between phonetic strangers.

As guest conductor I have not infrequently been confronted with the need of speedily devising a make-believe coordination of woefully unadjusted registers in the single choral lines. My only resource has been the shifting of dynamic levels to compensate for the lacking continuity of tone quality which should prevail in each part. An admonition to raucous sopranos to sing all notes above C″ at *piano*; to bleaters, a request for reinforcement from C″ to C′ especially in downward progressions; to murky contraltos, a suggestion for a modicum of quantity throughout; to reedy tenors, minimum volume in the high register, etc.

It is not only futile, it is fantastic to essay ratios of volume for interpretative effects until all the agencies have been balanced acoustically.

The most curious fact to be noted about many contemporary musicians who are well informed in the theory of music is their seemingly stubborn indisposition to acknowledge the influence of quantity on the validity of performances of music. Many conductors preside over potentially effective organizations. The number of units that rise to eminence as instrumentalities of true art is small. *Salvis salvandis*, the conductors and not the performers are to blame for inferiority and baneful mediocrity. All music depends, in many of its phases, upon the aesthetics of balanced dynamics. Choral and orchestral music relies on the conductors for the adjustments required to attain and maintain this balance.

CHAPTER VI

DYNAMICS (*Continued*)

Accidentals, Dissonance, Ornament,
Counterpoint, Canon, Fugue

OTHER aspects of the bearing of structural features on appropriate quantity ratios may be assembled under one caption, *tension*.

Accidentals engender varying degrees of strain against the tonality of a melody, thus modifying its simplicity and straightforwardness. Counterpoint exacts something from the *cantus* to which it is fitted. The dominance of melody and the consonance of harmony are challenged by dissonance, ornament, and every species of contrapuntal figure.

There are two opposite systems of dealing with accidentals, one keeping them quiet in the background, the other bringing them forward into trenchant prominence. One makes negligible dents in a melodic line, the other raises protuberant knobs. One originates in the diatonic simplicity of Gregorian chant and the modal expositions of the stricter polyphony; the other is related intimately with the growth of chromaticism which in the era of Beethoven had become not only a commonplace nostrum for curing melody and harmony of anemia but a source of luxuriant strength. Since the beginning of the Wagnerian epoch, diatony has been sitting in a rocking chair with little ribbons of flats or sharps pinned to its venerable head, watching the embers of tonic loyalty crumble into pathetic ashes.

The Gregorianists flattened B to eliminate harshness and lessen the likelihood of being trapped into a tritone. These *errores soni*, the term applied to scale intruders by Jean de Garlande in the thirteenth century, were not ornamentations. It is altogether reasonable to conclude, therefore, that the B flat was held *softly* to its negative service and not emphasized as a positive factor. The later accidentals of *musica ficta* were by diplomatic necessity surreptitiously introduced to "do good by stealth and blush to find it fame." One can scarcely conceive of the singers of the Sistine, St. John Lateran's, and the other lifetime choirs jeopardizing their endowments by flaunting heterodox semitones in the ears of orthodox custodians. The sub-semitone (the sharpened seventh of a modal scale) was probably timidly as well as disingenuously substituted for the righteous major second.

The medieval employment of accidentals did not change the essence of the melodies and harmonies to which they were permitted entree. Conductors must take cognizance of this fact and maintain these alien factors in subordinate rank. The later chromaticism, however, gives to these factors such preeminence that if a conductor fails to pay obeisance to it, he will misrepresent altogether the tonal ethos of a composition.

It has been stated already in this book that "a modern director . . . is required by the criteria of authenticity to present each melody with due consideration of the epoch of its origin. Otherwise anachronisms will rob a melody of its most distinctive features. This means that the modification of modal or tonic homogeneity by *accidentals* must be effected only in the degree intended by the composer."

Since it is beyond the scope of this volume to make a detailed study of plain song, it is sufficient to have indicated that the *errores soni* were intended to smooth rough intervals and to protect modality. To emphasize accidentals in early music is to ignore their historic purpose.

With the development of discant and more involved polyphony, the accidental began to assume greater significance in the devisings of composers. But the tradition of modality was so firmly established and so carefully guarded by ecclesiastical censors that candid chromaticism awaited the conclusion of the Palestrinesque era. The vagaries and uncertainties of *conductus* and the gropings of Leonin and Perotier le Grand were soon followed by a positive plan of polyphony which recognized only the diatony of the modes as the orthodox basis of music. The number of "smoothing" accidentals gradually increased, but their function was still negative. It was the revolt from polyphonic restrictions by Caccini, Peri, Monteverdi, and their contemporaries that gave chromaticism its start. In the Dufay-Palestrina period cumbrous progressions—especially awkward major seconds—were modified (by *musica ficta*). The progressions in Fig. 44 were found to be unwieldy. The reduction of the major to minor intervals, as in Fig. 45, promoted the fluency of the passages. But obviously the sharp was not intended to be made conspicuous. There-fore a conductor in setting forth such phrases of early Renaissance music must temper the quantity of the accidentals. Even in more

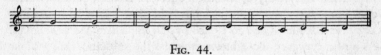

FIG. 44.

modern compositions flats and sharps, being frequently employed to the same end, should in this circumstance be delivered unobtrusively. Except in boldly chromatic styles, the aural impression made by a

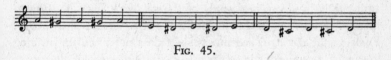

FIG. 45.

principal or prevailing tonality cannot be summarily altered and realtered without forfeiting aesthetic continuity. In polytonal and atonal music there are no accidentals.

If quantity is misapplied to accidentals in the classic scales, the symmetries of key relationship are disturbed. Even the notorious *tierce de Picardie* which raised a final minor to a major third called for an artful *piano*.

False relations, a delightful fancy of many Renaissance composers but interdicted in the nineteenth century, are subtle graces only when the conflicting semitones are softly opposed. The euphony of all music, save the modernistic mélange now soliciting admirers, requires that oppositions be converted deftly into apposition. I have tried the false relations both loudly and softly. In some striking passages of Aichinger and Byrd, alterations at *forte* were destructive, ingratiat-ing at *piano*, and haunting at *pianissimo*. I have never personally applied a *forte* to the raised interval of a *tierce de Picardie* because I was too often startled into disapproval by the raucous effect in my student days. The *tierce* at the end of a Bach fugue which has been naturally ascending to its dynamic as well as contrapuntal con-clusion, demands sonorous pronouncement. It is interesting to note, however, that in his latest fugues in the minor mode Bach usually concluded with a minor third or unison octave. The Phrygian cadence, with its abrupt employment of the dominant chord of the relative minor at the end of chorales, is so surprising itself that the sharpened note should be sounded lightly.

In the classical forms, simple modulatory accidentals should appear with modest simplicity. If theatrical effects in modern dramatic music depend upon the trenchant distinctness of notes borrowed from other keys, the conductor has no choice but to emphasize the accidentals. As a rule, however, a conductor promotes the substantial suggestions of a composition if he denies assertiveness to alien sharps, flats, or naturals. Accidentals, by the very fact of introducing new tonalities, qualify a prevailing atmosphere in the general manner of *subitos* (cf. page 120).

Charles Kennedy Scott, whose book about madrigals is the most authoritative and practical study of the subject,[1] favors the underlining of accidentals in the quaint fancies of the Elizabethan period. Probably the distinguished musicologist does not mean underlining to reach the degree of stiffness which the *forte* stressing of alien notes by many conductors imparts to these tripping conceits. Sharps and flats "drop in" on all simple music like visitors on a family party. They should be welcomed but without uncomfortable exaggeration. Their very appearance over the threshold tends to dispel the heaviness to which diatonic invariableness is conducive. Certainly the hauteur of minor thirds can be oppressive. But the tendency of modern performers to seize every special feature of a phrase as an opportunity for special sonority can readily make the substituted major thirds even less agreeable. I find no fault with a conservative definition of the functional contribution of accidentals, but I deplore the extravagant emphasis with which every altering note is greeted by a large percentage of practicing musicians.

The best procedure is to assign all (except Wagnerian) accidentals to the left side—the safe side—of the diagram of dynamic panels. It is easy to stress a particular accidental for a particular effect. It is difficult to temper chronic mismanagement to the needs of a general effect.

Dissonance, even the prepared dissonance of earlier music, is a weight on the freedom of melody and harmony. It needs to be counterbalanced by a compensating lightness of intonation.

Discussion of the essential difference between consonance and

[1] Charles Kennedy Scott, *Madrigal Singing* (2nd ed.; London: Oxford University Press, Humphrey Milford, 1931).

dissonance would be profitless. Perhaps there is no inevitable difference. The line of demarcation between the harmonious and the unharmonious is not clear. Some eras have designated certain harmonic items as discords; others have found them to be agreeable concords. Robert Schumann (1810-1856) wrote: "Nothing is wrong that sounds right." The whole subject of consonance versus dissonance is abridged in this axiomatic postulate. It explains the seeming contradictions of the past and may be alleged to justify the trend of modernistic tonality.

The curious (from our point of view) intervals of Greek music, with its descending scale forms, sounded right to the ancient Hellenes; therefore their system was right for them. Fourth-century Ambrosian forms delighted the Christians of Milan and thus the authentic modes of the formative chant were right for them. In the late sixth century the Gregorian modifications and additions were likewise satisfactory. The graduation of syllabication to melisma pleased the growing aural apperception of keener ears and increasing susceptibility. The three hexachord scales of Guido of Arezzo, with their octave and, in the *gamma* scale, two octave iterations, "indulged the taste which they created" of the eleventh and ensuing centuries. These hexachord scales are inadequate for current musical ends. They lack the *leading tone*, an influential member of the modern gamut, except by the subterfuge of transposition or "alteration." (Jean de Garlande in his thirteenth-century *Rules* shrugged his English shoulders in French ambiguity when he wrote about the Dorian finish: "Don't put the C sharp.") (Of course, our *leading tone* was the *subsemitone* of *musica ficta*, which, being destructive of modality, was roundly condemned at Avignon by Pope John XXII, 1322.)

Also the *tritone* and its tonal comrade the *diminished fifth*, although impressing listeners as right since the late sixteenth or early seventeenth century (Antonio Lotti made the interval celebrated and a normal feature of melodic progression, just as he foreshadowed the whole-toned scale for Debussy), were forbidden in the Guidonian days. A musical Satan was conjured up who would fain degrade the holy euphony of non-augmented and non-diminished correlatives. Medieval ears sensed the approach of evil communication when *mi* of one scale and *fa* of the next seemed to be contriving an apposition. An old rhymed Latin rule kept custody of intervallic probity:

> "*Mi* contra *Fa*
> Diabolus est in musica."
>
> ("If *Fa* joins Mi,[2]
> Ye faithful flee!")

That consonance and dissonance are two equivalently different forces in harmony cannot be gainsaid. In the fourteenth and fifteenth centuries dissonance and discord were frequently used as synonyms. But discord, in the more modern nomenclature, means univocally a continuous or irreconcilable clash between allegedly alien sounds, whereas dissonance implies only such a passing out-of-tuneness as may be restored, after a moment of pleasant tartness, in an ensuing consonance. We are dealing here with dissonance in this specific sense.

Beginning with Jean Ockeghem (Flanders, 1430-1495) the aimless discordances sponsored by Machault, Cesaris, etc., in the preceding century yielded place to the delicate interpolation of dissonances in the harmonic structure. These may be considered, broadly, as suspensions by which the monotony of consonance was reduced. There are two generic types of urbane dissonance, the prepared and the unprepared. The former, including retardation and anticipation, was a characteristic grace of polyphony and has since remained a resource of agreeable harmony. The latter began to attain vogue when dominant seventh and ninth chords opened the door to tritones and the vertical relations of other diminished and augmented intervals.

Both prepared and unprepared dissonances (except in full chords) affects the ear as *subitos*. It follows logically that they should be treated dynamically as unexpected agencies. They can serve gracefully to enhance the picturesqueness of harmony—to inweave intimations of latency—or they can summarily disorganize. Mere passing notes as such do not require special treatment, for they do not suggest interference with a consonance. But quantity ratios must be assigned with discrimination when a dissident note arrests or anticipates a chord.

A reasonable procedure in dealing with prepared dissonances is to keep the preparatory note, except in anticipated movement, more in evidence than the ensuing dissident. The preparatory note has claimed prior attention, establishing a tonal atmosphere. It continues to sound after the induction of the interfering factor. The latter

[2] *Mi* of the preceding scale.

sufficiently challenges the existing tonality by its simple appearance. To underline it is to assail the tonality, and to go beyond the intention of the composer which was to provide a piquant innuendo or a trifling ornament.

The secondary note, then, should be subordinate. In the present bookish *status quo* of approved harmony, the minor third is the lowest independent consonance, because major seconds depend for aesthetic ratification upon the associated notes of dominant seventh or ninth chords. Therefore, whenever seconds are apposed either at adjacent positions or in different octaves, *the dissonant must be softer than the preparatory note*. When minor seconds are involved, the secondary should be allowed not more than fifty per cent of the volume of the primary note.

Furthermore, a prepared dissonance usually gives a fillip to the rhythmical movement if, at the entrance of the dissonant, the preparatory note increases in volume and diminishes at the resolution. But the dissonant must not be permitted to share the *crescendo*.

In lieu of the illustrations of these precepts which could be readily given with a chorus during a lecture, the student is referred to the following examples for experimental examination. Students are invited to play (or better to have sung) the dissonant formations first, with no regard for the relations of primary and secondary notes; next, with the secondary note *marcato*; finally, in accord with the precepts given above.

A. "Vere Languores" by Tomaso da Vittoria (1540-1608, Rome and Spain) (cf. page 235).

Measure 3 affords an example of a passing note (tenor D against soprano C sharp.) Obviously the influence of such a note is negligible.

Measure 4, alto F sharp against bass G, the primary note appearing at octaves in 3.

Measures 6 and 18 the same relationship.

Measures 23 and 28, soprano B against tenor C sharp.

Measures 38, 39, consecutive dissonances, alto D and C sharp against tenor C sharp and B; etc.

B. "Recordare" (Requiem) by Mozart (cf. page 176)

Measure 15 bass G against alto F, the F being prospered by slight *crescendo* from the first beat of 14; at the resolution of the dissonance (second beat 15) the bass G takes over the function of alto F in 14, to prepare for dissonance in 16 (alto A against bass G).

This alternation of higher and lower measure-long preparation for ensuing dissonances is characteristic of the number; and unless the precept for quantity ratios is observed, the *genre* is misrepresented, a congeries of ill-sounding discrepancies magnifying simple deferments of consonance.

The oppositions occurring within the structure of dominant seventh and ninth chords, being universally regarded as consonant, need no adjustments of dynamics for orderliness except when, as in the following example, two trenchant timbres are pitted against each other, tending to develop a friendly disagreement into a hostile clash:

(A notably resonant dramatic or *mezzo-soprano* is presumed to be intoning the A, an assertive string-type of baritone the B, and less acute voices the D and F; or trumpet and trombone against strings and clarinet.) Obviously, the pungency of the timbres emphasizes an intervallic discrepancy which depends upon the other notes for compensation. Therefore, in such a circumstance, both dissident notes should be adapted to the chord by careful balancing of quantities. If the clash is marked for dramatic effect in the score, it is evident that purely musical considerations have been set aside by the composer.

The dissidence between major seconds which occurs when the notes are not part of a normal chord should be reduced usually by

Fig. 46.

softening the more startling of the two items, except, as above, in the case of dramatic intent. The dissonance resulting from C natural in the second measure in Fig. 46 is *musically* annoying and, unless otherwise noted, should be moderated. Evidently the C natural must be the least energized note in the group, or a cacophony, intensified by the *fermata*, will necessarily result. Examination of the harmonic context usually reveals quickly the note which will jeopardize the serenity of a formation if not tempered in quantity.

Sometimes even repeated minor second dissonances require the obtrusive note to be stressed for descriptive effect, e.g., the tenor B natural against the C chord graphically limning the idea of sorrow in the last few choral measures of the "Cantilena" number in the familiar "Gallia" by Gounod.

These simple suggestions would be superfluous if the average modern conductor were not regularly disclosing a disregard for the function of dissonant notes in the harmonic structure. The discords of *megasonica* (cf. page 159) are not brought into focus here.

Modernistic atonal composition, moving upon a new fulcrum, will eventually, if it survives, organize its own book of quantity logarithms. Meanwhile, the purveyors of the classical forms of music vis-à-vis with cubistic vagaries will lessen the strain for themselves and their audiences by restricting all cacodemons of discord within the secure confines of the *piano* panels. Until the classical conductor has understood and balanced all the implications of polytonality, atonality, and the new freedom of semitones, he will not be psychologically equipped to manage *forte* collisions. The standard bearer of *megasonica* claims that a narrow unenlightened tradition has created a difference between concord and discord, that in reality the aesthetic judgment of the race will presently approve the new relations in harmony just as it eventually repealed so many sometime prohibitions, and that music will henceforth be more rugged, more peremptory, and possibly increasingly louder. But the conductor whose musicianship stems from classical sources subconsciously condemns certain intervallic relationships not only as irregular but as antagonistic to the nature of music. His subconscious view is prejudiced and therefore insular, but a discord is clearly a "rift in the lute" to him. Ben Jonson's "all concord's born of contraries" and Robert Schumann's "nothing is wrong that sounds right" the classicist interprets as epigrams which were not meant to acclaim the loud concurrence of diametrical opposites.

The *general* conductor is uneasy in a whirlpool of strident discords. Therefore he is well advised to qualify their clangor by the only means at his disposal—reduction of tonal energy.

Let the fugelmen of *megasonica* blow their horns as loudly as the idiom, which they seem to understand, impels!

In all occidental music up to the time of Wagner, dissonance is an ally of harmony only when elements alien to a chord are presented with polite restraint. Conductors must develop a feeling for symmetry in the quantity balance of dissident sounds. Alexander Pope's counsel to writers is equally pertinent to musicians: "True ease . . . comes from art, not chance."

Dissonance is only an intercurrent feature of harmony which requires a momentary shifting of volume ratios. But ornamentation and counterpoint are broad orders of composition entailing characteristics which demand correspondingly singular adjustments of quantity. These orders are kindred species of writing, for both involve the enriching of a simple melody, the former by tatting loose lace to its edges, the latter by adding formal figures to the harmony which thereby assumes a horizontal and more or less independent concurrence.

Unskillful allocation of dynamic relations not only prevents embellishments from appearing as decoration but confuses the melodic theme itself in a muddle of unsorted accessories. How frequently is one amazed by the jumble of noises lumped together from the miscellany of choral or orchestral patterns! How difficult of comprehension that skilled theoreticians, whose pencils freely trace the positions of superior and subordinate material on paper, should ruthlessly destroy the correlations with their batons! Many a conductor, a master pedagogue of polyphony in the studio, converts it into enigmatic heterophony on the podium. *Fioriture* and figures gracefully woven into a score become puckering wrinkles and bulges when the searing iron of misapplied dynamics creases the texture at random.

Ornamental and contrapuntal devices can be faithfully and artistically translated into sound only by a well-studied plan for regulating the relative amplitudes of primary and secondary components. Without such regulation Palestrina is hodgepodge, Bach an inert and fortuitous concourse of vagaries, Handel turbid and opaque, Haydn and Mozart incoherent, and Beethoven unfathomable! Richard Wagner insisted that the first task of a conductor is to "find the melody in every bar." Of what avail to find it, if it be not disclosed? And how may it be disclosed save by carefully balancing the dynamic contributions of all associated notes?

Ornamentation is the self-adornment of melodies. This means that they embroider or otherwise decorate themselves independently of the synchronous melodic arcs of counterpoint. Lively silken filaments are sometimes woven into most congenial designs, graciously embellishing the melodic substance. Mozart and Handel come to mind at once as great masters of such ornamentation. Much of the music of these composers must be studied with a view to identifying the essential and the ornamental features. The framework of the texture is commonly formed by the notes which coincide with the beats of a measure, unless syncopation is in progress. During the sixteenth century melody was considered by some as the agency for expressing texts, by others as opportunities for ornamentation. In the eighteenth and early nineteenth centuries the custom of adding *fioriture* to the subject matter was widely prevalent. If the composer failed to provide the elaborations, the performers improvised them. Dr. Charles Burney, in his monumental *History of Music*, wrote in this connection: "An adagio in a song or solo is generally little more than an outline left to the performer's abilities to colour. . . . If not highly embellished they soon excite languor and disgust in the hearers." Dr. Burney was evidently recounting the fashion of the Mozartian era. Karl Philipp Emanuel, the fifth son of John Sebastian Bach, devoted many pages of his *Attempt at the True Manner of Keyboard Playing* (1753) to a study of ornamentation. In epitome we discover: "Nobody doubts the necessity of ornaments. They are quite indispensable. They connect the notes and give life to them. . . . They render the meaning clearer. . . . An indifferent composition is made tolerable by them and the best melody without them is empty and lacking in significance." He urges, however, that performers add their decorations with such conservatism as *to preserve the general expression of the composition.*

This adorning of rough drafts of melodic patterns did not begin at so late a date in the history of music. No doubt the vocal facility achieved by *bel canto* singers had lured them earlier to essay their laryngeal agility on improvised "divisions," coloratura flights and fancies, as well as on the diffuse tautology of cadenzas. But the tendency to add to the principal content of a melodic phrase began with the melismata of Gregorian chant. The simple songs of the Church were syllabic, i.e., one or two notes to a syllable, but the proclivity of the race has been to dress bareness. Thomas Carlyle found it a historical aspiration: "The first spiritual want of a barbarous man is Decoration."

Altars, baldaquins, choir stalls, and choir screens; spires, naves, transepts, and apses; plinths, columns, and cornices—these and the other integers included in ecclesiastical architecture have drawn upon all the known, appropriate, and available resources of decoration throughout history. Windows are stained with lambent colors. The Church encouraged and developed the science of artistic embellishment to invest her liturgy with an irresistible beauty.

There is a good distance between the substantial and the decorative. Intelligent artistry measures this accurately. Unskillfulness and ostentation mistake the distance. Rococo tends to defeat the purpose of decoration. Florid trappings readily arrogate attention which should be directed to principal features. In music, ornamentation usurps the place of true melody whenever maladjustment of dynamic proportions permits garnishings to become garish or arabesques fantastic. The prevailing indifference to the importance of quantity ratios has inhibited neat disclosure of the elegances of the *fioriture* school. The old-fashioned lace which hung modishly from the cuffs of Bach, Handel, Haydn, Mozart, *et al.*, has been sewed back upon the sleeve lengths of coats, becoming an integral and clumsy part of the fabric. Mozart still tries to *look* well to the trained eye, but he sounds like one lacking politesse, his *bons mots* and raillery being metamorphosed by *fortes* into uncouth solecisms.

If I were invited to propose a test piece for candidate conductors in this connection, I could find no more revealing number than the double fugue ("Kyrie Eleison") of that composer's "Requiem." It would disclose many things about their qualifications. It would indicate immediately whether a candidate has any or no practical understanding of the relationship of ornamentation, in its broadest meaning, to melody. The "Kyrie" presents its own severe criteria from the outset. The nonchalance with which these criteria are ignored in public performances deserves a George Bernard Shaw for satirist!

All notes which are added to the basic design of a principal melody, either to the theme itself—as Gregorian melismata, *divisional* inventions, coloratura pyrotechnics, *appoggiatura, acciaccatura,* mordents, and trills—or in the associated harmony—as contrapuntal figures against canonical antecedents and consequents, and countersubjects in fugues during the exposition—must be considered as subordinate material. What is more important, they must be rendered so that their dependence on the melodic design is unmistakably evident.

The *appoggiatura,* unlike the *acciaccatura* with which it is often confused, was deemed to be a feature of the substratum of melody in some schools of composition. During the era of Durante, Pergolesi, Piccini, etc., and even in some more recent styles, the *appoggiatura* was allowed one half of the time value to which it was prefixed. The *acciaccatura* had no positive time value, being expected to achieve as near simultaneity of sounding as the ensuing note.

Therefore, the conductor must familiarize himself with the recognized place of graces in the melodic structure at different times in the history of composition. Pergolesi's celebrated "Stabat Mater" requires the presentation of the *appoggiaturas* as substantial notes. Much music of the later eighteenth and part of the nineteenth centuries needs similar interpretation. Perhaps the *acciaccatura* and the *appoggiatura* are identified by some modern composers as identical graces. In any event the precise conductor will discover for himself the composer's intentions with regard to the grace notes. Sometimes it is difficult to arrive at a scholarly conclusion about these intentions. One has frequently to rely upon an alleged prevalence during a period. I remember being thrown into an eddy of wistful yearnings to play correctly the "turns" of Bach. Several tutors in organ playing, all claiming to have the Bach tradition, insisted on different readings. Whatever impressions, however, a conductor may accumulate by his study of period styles, it should be remembered that, with the exception of the Pergolesi type of *appoggiatura,* all graces, long and short, must be subordinated to the substance of melodic progressions.

The average performances of Gregorian chant, discant, fugues, and the eighteenth- and early-nineteenth-century styles, are cumbersome and burdened by excessive weight. They lack delineating emphasis of essential melody.

Wagner's advice to "find the melody in every bar" should be extended to include the simplification of ornate melodies, *for the essence of a melody is not in circumambient decorations, but in the sequence of those notes which furnish its contours.* Having stripped a melody of its spangles, one sees immediately the notes entitled to prominence.

Here on my desk are copies of the Gregorian *Liber Usualis,* Bach's "Mass in B Minor," and Mozart's "Requiem." A brief analysis of passages from these three sources will illustrate the application of the principle formulated above. The dynamic ratios between skeleton melody and ornamentation in the selected passages must be determined on the same aesthetic basis. The psychology of *artistic* decoration has not changed with the centuries.

The *machitotage* (eighteenth-century appetite for dressing up plain progressions) manifested itself early.

The Gregorian Tract assigned to the Wednesday Mass in Holy Week (*Liber Usualis*, page 614) is unmistakably a florid chant. Quite generally each of the ornamenting or "commentary" notes is given the same dynamic prominence as the basic links of the simple melody. The monks of Solesmes, and other chanters who have been set right by the monks, instinctively differentiate between the important and the incidental notes. It is a disagreeable and disheartening experience to listen to the average choir disorganizing the Tract (a very long one and, if mismanaged, insufferably dull) by designless stressing of supplementary features. The chant is in the Hypodorian mode and the depressing effect of persistent minor intervals must be mitigated, at least for modern ears, by lightening the weight of ornamental neumes. The simpler style of the melodic structure of this mode must be recognized (cf. *De Profundis,* page 1076) before any choir can make more of the decorative involutions than meaningless vocal divergences. Many final syllables are spun out in diffuse meanderings after the syllabic service of the melody has ended, e.g., the finals of *Domine, meus, veniat,* etc. Penultimates— *a(ver)tas, defe(ce)runt, (me)i,* etc.—monosyllables, *te, me, sunt,* etc., and the last syllable of each sentence are vocalized for the clear purpose of adorning a bald chant. These embellishments are obviously separable from the substantial communicability of the Tract, and should be sung as incidental material, lightly and perhaps more quickly than the neumes assigned to the required syllabic utterance. When the extraneous figures of the chant are glided over, as it were parenthetically, they contribute buoyancy, but when they are stressed note for note equally with the declarative *puncta* or neumes, they add more weight to the heavy mode. The melismatic flourishes appended to the alleluias throughout the Liturgy are presumed to underline the cheerful aspects of religion, but these comely ceriphs are usually so distorted by thick and loud intonation as to neutralize their value. When chanters emit the superfluous and meandering notes of melodies with the same dynamic energy as the principal phrases, their bluster does violence not only to the ancient Gregorian song but generally to music as a fine art.

The *divisional* curvatures of the eighteenth-century style are too seldom limned in accord with the criteria of ornamental composition. They are generally depicted too vividly, the substance of the melody being correspondingly obscured. The composers of divisional music found joy in interpolating roulades, runs, and ramblings in the context of a melodic sequence. They were intent not only on embellishing but on keeping the newly accepted time-pattern rhythms from becoming stiff through the oscillation of accents. They wished to guarantee fluency to the expanding forms of the art. Addison, commenting on the propensity to ornamentation, wrote (*Spectator*, March 21, 1710): "I have known the word *and* pursued through the whole gamut, have been entertained with many a melodious *the,* and have heard the most beautiful graces, quavers and divisions bestowed upon *then, for,* and *from* to the eternal honour of our English particles."

But the composers certainly did not intend the merry articles, prepositions, and particles to disrupt the expression of ideas or to impoverish themes by contrast. Probably, the distinguished essayist had suffered the familiar experience of hearing the decorative traceries promoted to undue prominence by boisterous bards, warblers, and choristers. The *fortes* of our modern choruses and orchestras addressing the flowery phrases would have evoked more stinging lampoon from that urbane Oxonian.

The passages from Bach and Mozart in Figs. 47 and 48, written first as completed by the composers and then with the melodic framework stripped of extras, *attest the aesthetic need of applying less*

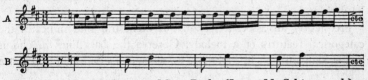

FIG. 47.—No. 20, B minor Mass, Bach. (Letter N, Schirmer ed.)

quantity to ornamental than to basic items (as written, A; without fioritura, B).

Differences of judgment as to the genetic notes are not important here. It is of signal importance, however, that conductors recognize *some* notes as the successive axes for the circumlocution. Otherwise primary and secondary material is consolidated in an unmusical density. Having himself ascertained the sequence of basic notes, the conductor should take time at rehearsal to clarify the impressions of the performers and to inculcate the stress and slack fluency of the

FIG. 48.—Alto Subject Kyrie. ("Requiem," Mozart.)

metric pattern. If each of the sixteenth notes in the Bach and Mozart is accorded equal dynamic stress, the delineation of both intervallic and rhythmical designs is prevented. Could the wraith of Handel be seen by human eyes, perhaps it would be discovered separating the ornamental filaments from the warp and woof of the "Messiah" and "Israel in Egypt." Maybe, long ago the spirit of Bach etched a diagram of divisional, subdivisional, and radical progressions to tempt conductors to "look and listen." If his noble spirit foresaw futility, perchance he whispered his disappointment to a sympathetic seraph, whereupon the whole angelic choir sang buoyantly the "Holy, Holy, Holy" of his much abused B Minor setting. What a real loss to music, that the cherubim and seraphim do not waft down to our rehearsal rooms, at least an echo of their lovely chantings! The *divisions* would be divisions!

Frequently an associated choral or orchestral line indicates the categorical features of a melody. Observe the bass lines in chorus and accompaniment in Fig. 49. The scheme of eliminating the extra

FIG. 49.—No. 19, B minor Mass, Bach. (10 measures before letter N.)

running notes while a unit is becoming familiar with melodic and therefore rhythmical outlines, is analogous to the general plan of silhouetting, for technically instrumental reasons, rapidly moving cello and bassoon parts for the slower-moving trombones and string basses.

In the second subject of the Mozart Kyrie fugue there are many pivots around which charming and animating extrinsicalities rotate. The altos intone a theme that scintillates with confidence in God's kindness. Their thematic subject will furnish a luminous sheen throughout the fugue, quietly insinuating that the first subject (announced by the basses) is too ponderous, self-conscious, and somber. The shimmer of the second subject must be kept aglow. The pivots must be sufficiently sturdy, but the pendants should be blithe darts of light. The sixteenth notes illumine the halves, quarters, and eighths; but they are merely the facets of these, by their sparkling showing forth the gems.

The tendency of conductors today is to confuse substantial and incidental features. Every note calls for stress. There is no slack. Decorative short notes and passages which should only gleam and shimmer are piercingly vivid. The subdivisions of quarter and eighth notes instead of enlivening movement make it sluggish with undue weight. Non-idiomatic performances of great choral works and the contrapuntal orchestration of the eighteenth and nineteenth centuries have become so general as to be judged traditional. The two "Glory to God choruses and "Lord, When Our Haughty Foes" of Bach's "Christmas Oratorio" are great welters of blatancy, and the elasticity of the perennial fugues of Handel's "Messiah" is caricatured by rigid immobility.

After many years of critical analysis of my own work and discriminating observation of the enterprise of others, I am convinced that the recommendation offered in the preceding pages should be accepted as a formal precept: *never permit secondary material, however enhancing and attractive, to usurp or encroach upon the eminence inherently vested in primary melodic elements*. The adjustment of dynamic ratios entailed in fulfilling this precept is a simple procedure. It is epitomized thus: *embellishments should normally be softer than the definite articles of a melody*.

In contrapuntal music the procedure, based upon the same principle, is substantially the same. Counterpoint involves tension, notes against notes, rhythms against rhythms, *crescendos* against *dimin-*

uendos. Tension is the activity of forces tending to dissociate parts from the whole, combined with the opposite activity—a system of cohesion—by which the parts are kept integral and unified. Carefully balanced proportions of tonal amplitude disclose the tension of counterpoint as one of the most effectual agencies of music. Unbalanced dynamics magnify the element of conflict. What was intended to be an amiable rivalry between choral or orchestral lines is too often at first a skirmish and after a few measures a free-for-all melee.

Counterpoint that delights the eye may torture the ear. The fluent equations and graceful feints of composers are transformed by motley *fortes* into irreconcilable factors and ugly lunges.[3]

The development of counterpoint, historically, connotes certain criteria for its performance. The escape from unison Gregorian was accomplished when *organum* attained vogue.

Organum, however, being merely the synchronous chanting of a melody at different pitches—fourths, fifths, and octaves apart—the *vox principalis* (tenor line) enjoyed a primacy of honor only. Since the same melody was in progress in the alto, tenor, and bass lines, there was no need of *protecting* the melody, and, except for acoustical reasons (cf. page 133) which were probably unheeded, a plan for balancing the parallel parts would have been useless. But in the twelfth century, discant, the art of improvising melodic accompaniment to the chant in oblique and contrary motion, brought forward the need of correlating two independent factors. One cannot prove indisputably that concern about the relative tonal strength of these was shown by medieval precentors, but it is more likely than not that discretion kept the inchoate counterpoints in the background. The ecclesiastical custodians of the chant were presumably on the alert lest innovations assail its inviolability. It is equally probable that acumen, if not artistry, subordinated the innovations lest they be ruled out by commissioners. One would be unmindful of the

[3] A good example of the defeat of a composer's intentions by the misapplication of volume to contrapuntal commentaries is the average performance of measures 124-154 of the Brahms "Requiem" (cf. page 111). At the start of this movement, the basses almost invariably promise a war to the death against the theme announced by the sopranos. And all the parts successively make good the promise. In the balancing of the basses against the sopranos at measure 125 *et seq.,* the conductor has the interesting obligation of establishing an acoustical as well as a contrapuntal apposition (cf. pages 161 *et seq.*).

thoroughness of the Church's supervision of the art of music in supposing that ornamental improvisations[4] or composed adjuncts would be allowed to arrogate attention to themselves, thus belittling the sovereign dignity of liturgical melodies. Toleration of furbishing fancies was as much as pre-Renaissance musicians could reasonably have expected. Therefore, one may intelligently assume that discants were not vocalized at such quantity levels as to obscure the characteristic phrases of the modes.

Polyphonic music attained maturity by growing *quietly*. *Forte* discants would have invited interdict. *Falso-Bordone* and *musica ficta* were naïve inventions to keep the gradual expansion of harmony "off the record." It may be posited with assurance that the commentaries of counterpoint were delivered at a relative *piano* until, in the fifteenth century, the figures of concurrent choral lines had been organized more candidly on the basis of symmetrical parity. This equality of parts became the structural constitution of *a cappella* polyphony. A definite system of rationing dynamic degrees to the horizontal lines was necessarily developed. This system is surveyed in the ensuing chapter. Attention is drawn here to the quantitative relations of contrapuntal figures in general and to the juxtapositions of canon and fugue in particular.

The degree of tension against the *vox principalis* which a contrapuntal figure involves must be estimated carefully if a conductor is to present the design as conceived by the composer. If the tension is forcible, the contending notes must be restrained, for notable quantity will tend to alienate the figure from the cardinal material.

Of the five species of counterpoint theoretically set forth in textbooks and more freely applied by composers, the first and fourth seem to imply the greatest tension, and therefore demand the most discriminating attention from conductors.[5] In the first species each

---

[4] The spontaneous improvising *alla mente* of solo instruments around themes in current swing music pays tribune to early discant. If the swinging soloist were fearful of someone, as the discanters were fearful of ecclesiastical censors, their extempore annotations would be less vagaries. Swing, if kept within aesthetic limits, might give promise—as discant did—for the future.

[5] The five species are listed to freshen the student's memory.

1. Note against note.
2. Two notes against one.
3. Four (occasionally three) against one.
4. Two, coupled for syncopation, against one.
5. Florid counterpoint, or a potpourri of the four species.

note of the *canto fermo* (C.F.) is challenged by a note of equal value. The movement of the C.F. is not lightened by extra shorter notes as in species 2, 3, and 5. The counterpoint is a weight thrown against the principal melody. Since this melody (the C.F.) furnishes the primary material, the contrapuntal progression must be lightened sufficiently to permit buoyancy to the C.F. This means succinctly that in the first species the C.F. should always be more prominent than the attending notes. If the latter are not literally *attending* they become aggressively *separatist*.[6]

In the fourth species, although the movement of the whole is eased by the two-against-one combination, the disturbance of rhythmical normalcy by syncopation brings the contrapuntal line into prominence. If the latter is stressed by impact instead of indirect attack (cf. pages 120 and 125), the passage as a whole is unsettled chiefly to the disadvantage of the C.F. (cf. syncopation, tied notes, in the Index).

Whenever a *canto fermo* is obviously the core of a design, the counterpoint must offer proper acknowledgment; and unless the latter is delivered in a lower dynamic panel, the whole period is frustrate. The precept for the procedure is then: *emphasize the* canto fermo *by a relative repression of the counterpoint*. This does not mean that the C.F. is always to be pronounced *forte* but that its eminence is to be assured by diminishing the volume of associated figures. (Cf. accentuation by *diminuendo*, pages 23 *et seq.*)

If a conductor has even a moderate flair for polyphonic music, he will experience little trouble in applying the foregoing principles to species 2 and 3, for the extra notes included in these figures *sua sponte* suggest motion and lightness. These and the florid species should be related dynamically to the C.F. in the mode of linear ornamentation being adjusted to its own melody.

During the great era beginning in the early fifteenth century with Dufay at Cambrai and culminating in the late sixteenth with Lassus at Munich, Sweelinck at Amsterdam, Palestrina at Rome, Byrd at London, and Vittoria at Madrid, the art of *imitation* engaged the talent and zeal of the masters. From imitation came *canon, ad fugam,* and fugue itself. The copying in other parts of melodic material set

---

[6] The special relations of *antecedent* and *consequent* in canon, *subject* and *countersubject* in fugue and the *synchronous* melodies of *a cappella* polyphony are not included in the coverage intended here. (Cf. index.)

forth by an initiating voice line became the richest structural resource of the contrapuntists.

The thematic arc or phrase comprising the material of the imitation is of paramount importance to a musical sentence, its appearance in each successive part demanding lucid definition. Canon and fugue (*q.v.*) depend ultimately upon such clarity for valid interpretation. Good musicians are aware of this need, *theoretically*, but many neglect to apportion due ratios of volume in performance.

Imitation invites the same basic interpretation whether it be a feature of Renaissance polyphony or of the freer contrapuntal writing of later generations, viz., each appearance of the norm should be stressed sufficiently to be easily discerned. Each copying need not be an exact dynamic facsimile of the pattern, except in the mathematical precisions of canon and fugue; but if a melodic figure is to migrate with enriching effect through the different voice lines, its journeyings should be duly recorded. In strict polyphony, the arsis and thesis requirements of the associated voice lines (*q.v.*) may demand dynamic modification of the imitating arcs, but in more modern music, themes may generally be underlined in their entirety. For example, the norm iterated from measures 24-58 in the Brahms' excerpt (cf. page 111) and that flowing through measures 39-50 of Vittoria's "Vere Languores" (cf. page 235) require clarification equally because the norm in both instances is the agency of a new progressive activity. But though the need of clarification is the same, the method of securing it is different. *Positive* underlining of the figure at each recurrence in the Vittoria motet is unnecessary because a thesis is already in progress or about to start in the associated parts, thus ushering other material to the background. Here again is evidence of the efficacy of accentuation by *diminuendo*. (Cf. page 111.) In the Brahms number positive emphasis of the figure at each entrance is indicated because there are no accommodating theses to clear the field and a steady *poco a poco* development of all parts to an important apex is prescribed both by the curve line of the melodic arcs and by the instructions of the composer. In Renaissance counterpoint (except in canon and *ad fugam*) the dynamic treatment is thus often negative, while positive reinforcement is usually indispensable to the worth of imitation in post-Renaissance styles.

Imitative phrases, inversions of melodic patterns, and momentary suggestions of thematic norms are the life of contrapuntal music. The relationship of such devices to the whole is determined by ratios of volume. Students who fail to convince themselves of this will never be bona fide interpreters of contrapuntal forms. Let them take along the scores to performances and judge for themselves the truth of this pronouncement. An average performance will amaze them by the obvious disparity between lucid writing and unfathomable rendition. Every note in a polyphonic *partitur* makes a mathematical contribution to the sum total of notes. If it is denied its full value it fails to function properly and automatically becomes a deranging factor.

Without a fine balance in the counterpoint of dynamics, no aesthetic value can accrue from listening to the counterpoint of notes.

Canon is imitation in its most formal procedure. The composer establishes a pact between the *dux* (antecedent) and the *comes* (consequent) and all movement is designed to the fulfillment of this pact. Canon is the strictest form of composition, and blundering in the apportioning of degrees of volume is immediately penalized by the travesty which it creates. *Forte* and *piano* must be juxtaposed with sensitive discrimination if the forging of a counterfeit is to be forestalled. Antecedent and consequent need adjustment to each other not only at entrances but throughout the duration of phrases. Furthermore, the commentaries of the non-canonical parts must be related carefully to both the antecedent and the consequent.

Canons at the unison, perhaps not necessarily but probably if one is guided by the code of artistic consistency, seem to require a continuity of timbre in the two components, as well as the same degree of quantity. Thus trumpets followed by violins, or vice versa, to me personally would comprise an inappropriate instrumental combination for unison canons. Clarinets and oboes may be regulated for canonical utterance; so too, violins and violas, violas and cellos, English horns and bassoons, and French horns. In choral canons at the unison, dramatic sopranos require much tempering before they can be successfully placed in apposition with lyrics. Canons at the fifth or octave presuppose different timbres in the antecedent and consequent, but not different degrees of dynamic stress. Conductors must first equalize the dynamic ratios of the canonical elements, and then as far as possible coordinate the qualities of contrasting colors.

The consequent, entering after the starting point of the canon, should reveal itself as clearly as the antecedent. This pursuit of the leader by the follower must be accomplished adroitly. Canons escape easily from the control of conductors.

The *dux* and *comes*, being identical and not cast as sound and echo, should make the same claim upon the hearing of listeners. But the advantage lies with the *dux*, the priority of its appearance naturally favoring its progress throughout. Usually the *comes* is slighted. In spite of their designed equality the *comes* just trots along, *also*. It is too often like an apologetic second fiddle. This humble participant in the orchestral ensemble needs more recognition if a true balance is to be achieved in the string choir. Likewise the *comes* must be made to rise to sounding parity if the correspondences of canon are to be organized. If either *dux* or *comes* is permitted to arrogate interest to itself, the other lacks opportunity for making its canonical contribution. If both are allowed vigorously to vie for eminence, making no concessions to each other's obvious prerogatives, the tension between the two is unmusical. It is reciprocal antagonism. Antagonisms are antipathetic to the nature of music. The mutual pleasant resistance conceived as the *raison d'être* of canon can be disclosed only by the timely parallelism of concurrent degrees of *piano* and *forte*.

When a strict canon is accompanied by imitative figures in other voice lines (these may be aptly termed *contrapuntal commentaries*), the construing and parsing of them should be postponed until the *dux* and *comes* have been balanced and then related to them as subordinate, superfluous, and separable accessories.

The notation of a familiar and illustrative canon by Palestrina is shown in Fig. 50.[7]

First, dissociate the strict canon developed by the two soprano lines from the imitative quasi-canonical material of the alto, tenor, and bass lines. It will be observed immediately that this soprano canon at unison can be sung independently of the lower contrapuntal material. When thus performed, modern ears will miss the major thirds supplied frequently in the accompanying parts. But major thirds were not essential to polyphonic structure of the late Middle Ages or the Renaissance, unsweetened octaves, fourths and fifths,

---

[7] To meet the exigencies developed by modern music habits, editors have found it expedient to publish the old polyphonies on G and F clef staves, and with bar lines. These latter create the false impression of time-pattern stresses and slacks. Likewise for expediency, I have numbered the anachronous measures.

Agnus Dei III

Fɪɢ. 50.

Fig. 50 (*cont.*).

Fig. 50 (*cont.*).

Fig. 50 (cont.).

blank and lacking though they seem to us, being quite delectable to the contemporary music perceptivity. We seem nowadays to need Keat's "lucent syrops tinct with cinnamon" to flavor our harmonies.

The antecedent (*dux*) entering at measure 1 is followed by the consequent (*comes*) at measure 3. The antecedent is already diminishing in a thesis (*q.v.*) at the entrance of the consequent; therefore free entrance is assured. The *crescendo* indicated (by indirect attack, *q.v.*,) for the consequent in measure 3 must be hardly perceptible. Otherwise there is no problem of dynamics involved in starting off both members of the canon. At the second beat of measure 4, the *rilievo* (*q.v.*) of the antecedent is raised. The increased pitch prominence underlines the antecedent necessarily unless the volume of the F, E, D is decreased. The conductor must be cognizant of dynamic ratios implied by the two *rilievos* a sixth apart. Furthermore, the consequent is diminishing in its thesis. When the consequent leaps the octave at measure 6, the need for the same degree of softening the F, E, D is not present because of the nearness of the antecedent. However, the softening should be *approximately* the same as with the antecedent in 4 and 5, because both antecedent and consequent must at all times arrest the ear with the same quantum of volume. The contiguity of *dux* and *comes* at 6 and 7, in fairly high *rilievo*, gives the underpart a natural fillip not offered the underpart at 4 and 5. The long descending *diminuendo* from 10-18 is easily managed, since the descent is accomplished gradually and concurrently by both members. Indirect attack at 10, copied meticulously by the consequent at 12, affords good chance to the conductor to prepare a well-balanced double *diminuendo*. One needs to be on the *qui vive* lest the *comes* at entrance usurp eminence and the *dux* at 14, 15, 16 be too attenuated. At 23 the B flat primary note of the dissonance (*q.v.*) must not be allowed quite the same prominence as in other dissonant circumstances, since the C of the *dux* is important as the first note of the contours prevailing from measures 18 to 33. The charming eight-note effect in descent at 25, 27, 29, 31 must be gracefully presented, a less than usual thesis-*diminuendo* being necessary to let the figure count against the baldness of the concurrent notes. (Cf. item 3, page 181.)[8] At 36, obviously, the *dux* should be amplified slightly to keep parity with the high *comes*.

[8] These notes suggest a chime effect to me. At about the time of the sung "Agnus Dei," the bells in the old campaniles used to ring for the *Domine non sum dignus* of the Mass. At any rate the progression is arresting and should be protected.

Other items might profitably be brought to attention if a complete analysis of the dynamic implications of this setting of the Agnus Dei were intended here. References to its structure as a piece of Renaissance polyphony are made in Chapter VII.

It is unnecessary to examine the different species of canon (*four-in-two, perpetual, cancrizans*, etc.), for these are generically the same, and the principles pertinent to the dynamic proprieties of the simple canon in unison (*two-in-one*) are applicable to all. The fundamental need is to maintain equality between all canonical members. Here is a helpful procedure.

1. *Dux* and *comes* make entrances with indirect attack (cf. pages 120 *et seq.*), thus avoiding excessive impact which inevitably magnifies the entrant. The contribution of *dux* or *comes* must never be overdrawn.

2. The entrant is *invited* by a slight decrease of volume in the other part or parts. The *gliding* attack of the entrant is thus assisted gently into the developing mosaic.

3. Every modification of volume in the *dux* is copied, in effect if not in facsimile, by the *comes*.

4. The degrees of increase or decrease in volume during concurrent motion are determined by the acoustical relations of the *rilievos* in which the canonical participants are proceeding. Thus, the upper notes in 4 and 5 should be softer than the same upper notes in 6 and 7 for the reason noted on the preceding page, and *pacem* of the *dux* in 34 requires less underlining than *pacem* of the *comes* in 36 since the *dux* is free of nearby tension.

5. In canons at the octave (cf. "Sancta Maria" in César Franck's "Ave Maria") cognizance must be taken of the acoustical differences of pitch and timbre which must be compensated by adjustments of the quantity ratios.

6. The special interrelations and naïve paradoxes of arsis versus thesis in *a cappella* polyphony sometimes must be waived (cf. Chapter VII) for acoustical balance, e.g., *comes* versus *dux* in 25, *dux* versus *comes* in 27, etc.

The directions for dynamic levels incorporated in many modern editions of old music—and especially of elaborate canonical forms— should be disregarded unless an editor is a recognized *practical* specialist in this field.

The student is warned here again of the futility of undertaking interpretative balances if acoustical equilibrium is ignored. Of this he must be certain: canonical and fugal symmetries cannot be conformed if entrances are made with impact, if high notes are accosted with striking amplitude, or if pungent timbres are allowed to bully their milder associates. (Cf. pages 171, 172, 179, 180 *et seq.*)

Free canonical movements associated with a strict canon, such as the alto, tenor, and bass *symphonizing* in this "Agnus Dei," must be considered of secondary importance. The canon can thrive mathematically and aesthetically without the supplementary features of the accompanying parts. Frequently such features are seen to comprise a motet in themselves. But in relation to the canon they must be made to serve as a harmonic *mise en scène,* a stylistic and enriching *décor.* Therefore the synchronous figures must be evoked adroitly. In this connection, adroitness means a fine discrimination between primary and secondary material, for the quintessence of contrapuntal and especially the older polyphonic music is in the equality of all the constituent lines. Certainly, the *raison d'être* of strict canon demands that the progress of *dux* and *comes* be made unmistakably clear. This is accomplished by the *finessing* of dynamics, i.e., by easing a part to the minus side of a panel while another part remains in the center; by allowing a *dux* to grow very slightly to the plus side while the *comes* awaits its turn; by creating a *feeling* for the momentary primacies of a figure which will make itself, therefore, sufficiently discernible (cf. chiaroscuro, page 131); by always maintaining the modifications in close proximity to a prevailing dynamic background; by a sort of rubato of soft and more soft, louder, and less loud; *never by impoverishing Peter to glorify Paul.*

Providing he keeps clearly in mind the duty of expounding the canon, the conductor will set off the number to best advantage if he accords every imitative figure in the other parts adequate opportunity for making its contribution. Thus, in the "Agnus Dei" the altos, tenors, and basses may be effectively invited to give their versions of the canonical theme. A gentle *crescendo* in the rising alto figure at 6 does not menace either *dux* or *comes* but enhances both by its contrary motion and fuller timbre. The tenor, from 7 through the first note of 10, is in strict imitation and, lying so far below the *dux* and *comes,* can, without jeopardizing either, add quality and substance to the whole movement. The alto at 32 proposes a new form which *dux* and *comes* seize upon and develop from 33 and 35 to the end. Tenor and bass at 40 make interesting comment on this in contrary motion without necessarily distracting attention from the sopranos. Multiplication of examples of serviceable underlining of the auxiliary lines would be superfluous. The safe procedure is clear. Having guaranteed the principals their rights, the conductor may freely—in fact, he is artistically obliged to—acknowledge the prerogatives of the concurrent lines.

Canon is usually presented without organization. It is therefore just as usually ineffective. Its distinctive disposition is lost in a random dealing of quantities. The flattery of imitation, by which one part ingeniously and suavely pays compliment to another, is one of the most gratifying amiabilities of music. The etiquette of harmony is urbane, the give and take between counterpoints being only nimble-witted repartee. If this repartee is guided by the refinements of dynamics, it never forfeits elegance to the gracelessness of retort.

Fugue and all music in fugal style require deft appositions of volume in the various lines which comprise its systematic procedure. Being more elaborate than canon on account of the countersubject, fixed relations of tonalities, exposition, *codetta*, *stretto*, etc., its effective dynamic treatment involves more sorting and allocating of elements. A well-devised and cleverly developed fugue is music's masterpiece—on paper. It is frequently, if not generally, music's most messy miscellany—in performance. The clarity which charms the eye in the score, ceding to the influence of some "noonday devil," becomes at first murky and anon increasingly obscure even to unintelligibility during its translation for the ear. Lucid as light on the clefs! Dark as Erebus on the tone waves! Ratio and proportion at the desk! Amorphous enigma on the podium. If all principles of contrapuntal relations—save in the new field of *megasonica*—are found exemplified in the complete fugues, it follows that the "compleat musician" must be a master of the aesthetics and technique involved in expounding them. We find here, as in so many phases of musicianship, a wide distance between theory and practice.

Uninterrupted observation of choral and orchestral performances over a long period of years has convinced me that conductors must learn to *raise* their batons. Having discovered the locale of melody and its distributed arcs and having foreseen the general tempo with its probable modifications, they need to concentrate eagerly and intently on all aspects of dynamics. The *upbeat* is the sesame to fluency. The absence of weight from fragile beats and less sturdy phrases must be prearranged if unencumbered motion is to ensue.

Anacrusis, diminuendo, *and the left panels of the diagram of dynamics are the plenipotentiary custodians of tonal concinnity.*

In fugal music the increasing momentum and ever-expanding inclusions of components require the philosophy of the *raised* baton and "easing off" to be applied with sensitive understanding. *Ricerare,* Fantasia, *Ad Fugam,* and *Fuga per canonem,* the fugal forms current from the sixteenth to the eighteenth centuries, were not constructed on the mathematical bases of our modern fugue and may be satisfactorily interpreted in the mode already set forth for ornamentation, imitation, and other contrapuntal devices and according to the further criteria discussed in the ensuing chapter. But the strict fugue requires special treatment. Since it is a composition with fixed tonal relations and fixed fashions of development, its equations must be disclosed by a correspondingly fixed scheme of dynamics.

Apart from the aesthetic advantage accruing to a clear definition of its integrants, a balance of its carefully juxtaposed parts is indispensable for acoustical compatibility. There are many more reciprocities to be compounded agreeably for hearing in fugue than in canon. If the multiple parts are allowed to assemble and evolve in the disorderly tumult of unrestrained *fortes,* a Donnybrook Fair of mixed noises results. Instead of co-operating in the definite plan of composers to vitalize subjects with smartening inlays and disposals, countersubjects and episodic strands, whole *codettas,* and enervated but raucous *strettos* seem intent upon providing "a nice derangement of epitaphs." The geometrical mind of Euclid would have found joy in the theorems, proofs, conclusions, and corollaries of great fugues, but the acoustical ears of Pythagoras would have been frightened to deafness by the din of conflicting forces.

In listening to performances of choral and orchestral fugues, I sometimes feel as though the conductor were directing the score at first sight. When I was a very young man, it fell to my lot to conduct a fugue with a great metropolitan orchestra without any preparation because of the emergency of the delayed arrival of the score and parts for a publicized performance. I said to the concertmaster on the stage: "What shall I do with this thing? I've never seen it, heard it, or met anyone who has heard it." His reply has remained in the foreground of my memory: "Don't worry; it's only a fugue. I've looked at the first violin part. It's all in four-four *moderato.* Just give us a good downbeat, and *you'll get what's there.*" I gave a good down-beat and kept squinting at the score so that I'd be sure to stop con-ducting when the players had stopped playing. I am sure that I did *not* get what was there, and I am equally certain that a large per-centage of choral and orchestral conductors rarely get "what's there" when the fugal furies are loosened in sound, when the fine juxta-positions of the score begin to mock themselves with truculent ridicule, and when landslides of *fortissimo* chunks, falling from on high athwart the lanes of avid inner and lower parts, invite them to hurdle the obstructions with their most extravagant efforts.

A fugue could perhaps be essayed more reasonably by a conductor "at sight" than some other forms of composition, *if he has worked out a definite plan of fugal dynamics.* Fugues proceed, substantially, according to established norms. The relationship of subject and answer to countersubject and collateral material does not vary intrinsically. Episodes are as discernible in one fugue as in another; exposition and counterexposition bear the same relevancies to a sub-ject in Bach, Handel, Mozart, Gaul, Dubois, and Chadwick. *Diminution* and *augmentation* declare themselves with unfailing insistence in Latin and Nordic idioms; the *stretto* "squeezes" in one fabric as in another.

Possibly the average conductor has not adverted to the dependence of the fugal forms on ratios of quantity. Probably many who have become aware of this have failed to *simplify and systematize in a brief code* the processes by which the principal interrelations can readily be served. Certainly, there is immediate need for oncoming conductors to apply dynamic equations to the written equations if the lambs, ewes, and rams in Handel's "All We Like Sheep" are not to go farther (with the increasing urging of modern stentor!) and very much farther astray.

The dynamic level at which a fugue is initiated seriously influences its effectiveness. Many conductors permit *forte,* with frequent invasions of the *fortissimo* panel, to prevail from the beginning. This bad judgment or inadvertence to the progressive movement of musical material to the summit of its possible eloquence tends to frustrate any mode of composition. (Cf. climax, pages 143 *et seq.*) Some sensitive conductors promote the general effectiveness of fugues by presenting the exposition boldly and modifying the volume of the material lying between this and the *stretto;* but the average fugal performance is futile, not only because of unsuitable ratios of volume between the contrapuntal members, but because it lacks a dynamic apex. It is the same at the beginning, in the middle, and at the end. Failure to pilot any style of composition to its intended consummation, slighting the potentialities of the number and the proposal of the composer, always cheats the audience. In so academic a form as fugue, this neglect is equivalently disparagement and misrepresentation. It is easy for all its graces to be engulfed by waves of monotonous sound.

Starting off and continuing obstinately in the upper dynamic panels, a fugue spends itself before the exposition has been completed. There is nothing left for myriads of ensuing measures to accomplish. The loud-mouthed orator "shoots his bolt" in a few boisterous sentences. Ennui or exasperation nettles the listeners. A noisy fugue, plowing its way through academic inventions and vociferously proclaiming dry formulae, is the most inept vehicle of musical utterance. It is Shakespeare's "full of sound and fury, signifying nothing."

The orderly procedure, in this connection, is to set a starting level of volume which will permit growth to the climax, or, if a high initial level for the sake of sturdy announcement, to lessen the vigor after the first exposition so that the *stretto* may not be robbed of the prerogative of emphasizing, in forceful epitome, the acoustical and artistic projects of the fugue.

As in canon so in fugue; the important melodies reveal their locale unmistakably. There is a definite place for each of these in the architectural structure of the fugue itself. The *subject* is obviously the primary motif. It should be marked accordingly for distinct delineation. During the exposition this theme should be clearly in the foreground. The *countersubject*, entering with the first *answer*, offers a contrapuntal melodic background against which the motif at the new pitch is to elicit increasing attention. Episodic commentaries interpolated before the third appearance of the subject matter are parenthetical and should be uttered as obiter dicta, viz., with less volume. If there is a counterexposition, the countersubject may reasonably be brought forward, since the subject and answer have already been given sufficient eminence and in the recapitulation or *stretto* will again assume first place.

If the counterexposition is a candid change from major to minor mode, or vice versa, the new harmonic atmosphere suggests a corresponding shift in the dynamic level. If from major to minor, the shift to a lower level is usually effective since the stressing of minor intervals in academic array tends to depress; if from minor to major, it seems opportune to raise the level slightly to welcome the new brightness. However, before the conclusion of the counterexposition, it is well to reduce the volume to the *status quo ante* in order to guarantee the *stretto* full opportunity for reaching the climax. When the subject theme appears in diminution, it needs reinforcement lest the theme be lost in the speed of the notes. When it appears in augmentation, the increased duration of the thematic notes, assuring time for identification, invites the accompanying counterpoints to greater freedom.

This procedure is indeed simple. It can be applied effectively to all types of fugue. Succinctly it may be epitomized in these precepts:

1. *Generally,* establish a moderate dynamic level for the exposition—(*minus mezzo-forte*).
2. Introduce the countersubject at a lower level, allowing it to *approximate* the volume of the answer after a few notes.
3. Similarly adjust the volume of accompanying parts at the third and fourth entrances of the primary melody.
4. Contrast the dynamics of exposition and counterexposition, underlining the countersubject in the latter as well as all imitative fragments and striking figures in all voice lines.
5. Regard the recapitulation or *stretto* as the climax of the composition, making proximate as well as remote preparation for a convincing culmination.

Since the successful apposing of quantity ratios in fugues and fugatos may thus simply be arranged, it is unnecessary to analyze here the notation of any particular composition. The relationship of subject and countersubject is the fulcrum upon which a fugue moves. This relationship is less rigid, note for note, than that of *dux* and *comes* in canon. In fugue it is segment abutting upon segment, paraphrases coexisting with phrases; in canon it is the identity of lines, artistically challenged by ostensible contravening temporal discrepancy. The genius of both canonical and fugal idioms is the simulation of disagreement between component parts. The skillful conductor makes sure that the dissidence is disclosed honestly as a pretense. The mere wand-wielder establishes it as a disagreeable reality. Proper ratios of volume are invoked by the former to read the roles aright. The latter is unconsciously lured by confounding *fortes* to "ham-act" and thus to misrepresent.

In rehearsal, a chorus may profitably be directed to sing all the parts through singly, as far as the compass of voices permits. Thus the relative positions of subject, countersubject, and all auxiliary contrapuntal figures are soon understood and enlightened co-operation is prearranged. When feasible, I propose the humming of all parts save one, which, each in turn, is sung in natural manner and observed by the others.

In accompanied fugues, I customarily invite the orchestra to listen to an *a cappella* performance of the choral score, and the chorus to listen to the instrumentation, each checking the dynamic needs of the number in its full length and the particular relationships of the structural members.

A double fugue should be read as the simultaneous development of two single fugues or, if a true countersubject is not proposed for the secondary fugue (primary and secondary are usually clearly indicated), as an elaborate single fugue with two running countersubjects. The principal of these is usually the subject to be expounded in due process by all the voice lines. In this circumstance the conductor must at first establish the ratios on this basis, e.g., (1) subject of primary fugue *mf*, (2) subject of secondary fugue *p*, (3) countersubject of primary fugue *p*. In the event of the double fugue providing a complete and independent countersubject to the secondary subject, the procedure is as follows:

1. Rehearse both fugues as separate entities, exemplifying the conformations of each according to *some* scheme analogous to the epitome on pages 221 *et seq*.
2. Place the fugues in juxtaposition and give dynamic priority to the primary fugue through its exposition.
3. When an ensuing *codetta* is finished, begin to stress the subject matter of the secondary fugue.
4. In all episodic figures, underline equally fragments of both subjects.
5. In the recapitulation or *stretto*, alternate stress between the contours of the duplex design until the finale is in sight, whereupon all forces should be assembled in parity for the *poco a poco* ascent to the summit.

The difficulty experienced by radio engineers in broadcasting involved contrapuntal music is enlightening and should be persuasive. In broadcasting and recording studios, the intonation of several sounds simultaneously, save in well-spaced vertical harmony, is an acoustical hazard; synchronous utterance of independent themes tends to rob each integrant of definitiveness and the whole of purpose, the ear of the microphone translating competitive elements into jumble; even a minimum of aesthetic value is unattainable unless discriminative ratios of volume are established between *rilievos*, timbres, consonance, and dissonance and all agencies which influence or are influenced by the paramount controlling force, quantity.

At the present writing, the comparative capacities of human and mechanical ears for receptivity and selectivity have not been satisfactorily authenticated, but it is reasonable and profitable to assume that a confusion of *fortes* disturbs both similarly.

Throughout this book quantity is proclaimed the chief trustee of quality. In this chapter, tonal amplitude has been seen to be the custodian of form as well. The good estate of contrapuntal factors is entrusted to the discipline of volume rationing. By the distribution of *pianos* and *fortes* the worth or worthlessness of the written conformities of imitation, canon, and fugue is determined for hearing—there being an inexorable nexus between cause and effect.

CHAPTER VII

A CAPPELLA POLYPHONY

Masses, Motets, Madrigals, Canzonets, Ayres, etc.

A CAPPELLA polyphony is the choral contrapuntal music which, after the adumbrations of discant, began to develop in the fourteenth and reached its rich maturity in the sixteenth century. Many excellent choral numbers have been written since that time which, by reason of structural similarity, seem to merit classification as *a cappella* polyphony, but the designation has come to identify an epochal rather than a technical type.

The terms *polyphony* and *counterpoint* are often used correctly as synonyms. Broadly, the two words have the same meaning, but the import of the latter is more restricted. *Polyphony* connotes the whole scope of many-voiced music, its relations with Gregorian scales, modal fidelities, and free and mensural rhythm; *counterpoint* alludes specifically to the note-against-note combinations of horizontal harmony.

Involving all the chief expedients for regulating the tensions inevitable to these *punctum contra punctum* dipthongs, successful interpretation of *a cappella* polyphony depends upon the application of a greater technique which is altogether proper to itself. In the preceding chapter effort was directed to making clear that it is one thing to recognize, analyze, and even compose contrapuntal music and quite another thing to make it sound like music. In this chapter the undertaking is to expound a simple procedure by which the polyphonies of the Renaissance may be performed agreeably and convincingly to modern ears. The Palestrinesque[1] style must be disembarrassed of the confusions in which general practitioners have enveloped it, and from which it rarely escapes under the guidance of specialists.

Listeners are not generally invited to hear what the composers fancied, pre-heard, and committed to notation. Modern conductors

---

[1] This word is chosen to denote *a cappella polyphony* in its inclusive implications.

cannot fairly be censured for not having discovered the secret of
disclosing the attractiveness of polyphony. The methods of the
masters were tossed into dark corners of seventeenth-century clerestories. Polyphony had ceded to accompanied monody, and the
horizontal line had capitulated to homophony. Abbé Baini made
valiant efforts to revive interest in the Palestrinesque style at the
beginning of the nineteenth century. He was disappointed with
meager rewards. He took dusty copies off the Sistine library shelves
and drilled choristers in Renaissance repertoire, but probably failed
to search the right corners of the clerestories for the method of
drilling. There is no record of his having found the interpretative
charts. If he had been fortunate in coming upon the code of the
cinquecentists his zeal would have been compensated more adequately, for the arcana would have been divulged and a simple
system passed on to Proske, Witt, and Haberl of the mid-nineteenth-
century *Caecilienverein*, to the *Chanteurs de St. Gervais* of Bordes
(César Franck), the *Schola Cantorum* of Guilmant and d'Indy, to
the twentieth-century Roman singers of Perosi, Rella, and Casimiri,
and to the Westminster Cathedral Choir of Sir Richard Runciman
Terry.

To the enthusiasm of Baini and these others, however, should be
credited the extensive repertoire of polyphony now available.
Although the protocol for converting written counterpoints into
felicitous sounds remains hidden above the aisle roofs of old cathe-
drals, we have lately been discovering keys to the code in likely
but long-overlooked places, the vocal parts themselves. At long last
we have stumbled upon the basic strategy of the *magistri chorales* of
quondam eras. If we cannot reconstruct their complete plan, we can
at least formulate an adequate technique from the data offered by
notation. Monteverdi's equivalent tossing of the records into seventeenth-century attics, by diverting the attention of singers from polyphonic traditions and presently dissipating memories of them, is no
longer of consequence.

The renewed but puzzled interest in polyphony of church musicians, choral leaders, and that signally influential sector of the profession, the teachers of music in elementary and high schools, will
be well served by the information now at hand.

Only those constitutional singularities which, differentiating *a
cappella* polyphony from other orders of composition, require correspondingly singular treatment for disclosure are considered here.

Academic aspects, having no direct relevancy to interpretative resources, are excluded.[2] Conclusions set forth in the preceding chapter about the general bases of contrapuntal conducting are assumed
to apply to the sacred and secular forms of the Palestrinesque and
Tudor schools except when and as noted.

A particular and nearly esoteric nomenclature has long enshrouded
polyphony. *Modality, horizontal line, the independences, metrical
mode, time, prolation and proportion, the honorary precedence of the*
cantus firmus, etc., are terms and phrases used volubly with aridity
by pedagogues. The wordiness savors of elegy—a sort of committal-
ritual of a personality to "the lone couch of his everlasting sleep."
Doubtless they furnish good enough captions for theoretical parsing.
But live definitions were chucked into the clerestories. The expressions need pointing up. They must be translated out of the abstract.
Modality; what does this convey of practical significance to a maestro?
The *horizontal* line with its implied three freedoms; does it connote
agenda for bringing it to the ear? *Metrical mode, time, prolation,
proportion*; of what import are these to leaders using the modern
scores of Breitkopf and Härtel, and Dr. Edmund Fellowes? How
make obeisance to the honorary primacy of *cantus firmus*?

Modality and the terminology of temporal arrangements are in-
timidating ogres. At no time did modality relate itself to performance,
and the symbols of Renaissance note values have long since been
simplified. Modality has frightened many a student as the ghosts of
Glareanus soaked through the walls of his cubicle. A multitude of
pupils have trembled before erudite inquisitors lest they confuse the
discriminations of verbiage about meters and rhythms which they
were never to encounter in tones. Reams have been scribbled appre-
hensively by examinees aspiring to Master's and Doctor's gowns regarding the parallelisms and separable-inseparable strata of horizontal
harmony with no hope, flunking or passing, of recognizing them in
the circuit of audible sounds.

The twelve modal scales (Ambrosian, Gregorian, and the four

---

[2] Students have access to an extensive bibliography on the theory of
medieval and Renaissance counterpoint. The *Gradus ad Parnassum* of
Johann Fux (1725) is of course the rich source from which more widely
read treatises stem. The indispensable book for English-speaking conductors
is *Contrapuntal Technique in the Sixteenth Century* by R. O. Morris
(Oxford, at the Clarendon Press, 1922). Another important though less
technical volume is *Palestrina* by Zoë Hendrick Pyne (New York: Dodd
Mead, 1922).

added later) to which Glareanus assigned Grecian misnomers in the sixteenth century do not imply twelve orders of dynamic ratios for intoning polyphonic octaves. These scales are different only because their respectively normal arrangement of intervals is different, minor and major steps being variously distributed. The strategic position of major and minor thirds is reasonably thought to influence emotional moods and thus to affect the temper of intonations. But, architectonically, each scale is a more or less arbitrary sorting of seven notes with the octave repetition of the lowest note.[3] Are there five distinct techniques involved in vocalizing the modern major, pure minor, harmonic minor, melodic minor, and whole-tone scales? Certainly, the most discriminating sensitiveness could prescribe nothing more consequential than the slight softening of notes party to augmented or diminished intervals, and this merely to reduce suspected harshness. As far as I have been able to perceive, it makes no difference to *performing* choristers or leaders whether a motet is cast in an authentic or a plagal, the Dorian, Phrygian, Lydian, Mixo-Lydian, Aeolian, or Ionian mode. A sonata in D does not need special interpretation because of the two sharps in the signature. Save for possible adjustments to acoustical conditions (cf. pages 181 *et seq.* other), the movements would be the same in F, A flat, or any key. For some years I used to try to persuade myself that a number in the Phrygian mode necessarily indicated a different approach from a number in the Aeolian, etc., but I eventually outgrew this unlearned and confusing credulity. The rhythmical processes of Gregorian chant do not vary with the modes. Certainly, knowledge of modal forms has a musicological value, probably whetting taste for archaic savors, but students are advised to dismiss summarily the unwarranted impression that the modality of polyphony is a determining factor in its presentation.

The *horizontal line*, on the other hand, does imply agenda for proper interpretation. The basic difference between polyphony and homophony is in the relationship of voice lines, each of these comprising a melodic independence in the former, but, save the *vox principalis*, contributing only to chordal support in the latter. Polyphonic parts are designed to move in parallel panels, each part pursuing its own course. The task of the conductor is to convey the reality of this parallel movement. The natural tendency of concerted

[3] Cf. modality, Appendix II, pages 280 *et seq.*

intonation being toward vertical effects, the problem has been to devise a technique which will guarantee the horizontal constitution. Harmonized singing began with a sort of homophony (*magadizing* and *organum*), and toward the end of the sixteenth century composers were showing an increasing interest in perpendicular organization. The fifteenth, sixteenth, and early seventeenth centuries—Dunstable and Dufay to Palestrina and Byrd—have been acclaimed the golden age of choral music, and it is in this period that the art of horizontal singing reached its perfection. From this period, too, we must derive, by deduction, the technique of its interpretation. If choirs are permitted to intone the polyphonies without a simple plan for manifesting the horizontal freedoms of the voice lines, their confused utterance inevitably creates the impression of badly composed homophony. Tenors wrangling with altos, basses challenging sopranos, and the latter with piercing truculence crying down the efforts of all the rest to displace them from arrogant and, of course, unwarranted supremacy!

It is unreasonable to suppose that the master polyphonists would or could have fabricated their concurrent melodies if the performing choirs were going to distort and misrepresent them in a jumble of vertical cacophony. Every slightest figure, every fragile arc of melody must have been intended for proportionate hearing. The coryphæi of the golden age knew that the choirs would properly elucidate their compositions; otherwise they would have had no purpose in spinning their contrapuntal textures. There would have been no incentive to their creative genius. Imagine Palestrina knowingly facing futility but exerting himself nevertheless in the enormous task of composing ninety-three *horizontal* Masses, thirty-five *horizontal* settings of the *Magnificat*, and a vast library of *horizontal motets, hymns*, and *responsoria*!

From the notation it is evident that each voice unit was endued equally with the prerogatives of essential melody, and that the federation of the units was neatly accomplished. It is equally evident that the proper distribution of degrees of volume will assure the autonomous livelihood of each line and simultaneously accommodate each to each and to the whole in harmonious synthesis. The predetermined freedom of each line is proclaimed (1) by definite contours of intervallic sequences, (2) by individual rhythmical patterns, and (3) by independent dynamic urges.

The practical problem is: how agreeably to impress these independences on the ear, the selective capacity of which is so much less sensitive than that of the eye.

I have already given the answer which comes directly from the implications of the notation: *by serving the dynamic needs of each line.*

Accentuation according to the free rhythm (in mensural design) of the era, exact adjustments of *piano* and *forte*, discriminating employment of the indirect attack (cf. page 124), and adroit balancing of *crescendo* and *diminuendo* make certain the discernibility of each horizontal sequence without prejudice to the symphony of the whole.

These items comprise a simple but ample method for *sounding* the polyphonies and are assembled here in a series of *axiomatic precepts*, each of which is examined for its practical worth and applied to accompanying excerpts for illustration. Five of the precepts concern accentuation, and five the undulatory motion of polyphonic voice lines. Each precept is a digest—*for use*—of principles and facts brought forward by academic analysts of Renaissance counterpoint.

1. *Stress first beats only when there is a better reason for stress than mere position in the modern measure.*

2. *Aim generally to establish syllabic accents.*

3. *Consider long notes, especially if preceded and followed by shorter ones, as conveying the impression of stress; therefore permit no dynamic underlining except in the manner recommended in Precept 4.*

4. *Evoke a slight crescendo from the first to the second note in tied couplets and from the first to the second half of a long note which overlaps the second and third beats in a 4/2 or 4/4 measure.*

5. *Whenever feasible (i.e., without inviting confusion among singers), give the triple rhythmical effect to short ternary groups in a prevailing binary pattern, and the duple effect to short binary groups in a ternary pattern.*

6. *Mark all ascending passages (arses) by a slight crescendo, and descending passages (theses) by a slight diminuendo. Favor the Cantus Firmus by a little more underlining in the arses and less noticeable decrescendo in the theses.*

7. *At the entry of a voice line, lessen the volume, momentarily, of the parts already engaged.*

8. *Conclude all phrases with a* diminuendo, *as well in the single lines as at synchronous points of repose.*

9. *Adhere to the general rule of softening final syllables of Latin and English words, in spite of occasional accentual intimations in the harmony and the position of such syllables at the apex of an arsis.*

10. *Emphasize inner parts in numbers of the* stile famigliare *to avoid conveying impression of straightforward homophony.*

The following excerpts from *Masses* and the complete notation of two motets are offered in addition to the *Canon Symphonisabis* (cf. pages 210 *et seq.* as typical examples of sacred polyphony for illustrating the application of the precepts. Madrigals are examined later.

COMMENTS ON THE TEN PRECEPTS

1. Most of the violent distortions of Palestrinesque rhythm and the resulting angular awkwardness of melody and harmony are due to unfortunate treatment of the first time units in the modern-looking measures. Hapless notes transcribed as downbeats have been singing "with wooden ladles in their mouths" for almost three centuries. When these notes are stressed habitually, the accent, more frequently than not, falls in the wrong place and a non-musical series of stresses and slacks is initiated which, knocking the text away, ignoring the punctuation of harmony, and disorganizing binary or ternary clusters, makes an all-out attack on the natural flow of phrases. *The first time unit in a measure must never be marked unless the syllabification of the text, the movement of the harmony, or the apex of an arsis demands underlining.*

The appearance of the old music in post-period editions invites unwary musicians to forget what they learned about the history of notation. Polyphony in modern attire has the semblance of modern music to a sleepy eye. Bar lines *seem* to separate polyphonic units into metrical measures whose fixed accentual design is announced by a time signature. The setup is misleading. From the long habit of associating downbeat weight with the time unit nearest the left bar line, one tends subconsciously to read temporal accents into phrases which falsify the polyphonic idiom.[4]

---

[4] Editors and musicians have seemed to agree that it is better, on the whole, to publish the old contrapuntal music in modern measure form than in what our singers would consider the archaic silhouette fashion of period

Fig. 51.

Fig. 52.

FIG. 53.

Fig. 53 (cont.).

Fig. 54.

Fig. 55.

Vere Languores

Fig. 56.

FIG. 56 (cont.).

Fig. 56 (cont.).

FIG. 56 (*cont.*).

O Bone Jesu

Fig. 57.

In Fig. 51, obviously, a downbeat accent on the top G, soprano measure 2, distorts the word *Kýrie,* for the misplaced stress warps it into *Kyriè.* The modern metric beat here flouts the dignity of the word which polyphony characteristically respects. Fig. 52 shows the modern metrical accent coinciding with the rhythmical beat in alto, second tenor, and bass lines (*lúmen de lúmine*), but distressingly out of step with the sopranos' correct pronounciation of *lúmine,* and upsetting the prevailing ternary effect of measures 1-4. (Cf. Precept 5.) An accent on the B flat, measure 2 (Canon, page 210), obviously impedes the natural progress of the text and melody of *Ágnus Déi,* for the B flat is assigned to a slack syllable and is the short note between two agogic influences, the longer C and A. In Fig. 56, time-pattern and polyphonic stress are in agreement on the first note of soprano measure 16 (text and agogic position), but are in conflict on the first note (tenor) in 15 and soprano 17, because the text is assailed and the clear ternary grouping the *ipse portavit*

I-pse por - ta - vit,   I - pse _____ por - ta - vit.

Fig. 58.

figures is disrupted. Vittoria's rhythmical pattern for this figure (from soprano part 15-19) must be interpreted (cf. Precept 5) as in Fig. 58. The word *benedíctus,* Fig. 54, measures 6-8, wrenches itself out of rhythmical shape if accented on the first notes of 7 and 8.

Downbeat accents start most of the trouble. A conductor, indicating the pulsations of the rhythm with the diagrams of baton tech-

---

days. The music is published to be sung by choruses of average competency; average groups of tenors and altos neeed to know exactly what is taking place in the bass and soprano choirs, and vice versa; therefore the editors, having abandoned old notation symbols in favor of our simpler signs, strewed bar lines through the scores at regular intervals as aids to concomitance.

A few publishers, however, realizing the adverse influence of the measure form, have offered divers compromise arrangements. The two best that have come to my attention set off the notes in *quasi*-measures, one separating temporal groupings by faint *dotted* lines and the other by sixteenth-of-an-inch spaces. But these and similar subterfuges are signally unsuccessful, for wherever there prevails inadvertence to the basic difference between syllabic and agogic underlining, on the one hand, and metrical accentuation, on the other, performers invariably favor the latter—if indeed, they can truly be said to exemplify any rhythmical scheme whatsoever.

nique suitable for modern music, is often conveying the wrong impressions to singers. It is safer, simpler, and suasive (in the interests of the polyphonic idiom) to beat the time after the manner of the medieval sol-fa (cf. page 2) who established order by merely wagging a little scroll for the tempo of the major units. I have adopted this old scheme and for many years the reactions of choristers have been gratifying.[5]

2. This precept follows as a corollary of Precept 1. Polyphony, like Gregorian chant, was primarily committed to the musical exposition of texts. Its resources were to be used to emphasize the words. Therefore the basis of its rhythmical structure was necessarily syllabic, its serials of stresses and slacks being determined by the length of vowels as used in correctly pronounced language. Therefore, again, it is evident that a modern conductor may direct his singers to follow the accentual organization of the text, secure in the knowledge that the polyphonic design will be disclosed in each voice line and that the crossing of rhythmical beats, so favored a fancy among cinquecentists, will thus automatically suggest the counterpoint of rhythms, which is further revealed by the application of Precepts 4, 5, 6.

Perusal of any polyphonic number will corroborate the above data. The fluency of the undulatory motion accruing from obedience to syllabic conventions is as unmistakable as the erratic wryness from disobedience in all the examples given. In Fig. 51, the text and music in all lines require and are satisfied with *Kýrie Eléison*; in Fig. 52, with *lŭmen de lŭmine*; in Fig. 53, with *gēnitum non fáctum*. In Fig. 54, *Bĕnedíctus[6] qui vĕnit* and in Fig. 55 *Hosánna in excélsis* are fixed in these rhythmical sequences by the prearrangement of words and melodic lines. In the latter figure the tension offered between *Cantus I* with Tenor I and *Cantus II*, measures 2 and 3, invites a charming accentual counterpoint.

3. Long notes arrest attention by their duration, for the prolongation of a sound, especially if the elongated tone lies between shorter tones, is itself a species of accentuation—*agogic* rather than

[5] When choirs are divided in the liturgical mode, the sol-fa scheme is not safe, for the group on one side of the chancel is frequently uncertain about the status of the other group and a clear modern downbeat seems necessary to assure both sides of synchronous activity. A chorister, keenly apperceptive of polyphonic rhythms and their ingratiating counterplay, dissuaded me from the sol-fa method in the sanctuary.

[6] × indicates the auxiliary (weaker) accent which is needed generally in words of four or more syllables.

dynamic stress. The symmetry of rhythmical contours is disturbed if agogic prominence is emphasized by vigorous utterance. Fig. 51 provides good illustration: the first note in the soprano line has both agogic and dynamic position.

A *marcato* attack of the long note is sure to overload the syllable *Ky.* Therefore dynamic stress should be avoided, save in the method of the indirect attack by which a *miniature crescendo* unobtrusively corroborates the agogic influence. In the case of *Benedictus,* Fig. 54 (*Cantus I* and alto, measures 1-3; *Cantus II* and tenor, measures 6-8), even a *miniature crescendo* is disruptive since the agogic magnetizes as much attention as an auxiliary accent can gracefully endure.

Agogics on final syllables must be tempered by decreased volume, lest durational prominence rob a word and phrase of inherent rhythmical effect. See Fig. 56, measures 39-49, where in all voice lines *quae šola,* if allowed by agogic suggestion to become *quae solā,* disturbs the textual organization, stiffens the melody, and prevents the contrapuntal sorting of rhythms offered in associated figures. Compare measure 43, in which the soprano C sharp should yield to the E of the tenor and the second E of the alto; measure 46, where the bass F sharp should diminish for the soprano A and the tenor A sharp. The management of agogic accentual impressions is one of the most arresting activities of a true polyphonic conductor. For the beginner the process seems involved, but a few months' experience will prove it simple and self-explanatory.

At first the young maestro will do well to follow a general rule of *decreasing volume on agogic notes.* Later he will be able to modify the rule with advantage according to Precept 4.

4. This precept aims at increasing the undulation in each part, eliciting hidden accents (sometimes in syncopation), and disclosing subtle patterns of crisscross rhythms. The quiet motion of waves imparts an impression of orderly yet free activity. Its counterpart in modern music is well illustrated in measures 158, 162, 164 of Brahms' "Requiem" (cf. page 118). The effect sought in applying Precept 4 is the same, viz., a barely perceptible swell, after a soft start, and a tranquil recession, as it were, *below the surface.* The *crescendo* involved hardly merits such designation for it is not a deliberate push to greater volume, but only the slight activating of the vitality latent in the note itself. The tied notes across bar lines and their equivalent, the overlapping middle notes in measures

have an agogic effect which is enhanced *by holding back the full accentual impression.* Thus, in Fig. 56, measures 5 and 6, the tenor and bass withhold their rhythmical contribution until after the soprano accent, giving the effect of modern syncopation. In measure 6, the alto, on the other hand, addressing F sharp lightly and swelling, synchronizes with the stress of bass and soprano in the third beat. In measures 8 and 9, the application of this precept sets off the *consecutive* approaches of alto, bass, and tenor-soprano to the rhythmically important second syllable of *dolores* and the first syllable of *nostros* in 9 and 10. Thus, the use of the indirect attack in such circumstances, by its gradual processing of stress, increases the sense of vitality in notes, invites less evident facets to sparkle, and gently crosses rhythms in the prismatic marquetry which is one of music's mystic skills. The procedure of the precept implies this sequence: *soft—slight swell—soft*. If the two *soft* fractions are properly arranged, the *swell* will take care of itself. (Cf. accentuation by *diminuendo*, page 23.) Dissonances require the primary note to develop enough intensity to regulate the tension of the discordant note (cf. page 192); it will be noted that this precept assures adequate preparation of the primary for the advent of the secondary note. In Fig. 56, the tenor F sharp, measures 10-11, grows sufficiently to hold the bass G, measure 11, in agreeable relationship to the harmony. In the "Canon" (page 210) the alto A, measures 7 and 8, becomes unobtrusively sturdy enough to withstand the tenor B flat in 8. The actively discordant intervals were permissible, in polyphony, only on strong rhythmical beats. Other good illustrations in the "Canon" are measure 30, where such treatment of the antecedent's F prepares for the challenge of the tenor G, and measure 32, where the consequent and bass are in the same apposition. Also, Fig. 51, measure 5, the soprano C manages the alto D. Fig. 53, measure 5, the tenor D accepts the tension from alto E. In the *stile famigliare*, Fig. 57, the alto E, measures 7-8, makes ready for the bass F, measure 8; and the soprano A, measures 22-23, for the tenor B, measure 23.

Furthermore, this manner of managing tied couplets and long middle notes prevents impact by voices entering at such junctures as would completely obliterate the horizontal character of a whole episode.

The horizontal line of polyphony and attack by impact are irreconcilable concepts. The hostility is that of the *vendetta*, and in every conflict the horizontal line meets instantaneous death. The average attempted performance of *a cappella* polyphony attests this fact. What a pity that the differentiating personality of polyphony must be slain so many times! Monteverdi at least respected it enough to ostracize it from an arena in which it could not escape lethal violence. In the clerestory it could sleep in dust—but intact.

5. Conductors are advised to postpone the application of this precept until choristers have become accustomed to processes epitomized in the preceding precepts. This particular counsel is implied in Precepts 1 and 2 and is given explicitly chiefly to illustrate the relationship of syllabic and merely time-pattern accent beats. A properly accented text usually takes kindly care of the principal rhythmical sequences. Obviously there are words which are ternary in syllabic structure. These frequently must appear in the course of a prevailing binary setting. Fig. 52 proves this admirably. The metric accents of the modern ¢ binary time pattern would destroy the musical as well as the syllabic continuity, for both the text and the music are clearly in ternary groupings, as in Fig. 59,

lu-men de lu-mi-ne, De-um ve-rum

FIG. 59.

soprano 1-4. See also the ternary arrangement and 5/2 sorting of *Ipse fecit*, Fig. 56, as given in the comment on Precept 1. Also the frequent ternary effect implied in the *Dona nobis pacem's* of the canon (cf. page 210), measures 48-52, as shown in Fig. 60 thus:

Antecedent

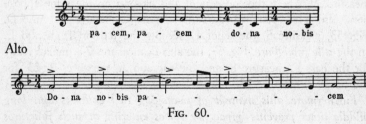

pa-cem, pa-cem, do-na no-bis

Alto

Do-na no-bis pa- - - -cem

FIG. 60.

Fig. 55 would need the arrangement of time signatures shown in Fig. 61 if metric accents and rhythmical stress were to concur.

The student may grumble here, complaining that the purpose of this book to simplify interpretative technique is defeated by such complex processes as are implied in Precepts 4 and 5. At first reading one does receive the impression of excessive delving, but careful study of these precepts should convince that the miniature *crescendo* of Precept 4 and the rhythmical patterning of Precept 5 are vir-

Fig. 61.

tually clarifying addenda to the simple instructions of Precepts 1, 2 and 3. If, after rereading and referring Nos. 4 and 5 to the inclusions of the primary precepts, the young *magister choralis* still senses a redundance of agenda, he is earnestly advised to pay no heed to the confusing items until experience has wakened sensitiveness to the more latent intimations of polyphonic movement. Therefore, lest ease of accomplishment be hindered by too many rules and the code of Palestrina threaten to remain hidden in the clerestory, abecedarians are urged to concentrate upon Precepts 1, 2 and 3. Faithful adherence to these simple counsels will, one day anon, find the seemingly more complex processes exemplifying themselves.

Precepts 4 and 5 may be set aside, but all the rest are indispensable, *ex necessitate rei.*

6. The procedure prescribed here accords with the natural tendency of all spontaneous declarative utterance, regular rising and falling of the voice. The words *arsis* and *thesis*, although variously employed since the beginning of the Renaissance, are used here in the strict historical connotations of Gregorian chant. Ascending passages were *arses* and descending passages were *theses*. Upward and downward movements of the cantor's hand (*cheironomy*) indicated to singers, who were chanting by memory, the rise and fall of phrases. Although the nomenclature is proper to Gregorian chant, it is fitting and profitable to apply the words *arsis* and *thesis*

to the corresponding sequences of polyphony, for the latter blends the free rhythm of the former with its own durational and mensural system. Basically, the rhythm of the several polyphonic voice lines is free (i.e., it is not regulated by bar lines), the absolute value of notes developing from the need of keeping the parts in harmonic accord. One of the characteristic features of free rhythm is its gentle rotation from a *lower to higher to lower* dynamic locus. Aristoxenes explained the greater satisfaction in circular than in straight linear formations by the fact that we know intuitively that a circular line may return to its point of origin, i.e., it intimates the natural intimacy of cause and effect.[7] Thus arsis and thesis are the circular coordinates of free rhythm. The urge to mount an arc is balanced by the need to descend on the recurving.

The art of tonal expression is necessarily concerned with the apposition of rises and falls. The curve line (cf. pages 161 *et seq.*) is generally a guide to the degree of excitation animating a melody. The curve lines in Gregorian chant and polyphony are characteristically limited. The emotive character of both is therefore relatively restrained. And, therefore the *crescendos* and *diminuendos* of arsis and thesis should be proportioned in sparing quotas. It is important that the variations be slight and the *poco a poco* element conserved. Hints of *subito* louder or *subito* softer inhibit the *aura* of nuance. Since this precept is a simple instruction par excellence, singers soon develop facility in setting off the arses and theses against one another, heightening the melodic fluency of each voice line and by means of this *counterpoint of dynamics* assuring to the concerted whole a polychrome iridescence, "iris all hues, roses and jessamine."

This precept guarantees proportional balance without imposing an elaborate system for compounding effects. The suggestion regarding favoring the *cantus firmus* by somewhat bolder underlining in the arses and less fall-off in the theses is not of the essence; it is a polite method of taking cognizance of the C.F.'s primacy of honor. Since the C.F. is most frequently in a tenor or alto line, such politesse is rewarded by the extra sense of solidity and coordination which careful attention to the inner parts always promotes. It is true that the tenor was the original pivot for contrapuntal revolvings, but it is also true that before the culmination of the polyphonic

---

[7] Cf. *Paléographie Musicale,* by the monks of Solesmes (Tournai, Belgium: Desclée & Cie.), Vol. VII.

school composers had ceased to pay more attention to one voice line than to another. Therefore it would be unreasonable to press the point. The tendency of conductors, however, to permit excess of treble quantity to mar choral and orchestral performance warrants inclusion of the suggestion in this precept. And a gesture to St. Ambrose, St. Gregory, Hucbald, and Guido, for the modal and hexachordal scales over which the *cantus firmus* is presumed to stand sentinel, rouses a feeling of understanding loyalty which in turn makes the gallant conductor more sensible of the ancient progressions, the clerestory rhythms, and the spirit of masters long lying in tombs.

Students are advised here to adopt the plan, proposed elsewhere in this book, of listening to two renditions of the same material, the first without the guidance of a particular precept and the second in compliance with it. Thus, in the present connection, the young maestro is urged to judge for himself the relative aesthetic values (without and with arsis-thesis treatment) of such passages as:

Fig. 51, soprano, measures 3-5.
Fig. 52, soprano and bass, measures 5-6.
Fig. 53, tenor, measures 3-5.
Fig. 54, *Cantus I* and alto, measures 3-8.
   "Canon" (page 210), antecedent, consequent, and alto, measures 5-9.
   Consequent and bass, measures 31, 32.
Fig. 56, tenor and bass, measures 10, 11.
Fig. 57, tenor and bass, measures 3, 4; soprano and alto, measures 12-18, etc.

7. The reason for this precept has been intimated in the comment on Precept 4 and in the treatment of fugal entries (cf. page 221). The entering voice line must establish itself, its appearance being essential to the harmonic scheme. If the parts already engaged do not step aside sufficiently to assure a graceful entrance, the incoming part must force its way. Impact, collision, and contention ensue. The polyphonic independences are burked and the horizontal line is garrotted again. The momentary *decrescendo* of the other parts welcomes the entrant to its prerogatives.

All of the rhythmical ratios must be carefully sustained at the temporary lower level.

Besides providing proper access to entering lines for musical reasons, this precept promotes the intelligibility of texts which, with multiple voice parts uttering different vowels and articulating different consonants simultaneously, more often than not are sorry muddles. The choral virtue rather loosely described as good diction has only two opportunities of manifesting itself in *a cappella* polyphony or later forms of contrapuntal music; neither can be ignored if the text is to be made apprehensible to listeners.[8] One is the opportunity afforded by the synchronous movement of all parts which establishes unison enunciation of the same syllables. The other is the moment of entrance when the words of the joining member can attract attention by the very fact of ingress. The majority of the measures in Fig. 56 illustrate the one, and Precept 7 is designed to protect the other.

In the beginning, the conductor is advised to apply this precept only to entrances after notable rest periods, such as the reappearance of the bass in measures 14 and 45, Fig. 56; the soprano in measure 61, Fig. 56; bass and tenor leads in the "Canon" (page 210) measures 7 and 8; the *dona nobis pacem* of the bass in measures 40-42; the tenor entrance in measure 6, Fig. 54. After choristers have had experience in singing polyphony according to the basic requirements of these precepts, they will gradually learn to sense the approach of reappearing lines and instinctively to welcome them with the proper graciousness.

I have found the practice of having all voices sing each of the contrapuntal parts in turn (as much as is feasible for vocal range) most helpful in inculcating aural consciousness of what is in progress when the associated lines are functioning together in harmony. Choristers must be convinced of the doctrine that each part is

---

[8] The intricacies of rich polyphonic composition were such a menace to the expression of the liturgical text that Palestrina was appointed to prove to an ecclesiastical commission headed by Cardinal St. Charles Borromeo (1565) that counterpoint did not necessarily prejudice the hearing of the text. The Good Friday "Lamentations" and the "Missa Papae Marcelli" are alleged to have been composed by Palestrina for that purpose. The commission approved and "modern" music was saved to the Church, but of course the great master was delightfully naïve in composing the test numbers with synchronous syllabic movement prevailing throughout the voice lines. Probably the delicacy of polyphonic singing had been neglected for a decade or two. It is quite likely that a few of the professional *cantores* were beginning to feel the importance of their personal contributions and ignored the caveats of ensemble singing. Perhaps a *tenore* or *basso molto robusto* was planning a remote clerestory a generation ahead of Monteverdi!

independent and equally essential to the complete texture, that no part is supporting another in the sense of vertical harmony, and (this is particularly relevant to the purpose of Precept 7) that "clearing the way" for arriving voice lines is a prerequisite of polyphonic virtuosity.

8. This precept is an extension of Precept 7. Vocal utterance, except in very dramatic music, normally loses intensity at the end of sentences and phrases. The important thought is usually described in the middle rather than at the end. And so, having "rolled up" to its fullness and having disclosed its principal idea logically and musically, a polyphonic melody declines to complete rest or to the starting point for a new disclosure, the circle of the arsis and thesis, the up curvature, coming down again to the point of origin. Charles Kennedy Scott[9] argues, too, that "it is generally necessary to taper the ends of sub-phrases by means of a *diminuendo*. . . . The tapering of ends of phrases is a most important point."

It is unnecessary to discuss this precept at length for its implications are evident. The reader is again urged to examine the point by listening to two readings of polyphonic phrases, one without and one with the softening of phrase ends. It will be immediately clear that the first lacks the *natural temperament* of the second, since the uninflected style affects to substitute a notchy angular design for the fluent roundness of a circle. Furthermore, since phrases throughout the voice lines are frequently overlapping, the entrance of parts is eased by the *diminuendos* of finishing lines, and the disaster of impact is thus avoided. (See the comment on Precept 4.)

9. Precept 9 provides an easy slogan by which the conductor may recall the instructions in Precepts 1 and 2 to the singers. If the latter are on the alert about *final syllables* the proper syllabic accent almost invariably is served. Frequently during the course of a polyphonic program I remind choristers of rhythmical proprieties by the terse admonition: *no accents on final syllables*. The broad sweep of a polysyllable is practically guaranteed, and the anacrusic relation of prepositions, articles, particles, and conjunctions to more important words is soon appreciated.

10. Many conductors who have developed facility in disclosing the independent horizontal lines of diffuse polyphonic writing are

[9] Charles Kennedy Scott, *Madrigal Singing* (2nd ed.; London: Oxford University Press, Humphrey Milford, 1931).

tempted by the vertical appearance of the *stile famigliare* to set forth such compositions as that in Fig. 57 as candid homophony. It is true, certainly, that synchronously moving parts tend to emphasize the impression of chords supporting a *vox principalis*, but the differentiating traits of polyphony, being essentially connected with the idea of strata of melodies producing harmony, are altogether forfeited when a vertical effect is the deliberate aim. A cursory examination of Fig. 57 will persuade the student that each voice line of the *O Bone Jesu* is a melodic unit in itself and that its vertical accord with the other lines is by polyphonic coincidence.

Each of the four melodies in this figure is a musical entity, proceeding for the most part in rhythmical unison with its associates. But the structural independence of each is clear, each contributing to the series of gentle dissonances and each imitating in some degree the patterns of the others. In order to dissuade singers from being satisfied with a homophonic presentation, it is excellent strategy to minimize the importance of the soprano line, directing attention to the tenor and alto lines, urging each line to be especially careful in the preparation of dissonances. Thus tenor and alto will be on the *qui vive* at measures 3 and 4, alto and bass at 7 and 8, alto and soprano at 14 and 15, and tenor and soprano at 22 and 23. Another device for lessening homophonic effect is to distribute primacy in turn throughout the parts, thus by slightly elevating the dynamic level to focus the singers' attention on the tenor arsis, 1-3, the alto figure, 5-9, the bass arsis at 10-13, the alto at 17-18, etc.

The application of these ten precepts is sure to disclose the horizontal character of polyphonic harmony as far as it may be clarified for the ear. At points where all voices meet, as at oases before making fresh starts in different directions, the conductor has opportunity for rebalancing the voice lines. Frequently after much free gadding, one or more lines is inclined to strive for individual eminence and needs tempering to be reassembled into the tonal picture. Oases abound in all polyphonic compositions, and while parts are enjoying a short rest from independent rhythmical activity, the conductor should convey his impressions of the adjustments needed. When all has been proceeding well I generally affect to blow a will-o'-the-wisp off the baton, but if a voice line has been threatening polyphonic parity I make appropriate gestures of disapproval to the restive group.

Musicologists delight in pointing out that there are two ways of listening to polyphonic music: one, by attending to the number as a whole without effort to identify single parts; the other, by selecting one voice line and following its migrations with little reference to the cohesive principle of the ensemble.

But there are not two ways of singing polyphony.

There is no *ad libitum* treatment feasible in major features, if the implications of horizontality are to be delivered. Rhythmical independence in the constituent parts becomes flagrant disorder, an olio of meaningless stresses and vocal collisions, unless the progress of each line is guarded and guided by the timely use of *piano*. Disregard of dynamic rationing is sure to bring about the noisy confusion which has demoted *a cappella* polyphony to a low place in popular approval. The revival of interest in this old music, now apparent in schools and colleges, will not persist if the delicacies of the interlinear relations are not observed. Dilettanti will always be interested in all archaic savors, but the musical sense of the public will not be arrested by the beauty of the Renaissance idiom until conductors have acquired skill in its revelation.

Mere academic discussion of the forms and rules of composition are fruitless. In common with a large number of aspiring young conductors, I had learned that the sixteenth-century music was still modal, harmony was horizontal, the dissonance came on the strong beat, etc. But what of all this for practical purposes? In England, Italy, Holland, France, Spain, or Germany, I could not find a basis for a plan adequate to bring *life* from the elegiac monologues of maestros. I had been struggling with disheartening futility to recreate the realities of Palestrina, Lassus, Aichinger, Tallis, etc., when in the mid-1920's Horatio Parker, dean of music at Yale, unwittingly provided the opportunity which I had subconsciously known would some day present itself. Horatio Parker was well versed in the lore of medieval counterpoint and at his suggestion I presented an exclusive program of *a cappella* polyphony at the great Wolsey Hall of the University. There was to be no straightforward homophony. The recital should establish a Renaissance atmosphere —free rhythm, modality, etc. After the recital had been in progress for half an hour the horizontal line began to disclose itself. I had never really heard it before. The singers were accidentally pursuing the right course—the course which theorists had not made plain. As one number followed another it became evident to me on the podium that a practical technique was being unfolded. And so during the intermission I jotted down the items which had differentiated this performance from all others in my experience. From these came the ten precepts. Succeeding years have attested the validity of the precepts, and I make no apology for insisting before the fraternity of maestros that only by their application can the musical values of this school of music be conveyed to modern audiences.

The technique for interpreting sacred and secular polyphony is substantially the same. Madrigals, ballets, and ayres are probably easier for most American and English singing units than masses and motets. It has been pointed out that Precept 2 is the principal custodian of polyphonic correctness. The rhythm of words in the vernacular is obviously more apparent than that of Latin words. Therefore it seems reasonable to drill a chorus in several of the more serious types of English madrigals as well as motets before addressing the less familiar syllabification of liturgical texts—such numbers as "The Silver Swan" by Orlando Gibbons, "When Shall My Wretched Life" by John Wilbye, "In Deep Distress" by Johy Mundy, "Let not the Sluggish Sleep" by William Byrd, etc.

Synchronous movement in the parts tends to give the Tudor ballet the general effect of a vetrical part song. Precept 10, applied with special care, will help to preserve the horizontal procedure. The student is referred to Charles Kennedy Scott's fine epitome of madrigal singing[10] for traditions and special points of interpretation which are needed to give authenticity to the performance of these charming creations of the poetic age of music.

The young conductor is urged to exercise great care in appointing the tempos for madrigal singing. The greater part of the large library of these quaint songs exploits the gay, blithesome, and satirical. Someone said that a madrigal played on the piano was the greatest caricature of music. I have often felt that a choral society undertaking to voice the persiflage of the Elizabethan lyricists with ponderous slowness and heavily guttural proclamation heaped more ridicule on the style than the most mechanical cartoonist at a pianoforte. In the *fa-la* ballets, and frequently throughout the madrigal repertoire, the text is not meant literally to express a conviction. The madrigalist is often—more often than not—the court jester of music. Silly lampoons, extravagant repining, squibs, skits, and

[10] Charles Kennedy Scott, *Madrigal Singing* (London: Oxford University Press, Humphrey Milford, 1907).

metaphor! Lyrical arrows with make-believe barbs! Once I heard Morley's "My Bonnie Lass, She Smileth" intoned in the tempo and mood fitting for "All Flesh is as the Grass" of the Brahms "Requiem." (A post-mortem rebuke to Morley for having been lighthearted?) Lightness in vocalism, brightness in tempo, spiciness in dynamics— these qualities are indispensable to the proper delineation of secular polyphony.

The assignment of proper tempos and ratios of volume is the only resource by which a conductor can unfold the aesthetic and psychological content of a piece of music. Careless employment of these resources necessarily sponsors indifferent performances. Altogether misguided application is inevitably destructive. In no phase of musical exercise are these facts so abundantly corroborated as in the sovereign school of *a cappella* polyphony.

CHAPTER VIII

HOMOPHONY

*Hymn Tunes, Part Songs; Face and Concomitant Melodies in
Vertical Harmony*

IN HOMOPHONIC music the outstanding melody is usually
assigned to the high treble line if the choral unit is a standard
S.A.T.B., and to the top tenor if the choir is *T.T.B.B.* But the melody
may be entrusted to any line. Sometimes it shifts from one locale to
another. Generally, however, a melody remains in the line of its
origin, at least until a rhythmical sentence has been completed. To
avoid the monotony consequent upon much reiteration, composers
frequently transfer candid tune melodies to other voice lines in
repetitions. The different *rilievos* at which themes thus present themselves, plus the modifications effected by change of mode and incidental harmonic treatment, lend freshness to each repetition of a
melodic sentence.

The place of a melody in a homophonic structure is discernible
to a tyro at first glance. Its migrations are also manifest. Therefore,
salvis salvandis, a conductor's task in setting forth this uninvolved
music is relatively simple.

Specifically: first he is obliged, by canons of blend and balance,
to acclimatize each melody to its harmonic atmosphere. Neither
melody nor harmony is effectual when either usurps or trespasses
upon the prerogatives of the other. Melody requires definition. So,
too, the harmonic characteristics of a number must be elucidated.
Homophony is equally unconvincing if a melody is overstressed or
if the supporting chords assert themselves with intemperate vigor.
Secondly, he should study the repetitions to ascertain how to sustain or renew the interest of listeners.

Another resource which enriches the performance of homophonic
choral music is the occasional use of sopranos as harmonics when
the melody is written in unison octaves (cf. pages 133 *et seq.*).

Short contrapuntal arcs, when encountered in a characteristically
homophonic composition, should be treated as momentary and re-

freshing digressions from a principal melodic topic. A conductor proves his skill by the ingenuity with which he italicizes such passages, at the same time keeping them subservient to the primary material.

May the face melody of a musical phrase yield primacy to a concomitant melody upon repetition of the phrase?

By the *face* melody I mean the series of notes which appears on the surface of a homophonic phrase, as distinguished from other melodic material which may be discovered below the surface. A face melody gives a phrase its personality. It is the aspect of a composition which is retained most vividly in the popular memory; it is the identifying countenance.

If the phrase is to be performed only once, or several times in strikingly different harmonic attires, the face must always be visible. If, however, there is not in the accompanying harmony a change or variety of tonal effects sufficient to contribute new vigor to a repeated tune, an interesting concomitant melody may advantageously be brought to the surface. But this melody must have an arresting profile of its own; it must be worth looking at, presenting an obvious orderliness of musical qualities.

The relatively recent vogue of superimposing discants upon hymn tunes attests the eagerness of musicians to avert the ruinous monotony deriving from the unembellished reiteration of face melodies. Although a concomitant melody may not be coextensive with the primary theme, being perhaps only a melodic segment of short duration, added interest accrues to singers and listeners alike if it is granted opportunity for exhibition. Monotony is disastrous to aesthetic purposes. Music speaks to the imagination, and the imagination tires quickly of monochrome intonation. Thus an interior voice part, if written melodiously, can be made to enhance the whole movement of which it is a part, when fittingly and opportunely accentuated. Many straightforward hymn tunes are composed so *vocally* for all the choral lines (the alto being usually the least fortunate) that often segments of melody are found in the subsidiary parts, and may be substituted profitably for the face in repeated passages, unless it is evident that the composer had only one melodic idea in mind which he purposed to stress by reiteration.

The face melodies of short folk songs may not generally be replaced by associated melodies lurking in the harmonic background, because the distinguishing trait of a genuine folk song is its graphic delineation of one simple tune.

As a rule, hymn tunes and carols, as well as themes made popular by wide use (e.g., the Moore melodies and the simple songs of Stephen Foster), may correctly be classified as species of a broadly defined folk-song genus. Folk songs in the more precise meaning of the designation, however, were conceived as pure melodies without the qualifications of harmony. It is true, of course, that the folk lore of many races and eras is now presented as accompanied monody, but the property which differentiates bona fide folk songs from modern hymn tunes and other kindred melodic simplicities is the fact that the majority of the former were designed as unison progressions, while the latter were and are habitually conjured up in association with harmony.

The folk songs of the people are the musical kin of the Gregorian chants. Musicologists find many points of similarity if not identity in their structure. Ancient and medieval folk songs were composed according to the modal system necessarily. The most frequently recurring modes in the authentic folklore of the West, as far as may be ascertained from the specimens preserved, are Hypo-Dorian and the Hypo-Lydian, which, like the Aeolian and Ionian (there is an academic but not an actual impressive difference between the Hypo-Dorian and the Aeolian or the Hypo-Lydian and the Ionian), create respectively the effects of our minor and major modes.

The probability that the Gregorian melodies stimulated some measure of intimated harmony in the subconsciousness of experienced chanters has been suggested by musicologists.[1] Probably the folk song tunes also carried to the imagination a silhouette of consonances. Consideration of this item, however, is not pertinent to our immediate purpose, except to the extent of indicating that a conductor who is intent upon giving authentic performances of folk songs, no matter what improvement has accrued from harmonic or contrapuntal re-formation and enrichment, should always keep the face melody to the fore. Many of the Teutonic melodies which

---

[1] Research has brought to light many facts about ancient instruments which corroborate the feeling that certain relations of synchronous sounds were not only suspected but sometimes employed before harmony was historically recorded; and further that ethnologists claim to have found indications among primitive peoples of a certain type of part singing in a style savoring of modern tonality. The bequest of earlier generations to the Bushmen of Australia is offered in support of this claim.

Bach so ingeniously furbished with counterpoint seem to suggest the genre of the folk song; they sacrifice something of their character-istic Nordic sturdiness if the conductor, yielding to the lure of the counterpoint, veils the strong features of the faces.

Short carol airs, daintily arrayed in the sheer harmonies of French and Walloon fashions, should always show their pretty visages, else they become mannequins upon which are draped the silks and satins from *conservatoire* patterns.

The treasured content of true folk songs, of folk hymns and folk carols, and "The Last Rose of Summer" class of airs is their bequest of single melodies from one generation to another. The occasional scraps of melody which may be hidden within the chordal euphonies accompanying these single melodies must remain latent. If the conductor substitutes a melodic segment essaying to emerge from the harmonic block for a familiar face motif, he can justly be charged with favoring distortion and anachronism at the expense of verisimilitude or authenticity. Overimaginative conductors would profit from reflection on this trite axiom: "Facts are stubborn things." Imagery, indeed, is the wellspring of the fine arts, but its concepts must conform to facts, they must reveal beauty as the "true," or they hint at Galsworthy's "visionary mania," expressing only the chimeras of disorganized thinking. One of the inexorable facts to which a con-ductor must make obeisance, in directing music of the folk song species, is the self-sufficiency of primary melodies. Therefore, as a credible artist he must allot to face melodies the preferred positions in the perspective of the ensemble.

There is unquestionably a fundamental dissimilarity between melodies conceived as unison music thoughts, dressed up later in the fashions of succeeding epochs, and the monody which was pre-arranged to function as the principal part of a harmonic unity. It is not always easy to distinguish between these two species of monody. Many conductors evince little interest in the difference. Perhaps, if they advert to the topic casually, they conclude that its implications are overvalued; they exempt themselves from serious inquiry on the basis of "much cry and little wool." But however little wool is gained by much shearing, no master conductor can safely consider as rodomontade the suggestions of musicologists which bear upon the authentic presentation of melody.

Wagner insists that the conductor "find the melody in every bar." His precept must be accepted, for it derives from the essence of music. *Music* without discernible melody is a misnomer for some other exercise of the imagination and is a curious craftsmanship as yet incorrectly named. *Melos* is the animating spirit of the art form which during many centuries has been identified as *music*. All conductors, then, choral and orchestral, have *melody* to consider, study, and master in all its styles, differentiations, historical appositions, and psychological reaches as their paramount interpretative obligation.

The question under examination here involves important subject matter. The items included have not been adequately discussed in the available literature on conducting. Just as the finer, more subtle, and therefore more distinctively musical phases of tone quality, rhythm, tempo, and dynamics have been treated cursorily by many pedagogues, so, too, have many aspects of melody been left to conductors to discover upon their own initiative. Initiative and spontaneity are invaluable assets in the pursuit of any vocation. In the exercise of the art of music, they are prerequisites of superior importance. No conductor can grow out of a textbook or fashion a perfect product upon another's pattern. The very nature of his art requires that in some degree he be self-taught by personal research into the mystic arcana of a vaguely understood medium of expression. One cannot help lamenting, nevertheless, the meager bibliography to which students and professional conductors have access in their search for answers to many questions. The majority of convincing maestros have eventually answered their own questions by the uncomfortable process, as I can attest by my own experience, of making egregious blunders.

For a full quarter of a century I conducted (with the nonchalance of misunderstanding) an ancient folk melody which, in spite of its brevity, had later been overloaded with harmonic costume-jewelry. It entertained me, so it seems in retrospect, to focus the spotlight upon the *bijouterie* of the harmony, permitting inferior facets to glisten and thus to distract attention from the theme which they were meant only to adorn. Professional critics failed to call me to account, although they were conscientiously and volubly stern about other matters, and so the unseemly trifling with the prerogatives of face melodies went unchallenged. Eventually, however, the eccentric properties of a small auditorium made me aware of the fantastic distortion which I had accidentally been provoking. In this particular hall the intonations of the basses concentrated in a direct channel upon the podium. I signaled the basses, as usual, to emphasize their line in the second repetition. The effect was grotesque. I heard the number for the first time as many probably had heard it in the stalls and balconies; it was the denaturalization of a plain short sequence of notes in the Hypo-Lydian mode. Therefore the performance was counterfeit. Having donned sackcloth, I apologize now, in vain, to many audiences.

I learned from this salutary experience that a conductor can unwittingly take liberties with style melodies which rob them of their idiomatic and historical worth. The search for the "melody in every bar" will disclose it to be always the face melody in such music. Figures drawn from auxiliary parts usually betray the candor of brief traditional tunes.

But all simple and familiar tunes are not so short or self-sufficient as to endure much reiteration, even when transferred to the various choral lines.

If they originated in the epoch of unaccompanied monody, obviously their later association with harmony should not deprive them of their unisonous vigor. Vocal or instrumental accompaniments are, in this circumstance, only vassals, and, as such, must humbly serve. The Moore and Foster styles of accompanied monody allow the conductor no choice but to keep the well-loved tunes in evidence. The Welsh air "All Through the Night" would suffer intolerable alteration if its three-note pattern melody were to retire in favor of some tuneful succession discovered in the supporting consonances.

The most extreme example of ruthless attack upon melodic integrity and propriety that has yet been achieved is the ripping of themes from their classical settings in the current form of musico-sadism, swing. So many of the motifs of sonatas, symphonies, and operas have been abducted from their honored niches by emissaries of Vulcan and constrained to dance with ugly caperings to hammering improvisations in the dire den on Mt. Aventine, that perhaps the merciless kidnapers will presently survey the Gregorian and polyphonic fields for new victims. Then indeed will the public be regaled by an orgy of highly spiced kickshaw; the "Crucifixus" of Lotti, the "Lamentations" of Palestrina, the "Jesu Dulcis Memoria" of Vittoria, and the chants of the antiphonary may be heard in night-club versions, mocking and ridiculing themselves in a corybantic frenzy of screaming reeds and impetuously clamorous horns.

Were Sir Walter Scott and Sir Alfred Tennyson possibly thinking beyond their respective contexts while penning "with bark and whoop and wild halloo" and "with us no language but a cry"?

Impresarios, arrangers, and conductors who are party to such desecration of the holiness of good music (the spiritual and the aesthetic are closely allied) are either wanton despoilers or un-reasoning disciples of a spurious philosophy of art.

Let swing have its day and make whatever valid contribution it may to the development of new concepts of music, but let it, by every canon of authenticity and seemliness, fashion its own forms and leave unmolested, in full dignity, the great figures of a reverent art. *Noblesse oblige!*

Melodies however, which were preconceived by their composers to be confirmed by or to rely to a degree on harmony are of a different order. It is clear that such inventions should be interpreted in apposition to the reinforcing components. The melodies of the past few hundred years were formulated as the integrants of a concerted whole; in the companionship of other attributes, they were naturally endowed with greater prerogatives. This does not imply that the less important features were always to hide in the background. Often one of these can save a face melody from becoming flabby and sluggish.

In the characteristic relationships of polyphony, complete melodies or segments of melody, proceeding with horizontal independence, are found in all the contributory lines of an ensemble. The resulting intricate texture of melodic threads has already been discussed. The specific topic for inquiry here is the relationship of a melody over chordal harmony or casual contrapuntal commentaries, to figures appearing in the other concomitant parts.

When, then, may straightforward tunes or striking melodic for-mations be replaced temporarily by simultaneous melodies which are found in the supporting harmony?

It would be presumptuous and arrogant to usurp the privilege of dictating rules in a phase of musical exercise which, perhaps more than other phases, is a "conductor's choice." Therefore I propose no fixed criteria by which interpretative orthodoxy may be rated. Many conductors of deservedly high repute are steadfast in their opposi-tion to the veiling of a face melody under any circumstances. A smaller class of maestros, impelled by a restless quest for variety, seem avidly intent upon adorning the face, or withholding it from view whenever they profess to discover melodic bits which they can chip off the harmonic block. Sometimes, discomfited by a dearth of applicable chunks and oddments, they resort to stucco dynamics and indecorous agogics to cover the natural features of a *vox principalis*. The extremists of this fortunately inconsiderable group, seeming to delight in artificial effects, have ever on hand a varied assortment of "transformations."

But the majority of conductors are too sensitive to the inherent sincerity of music and too well schooled in its authenticities to adopt the puritanical attitude of the excessively stern school, and much too sane and normal to join the "transformers" in their "not conventionally unconventional" whimsicalities. The policy of the ultra-conservative conductors is always too restraining; it tends to deny adequate freedom to the poetry of music, while indiscriminate efforts to reform homophony by an apocryphal gospel of polyphony promote only jejune heterogeneity. Great conductors are neither tyrannical with misunderstanding nor capricious without understanding.

Hymns and secular part songs written in the longer modes of versification are often rendered more convincing musically by bringing to the front, occasionally, a concomitant melodious figure. This secondary figure indwelling the harmonic structure must have a striking form and a personality of its own. The more vigorous the primary melody, the more satisfying must be its substitute. On the other hand, a weak face can be advantageously veiled by the sheerest material.

Unfortunately, puritanical rigorists seem to take sardonic delight in begrudging colorful musical settings to religious texts. "The beauty of the King's daughter is within" is a scriptural phrase which may be applied, without irreverence, to certain hymn tunes the comeliness of which lies only in the character and disposition of the harmony. Tradition and an ecclesiastical nudge or two keep many paltry airs in vogue. Perhaps someday a musical Savonarola will build a bonfire which will consume the compilations of hymnbooks whose chief virtue is their combustibility.

Fig. 62 is a sample (admittedly extreme) of a hymn tune which implores a conductor to come to its rescue. He cannot "service" the impotent thing if it is assigned to the list of congregational hymns (unless by sonorous discants on the organ), but he can, in some degree, re-create it from its own material if sung by a choir in harmony. I propose this example because it was a *bête noir* of my youth, and I was driven by an overwhelming urgency to resort to whatever and sundry means of reconstruction available.

The face is colorless. Symptoms of anemia appear immediately in measures 1-2; they are corroborated in measures 5-6 and 13-14. Measures 3-4, 7-8, 15-16, and the entire line 9-12 insist upon a diagnosis of melodic infirmity.

FIG. 62.

The ashen countenance of the tune should not be in evidence for more than one stanza.

Polyphony and homophony are organized on different conceptual bases; the former, by the parity of the component lines, is characteristically involved, recondite, and furtive, and the latter must be explicit, clear spoken and declarative. This means that the element of sturdiness is more necessary in the melodies of harmonized monody than in the horizontal themes and imitations of polyphony.

Here is an arbitrary—whimsical if you will—formula by which the pallid *face* may gallantly be shielded through portions of the ensuing stanzas. It tends to impart something of strength and color by making the lower parts expressive.

In the second stanza:

Emphasis of the alto line, 1-6, introduces at least a modicum of strength which has been wholly lacking; obviously the sopranos must give the shape to 7-8; the tenors may carry-on 9-10, sharing a duet figure with the sopranos, 11-12; the last two verses of the stanza may fall to the altos.

In the third stanza:

The tenors may profitably assert themselves to measure 8, the altos taking over to measure 12; the last two verses may with fair effect be divided among tenors and sopranos, in that order.

Or the basses may add substance, 1-6, ceding to the sopranos, 7-8; the soprano and alto thirds, 9-10, followed by the soprano and tenor combination, 11-12, and the basses intoning the tonic broadly, 13-14, introduce the face, 15-16 for a last glimpse.

Such a crisscross of melodic striae presents a kind of patternless pattern, but probably even so curious a series of detours is less trying than the direct route indicated on the soprano line. Certainly, the aggregate of such a mixture of ingredients is at best nothing more than an emergency arrangement, but it serves to improve the effect of the hymn as a whole.

This example was selected because of the dire need of reinforcing the treble tune. The harmony provides a somewhat clumsy *deus ex machina.*

Many a sturdy theme may be confirmed, and many a winsome melody of ceramic delicacy may be further enhanced, by inviting the cooperation of certain excerpts from the chordal accessories. A virile melody is reinvigorated if, during some of many repetitions, one or more strong themes are abstracted from the harmony and given equal if not primary responsibility for a stanza or two. Rarely will any tune, in spite of its sinew and energy (perhaps, indeed, because of these), hold the comfortable attention of listeners once redundant reiteration has played its age-old trick of teasing the consciousness to tedium. Sometimes, much encoring of a striking sequence of notes contrives the eccentric prank of urging a melody so forcefully upon the subconsciousness that one helplessly purrs it through many days.

The first unwitting purrings of such a strain are, of course, evidence of pleasure, but, anon, the persistent rote provokes annoyance and finally disquietude. How often would one escape from the ghost of a tune that haunts the resonant caverns of the subconscious mind!

Reiteration is an essential factor of effective pedagogy, but in the fine arts, especially those which produce their aesthetic effects by poetic movement (drama, pageantry, poetry, music, and the great all-embracing sacred art of liturgy to whose service the Church has directed these others since the fourth century), it is a difficult something to manage.

Knowledge of the essence of *poetic movement*, its sundry aspects, and its psychological influences is an invaluable asset to a conductor. It is a passkey to freedom from confining bars, clefs, signatures; it is emancipation from the tyrannies by which so many musicians are constrained; it is the guide to the lonely outpost where truth and beauty, aspirations and intuitions make mystic rendezvous, where the arts transcend technique, where the approaches to the Eternal are sensed. "I learnt life from the poets," wrote de Staël.

The reorientation which a conductor may achieve by even speculating about the profundities on which the art forms are necessarily only vague commentators, will make secure the reality and therefore the validity of his musicianship. The philosophy of art as well as the technical phases of his specialty should be the major subjects in the lifelong curriculum of every conductor.

Much reiteration has already been designated as an awkward constituent of the arts that proceed by *poetic movement*. The psychological reaction to it cannot be predicted. Therefore, genuine artists, when uncertain sometimes as to the artistic propriety of reading oft-recurrent themes with monotonous uniformity or with discriminating variety, are at a loss how best to proceed.

Thematic material in the symphonies, overtures, and tone poems, if repeated often with the same instrumentation in one monochrome interpretation, may become increasingly less effective upon each repetition. It is evident, then, that conductors should mark off each repetition for study as a possible asset or liability to the whole.

Poetic movement involves fluent continuity in the unfolding of an idea, and any interrupting factor is a liability. Poets, playwrights, composers, readers, actors, soloists, and conductors should regard the influence of repetitions upon the subtle efficacy of their cognate undertakings as materially important. The poet must have a care lest a periodically recurrent refrain traverse the progress of his fancy; the dramatist needs to provide against too much similarity in successive scenes as well as against the probable monotonies of stylists in elocution; the pageantist should be a *ne plus ultra* master in varying the color scheme and the processional rituals of his spectacles; composers could profitably erase many ditto marks (they rejoiced when freed from the A.B.A. type of aria which Scarlatti and many followers bequeathed to oratorio and opera); readers, actors, and soloists must shun frequent employment of singular inflections and mannerisms; and, finally, conductors, timid about deleting the dittos left in scores, should take counsel with judgment and imagination in selecting attractive frames for reappearing pictures.

To revert to the simple hymn, carol, or part song form of homophony: a prescription is given for Fig. 63 by which a sturdy melody not only may escape gradual enervation but may accumulate additional vitality.

First stanza:

Set forth the treble melody throughout, slightly more in evidence than the supporting harmony; there are no accidentals to color the eight-bar tune which is repeated twice; the three appearances of this straightforward sequence in diatonic severity indicate that some modifications must be introduced in the ensuing stanzas if one or other of the reactions to excessive reiteration is to be averted.

Second stanza:

Underline the tenor line X-16; from the upbeat of 16 through 20 raise the dynamic level of all lower parts slightly above that of the treble, especially the oblique ascent of tenors and basses, 19-20; conclude the stanza with all parts in dynamic parity.

Third stanza:

Soften the altos, X-8, while the tenors and bases are singing the treble melody, the sopranos functioning as harmonics (*q.v.*)

The First Nowell

Traditional

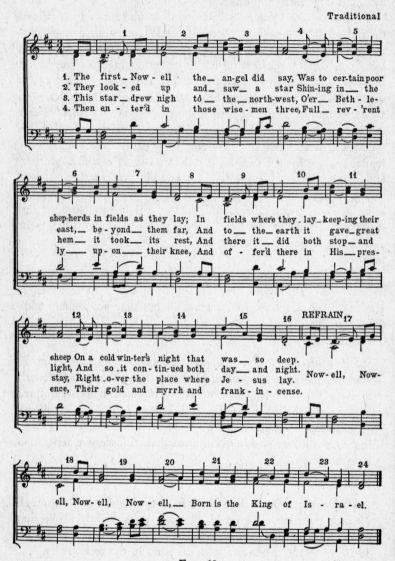

1. The first Now-ell the an-gel did say, Was to cer-tain poor
2. They look-ed up and saw a star Shin-ing in the
3. This star drew nigh tó the north-west, O'er Beth-le-
4. Then en-ter'd in those wise-men three, Full rev-'rent

shep-herds in fields as they lay; In fields where they lay keep-ing their
east, be-yond them far, And to the earth it gave great
hem it took its rest, And there it did both stop and
ly up-on their knee, And of-fer'd there in His pres-

sheep On a cold win-ter's night that was so deep.
light, And so it con-tin-ued both day and night. Now-ell, Now-
stay, Right o-ver the place where Je-sus lay.
ence, Their gold and myrrh and frank-in-cense.

ell, Now-ell, Now-ell, Born is the King of Is-ra-el.

Fig. 63.

in the octave written; eliminate sopranos here, assigning altos to the treble line, 8-16; sing the "Refrain" in unison-octave arrangement as in X-8.

Fourth stanza:

Proceed as in first stanza, at a lower dynamic level and slightly slower tempo, X-16; conclude as in the second stanza.

The dainty melody in Fig. 64 finds in its harmonic alliance an equally dainty catenation of contrasting elements. The piece is homophonic, of course, but it can be made to proceed after the fashion of the rhetorical *chiasmus*. The latter is merely an inversion of order in a statement, e.g., "I cannot dig, to beg I am ashamed"; its musical analogue inverts and reinverts the melodic utterances without altering the meaning of the sentence.

Here one finds the top-soprano line to be an undulating flow of notes. The continuance of the dactylic rhythm and the consequent subservience of the eighth notes for so many measures conspire to suggest the brook that goes "on forever," its ripplings at first delightful with pastoral poesy, but presently monotonous. The face melody will evoke increasing interest if it is gradually unveiled. Just visible in the background for two stanzas, its approach to the front in the concluding stanza has the element of drama about it that is indispensable to the modern appreciation of music. (Even a thousand years ago, ecclesiastical poets and the composers of Gregorian hymn melodies were uneasy about the repetition of metrical and musical norms, and probably from this uneasiness came the most striking poetic and melodic combinations of the liturgy, i.e., the sequences.)

Whereas it is impracticable to formulate canons to guide one in the different treatments to be accorded the virile tune and the more fragile melody, it seems logical to suggest that the "Nowell" type should proclaim itself at the outset, the qualifications to ensue, while the full grace of a flowerlike melody such as this should be revealed *poco a poco*. This carol is a good subject for laboratory experimentation. Perhaps it is not extravagant to claim that the greater number of effective homophonic songs in which a single picturesque theme is frequently reproduced is prospered by a tactical postponement of the full appearance of the theme until it can show itself to greatest advantage on the dais of a moderate climax.

The Angels and the Shepherds

Cordelia Brooks Fenno   Bohemian Carol

FIG. 64.

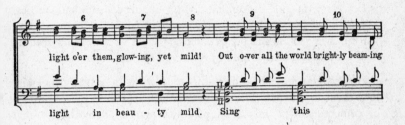

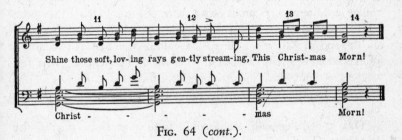

FIG. 64 (*cont.*).

Following conclusions derived from the foregoing considerations, I propose the following interpretation of this carol:[2]

First stanza:

A broad effect by the altos, 1-8, the sopranos keeping the face melody in the background, as muted violins; after the unison, conclude with first altos again in evidence, 13-14.

Second stanza:

The tenors should stress this graceful figure, 1-8, with a smooth cello *legato*, the sopranos still remaining in the background, a slight increase accruing because of the combining of first and second sopranos; accentuate the drone of the double pedal point,

[2] The rhythmical and minute dynamic graces are not included. Cf. chapters on Rhythm and Dynamics.

with special attention to the D of the baritones, 9-14, the parts hovering quietly above. (The musical and mystical value of emphasizing double pedal drones was sensed by the Russians and is characteristic of much of their *a cappella* music up to the revolution.[3])

Third stanza:

Allow the face melody now to present itself *poco a poco* more clearly, with the concomitant tenor sequence supplying a less prominent *cantus*, 1-8; over the triple pedal drone, the sopranos, 9-14, bring to an effulgent conclusion what in a uniform reading of the three stanzas would have been a colorless dénouement.

At first glance, such processes of dealing with primary melodies may seem to conflict with straightforward fidelity to the intentions of composers. Certainly such processes are not agreeable to that limited musicianship which evolves solely from mathematical formulae and the more rigorous conventions of form. Perhaps they even appear to transgress a major premise posited in the early pages of this book: "In all well-written music, the aesthetic concepts of the composer will discover themselves to listeners, if given fair chance, without much importuning from the conductor. Admittedly, however, the conductor must know how to accord the music its fair chance."

This knowledge will accrue only from a careful study of the fundamental property, melody—what guarantees its effectiveness in some circumstances, what handicaps it in others. The periodic repeating of a leading motif, if the dynamic level of each recurrence is varied, is generally a guarantee; it is the orator's emphasis on his main point. But in simply constructed pieces, persistent emphasis of sameness weakens melody; it soon becomes the whirr of a spinning top; it is defeat by monotone. Music is sure to thrive on a "fair chance," but unmodified reiteration is among the agencies that prey upon its rightful opportunities. The analysis of the conductor's responsibility to melody leads inevitably to the conclusion that face melodies must frequently be tempered by concomitant melodies, lest the purpose of music be, in some instances, altogether frustrated. Addison wrote (*Spectator*, November 6, 1711), "What

[3] The frequent use of the tonic and dominant in this position by the Russians has suggested the "Russian Fifth" as a new designation in the nomenclature of chorophony.

sculpture is to a block of marble, education is to a human soul," and (I presume to add) *interpretation is to music.*

In compositions of greater length than the short metrical styles already discussed, and especially in choral proses involving several movements, the danger of tune tedium is circumstantially averted. Nevertheless, a conductor will often find the repetition of a primary theme to be enriched by expounding a secondary figure which in the first statement was permitted to remain obscure. One example (No. IV, Brahms "Requiem," cf. page 111) will serve to indicate the validity of this opinion.

There are 180 measures, over all, in this chorus. The primary choral melody (9 bars) appears in some form at least seven times in the soprano line, twice in its full span, and partially or by imitation in the other instances. The same theme is found winding its way through the orchestral ensemble a minimum of nine times (probably more in inverted fragments), twice synchronously with the chorus, twice (4 bars) without chorus, and five times by suggestion.

At measure 90, the repetition of the choral introduction furnishes excellent opportunity to counteract the growing monotony of the soprano melody. The tenor figure which was properly subordinated in the first instance may be brought forward here with excellent effect. This figure is descending and in contrary or oblique motion to the treble. Reaching its apex two measures later than the treble, it may be broadened to give greater sweep to the passage. The main theme of the choral writing being an upward progression, the conductor will find descending figures or even small arcs suitable material for underlining; thus the orchestral passage 85-90. Since the treble line 116-123 is a reminiscence of the development at 25-44, the alto line from 116-124 may advantageously be invited to contribute a new though cognate element.

Generally, effective interpretation of homophonic music requires more imagination than is needed for polyphony. The structure of the latter provides its own criteria for artistic performance. In homophony, a tune can easily become banal, and it is a duty of the conductor to prevent this if possible. On the other hand, it is easy to overdo the adorning of a tune by its harmonic investiture. Here real artistry is indeed necessary. No rules of procedure may reasonably be established. Two extremes must be avoided: the

insipidness of unnecessary monotony and the capricious oversea-
soning of too much stress of concomitant melodies.

I have often thought that a conductor's practical knowledge of
music is manifested in his treatment of counterpoint and that his
taste and poetic sensibility are shown in his reading of a hymn tune.

The repertoire of church choirs, concert societies, and school
choruses nowadays is drawn from such a variety of styles that it is
important for young conductors to develop facility in selecting the
right approaches. He must always expound melody. But the estate
of melody is not always the same. The conductor must be both
academician and aesthete.

There's many a secret passage behind the façades of music. *Frons
est animi janua!*

THE LOCALE OF MELODY

MELODY AND SCALE CONSCIOUSNESS

By *scale-consciousness* I mean quick recognition of what is occurring or is meant to occur in any of the voice lines, contrapuntal or chordal, at any given point. If there is an arc of melody in an inside line, the conductor should be aware of it; this is "finding the melody in every bar." Without awareness of the modifying influence actually or potentially exerted by inner factors, he will necessarily miss much of the material by which a composer intended to enrich or even to make plain his musical thought. Every series of notes, no matter how short or subordinate, is a melody of a sort if the notes are related in orderly artistic fashion, and is therefore entitled to appropriate disclosure. Obviously, if the conductor fails to sense the activity of these subordinate entities, their contribution to clarity or adornment is sacrificed.

Many student conductors of the present era lack facility in identifying these arcs of melody. Perhaps they are distracted by principal (top-line) melodies or by the vague relationships engendered between voice lines by polytonal and atonal music. Whatever the explanation, it is evident that many young and talented maestros disregard much of the less obvious material. Frequently it is this material upon which the convincingness of a composition depends. Witness Wagner and the Colonne performance of Beethoven's "Ninth" (cf. page 8).

A long melodic phrase beginning in one voice line and extending through others, as in the "Requiem" of Brahms (cf. page 111, measures 49-57), insists upon recognition. It is melody's *top-line continuo*, a sort of correspondent to harmony's *basso continuo*. It will reveal itself unless a conductor altogether mismanages the phrase. But self-training in the kind of acumen designated as *scale-consciousness* is necessary before a conductor will feel the need of drawing attention to inner fragments of melody that are modestly veiled by their small dimensions. Such bits are like adverbs in a sentence; they qualify the activity of the verb. The activity of the verb frequently determines the force of a sentence. In music the principal melody is the verb and the oddments in associated parts can be made to add to or subtract from its vitality. Refer to Brahms' "Requiem" again: bass, measures 10-12, 20-23; alto and bass, 37-38; bass, 53-57; alto and tenor, 71-73, etc. These melodic sparks are intended to activate the glow of the principal theme. They are there to accomplish something. Therefore, if they are denied opportunity to function, they are purposeless. Such little figures should be rated as ornaments and be exposed adequately for perception.

The necessity of developing facility in pre-hearing latent melodic figures is essential to validity of interpretation. The master conductor lets the light shine on every facet in the score. Some young conductors have admitted to me during the many courses which I have given for post-graduate students, that they lack sensitiveness to less evident and concealed factors not only in scanning scores but even while a chorus or orchestra is sounding the notes. Such individuals are wanting in scale-consciousness. They need to exercise their faculties in discovering and identifying all the agencies in operation at a given moment. Scale-consciousness means sensitiveness to the contribution of every item in the melodic and harmonic structure.

It is easy to measure one's facility in this field. Invite a colleague to play for you, more or less at random. How many notes were in that chord? How many of these were octaves of fundamentals? How many and what major, minor, and augmented intervals? Were there accidentals or only dissonances in that progression? If dissonances, in what voice lines were the preparatory and dissident notes? If accidentals, where, and did they effect a modulation? Identify the modulatory processes involved in a peregrination from a given key to another. Ask the pianist to play in one key, e.g., E natural; immediately afterwards try to think the major and minor triads of another key, e.g., B Flat.

Listen to a slow movement broadcast by an orchestra. What timbres dominate the alto and tenor lines? Which instrument effected that modulation? Are oboes or clarinets playing the upper part in that wood-wind phrase? Is the harmony distributed for four or fewer French horns?

Listen to the pipe organ. Is the manual registration coupled to the pedal? Was that *crescendo* accomplished by adding more registers or merely by opening the *swell* shutters? Can you detect the cancellation of unison pitch, e.g., of a *stopped diapason* and the use of *super* and *sub* couplers? Can you analyze a synthetic cello effect such as *gedecht* 8 ft., *salicional* 8 ft., and *vox celestis* 8 ft.? Can you determine, after having had opportunity to hear the individual stops, whether the *vox celestis* is apposed to the *salicional* or *aeoline*?

Listen to an *a cappella* chorus. In what voice line is the greatest tendency to flatten? To sharpen? Where, in a phrase of eight bars, was attack by impact most disastrous? In which voice line were most of the figures announced for imitation? Which line in the harmony of that homophonic number contributed most to its general effectiveness? Was the juxtaposition of *crescendos* and *diminuendos* balanced to the prevailing dynamic level? If not, in what voice line was the irregularity most noticeable? Etc.

In my early days in the lecture hall, the difficulty experienced by many well-trained musicians in meeting such tests of scale-consciousness used to amaze me and the students. The result of the tests has usually been the resolve on the part of eager young aspirants to the podium to develop a quick and comprehensive alertness to a complete musical structure. The arc of a melody will not curve incognito through a series of chords if the conductor has cultivated such alertness. But if he is a top-liner, much, if not most, of the inner material will escape his attention.

It is not even doubtful, *it is certain* that no conductor can consistently bring inner melodic figures to the surface until scale-consciousness has become equivalently intuitive, just as the implications of a syllogism are instinctively sensed by a logician.

All of these foregoing considerations lead to the conclusion that the master conductor has developed a definite philosophy of music, that he is not drifting unawares through uncharted speculations or eliciting from his performers a series of spasmodic irrelevancies. Music has, indeed, a profound philosophy which accords to it a dignity and efficacy not suspected by those unacquainted with its principles and dogmas. The ratiocinations of speculative philosophy take due cognizance of *motion*, which is a universal attribute of everything created, of *cause and effect*, and of *teleology*, which means a preconceived purpose carried out by well-ordered means.

ADDITIONAL MEMORANDA CONCERNING MELODY

Straightforward unisons are usually melodies developed into tunes, if they are measured in time-pattern rhythms. In harmonized music, they may or may not be tunes. *Melody* is a series of pitch vibrations proceeding with some sort of rhythmical form. *Tune* is a melodic sequence with a definite rhythm mensurable by temporal values or accommodated to strict metrical scansion, as in the simpler hymns of Gregorian chant. If a melody in modern music remains in one single part throughout a movement, it is generally a tune. Melodies which appear in one locale for a phrase or two, migrating elsewhere thereafter, are too fragmentary to be considered tunes. The tendency to confuse the two words is so widespread, even in the fraternity of professional musicians, that the distinction should be noted. The term *melody* is used throughout this volume in its strict meaning, except when it is used figuratively as suggesting the aesthetic sum total of the musical art. Identity of tune and melody is found usually in homophonic music. The homophonic conception of the art tends to project a tuneful air out and beyond but not free of the harmonic support of other choral or orchestral lines or instrumental accompaniment. This harmonic association of other notes with an obvious tune which is more frequently than otherwise, although not always, on the top line, provides the key to the categorizing and placing by which the character of the tune is determined for listeners.

Variously, according to the category to which harmony assigns a tune —major, minor, diatonic, chromatic, or whole tone—a tune will invariably assume different aspects. The tune of "Yankee Doodle" played in slow tempo and on top of minor-mode chordings loses altogether its traditional war-song flavor and élan, taking on the features of a *marche funèbre*. The forthright airs of Stephen Foster, the much-beloved progressions of the Thomas Moore settings, the classic English ballads and folk songs generally can readily be translated to a new category, in which they may be unrecognizable, by the substitution of unfamiliar for the customary harmonizations. Gevaert, of the great nineteenth-century Conservatoire in Brussels, Belgium, used the same thematic material for two Christmas carols with surprisingly singular and dissociated effects, "The Sleep of the Infant" and "Shepherd Neighbors." Even candid hymn tunes, by slight alterations of harmony—and perhaps tempo—can be transformed into musical agencies of absurdly disparate values. Thus, many of the 3/4 hymn tunes can be made easily to degenerate into what were known, in my youth, as Mexican glide waltzes.

The Gregorian chants are not tunes in the modern sense, for they are free of time patterns, with the exception of some strongly metrical hymns, viz., "Adoro Te Devote," "Creator Alme Siderum," "Iste Confessor," "Veni Creator," "Veni Sancte Spiritus," "Lauda Sion," etc., and some short proses, viz., *Rorate Coeli, Attende Domine*, etc., they proceed without the balanced number of measures of a tune.

Melody has been called the surface of music. But sometimes, literally it is below the surface. This means that it may be found in the inner parts or even on the bass line. Marches composed for military or brass bands frequently assign the most telling effects to baritones and trombones, and in many glees and part songs the bassos bring the melodic content to its climax. The hiding of melodic arcs in inner parts indicates usually, although not always, the presence of contrapuntal movements or figures.

As to the hiding of melodic arcs in interior parts, in candidly contrapuntal music there is no hiding of such important structural features. But much modern music (from the mid-eighteenth century on) is a sort of ragout in which composers have mixed many oddments. Accompanied monody, homophony, and polyphonic similitudes are frequently stirred into a single movement. In such a potpourri one must seek, if he expects to find, the locale of complete melodies or the single arcs which, picked up here and there throughout the voice parts, will provide a necessary continuity. Accompanied monody, forthright homophony, and formal polyphony show their melodic sites to a first glance. Even the polyphonic melodies are clearly disposed, proceeding independently of one another, the conductor's task being the regulation of their inter-relationship. It is the medley of styles that confuses. Ralph Waldo Emerson wrote that "one must be an inventor to read well." This naïve bon mot may ease the strain of searching for the substance in much of the music that the modern conductor must analyze. Generally, a little patient persistence will discover the melody and trace its roamings through the various voice lines. It must be taken for granted as a most interesting and artistic vagary of mixed music that, *in styles of compositions which make free use of figures and tensions as well as of simplicities, a melody rarely remains long on one single line*. The restlessness of melody does not make music wayward; rather does it add charm.

The general repertory which conductors are called upon to interpret teems with mixtures of vertical and horizontal effects, melody thus being afforded unlimited opportunity for disclosing the elasticity of music. One style follows and mixes with the other naturally and therefore artistically. The natural and the artistic cannot be in conflict. A conductor must be on the alert to recognize the moments when the vertical or the horizontal is in the ascendant. When is music vertical? Whenever, indeed, a melody is stretched like a single strand across the skein of straightforward supporting harmony. When is it horizontal? Whenever each vocal or instrumental line of a composition reveals its own melodic formations, contributing, as it were, incidentally to the harmonic structure.

If little arcs of melody are found drifting through other parts while a principal theme is in progress, the music is obviously borrowing from the horizontal style. This means that the conductor, taking cognizance of the drifting arcs, must underline them appropriately and adroitly correlate them to the whole. But he must not miss them. Horizontal music does its share of borrowing, too. Whenever the independent melodic formations and figures of counterpoint merge in chords or chordal effects (these are called *synchronous rhythms* in the terminology of Renaissance polyphony), an impression of vertical structure is imparted.

Many examples of the mixture of styles in modern music are not necessary to substantiate these premises. Even if not always guided by them, the majority of professional conductors are aware of their validity. It will suffice here to refer the reader to Chorus No. IV of the "Requiem" by Brahms (cf. page 111). Measures 1-5 give a vertical impression; although the cellos are assigned a melody in contrary motion to that of the flutes and clarinets, the melody of the latter is obviously primary and must be set forth as such; measures 5-14 suggest horizontal movement on account of the quasi-independence of the choral lines, arcs of melody appearing notably in the tenor line, 6, 10, 11, and in the bass line, measures 10 and 12; these arcs need delineation.

A series of notes, the conformation of which is sanctioned by canons of art, may constitute a true melody, regardless of their adequacy-aggregate for a complete tune.

A melodic arc may be as short as two notes; cf. the leitmotif of woe in Richard Wagner's *Ring of the Nibelung*. This is probably the shortest

melodic instance in the repertory of music (perhaps the two-note "Amens" at the end of hymn tunes also deserve recognition); but because it expresses a musical as well as a dramatic idea, the two notes being in artistic placement, a conjunct melody presents itself and must be projected beyond its harmonic and contrapuntal investiture upon its every recurrence.

The quotation from Wagner's monograph *On Conducting* on page 8, namely, that the orchestra in Paris "had learnt to look for Beethoven's melody in every bar," is an unmistakable indication that in the "enigmatical Ninth Symphony" the Parisian musicians and eventually Wagner himself discovered the melodic line to be a nomad, wandering, every other bar or two, through the various string, wood, and brass choirs of the orchestra. Evidently the Leipzig musicians, with whom Wagner was dissatisfied after listening to the performance in Paris, were top-line players, or perhaps devotees of that type of ensemble performance which projects and underlines nothing in particular. Personally, I have listened to performances of the masterpieces of Haydn, Mozart, Beethoven, Brahms, César Franck, etc., during which the top line persistently arrogated attention to itself, as if altogether unmindful of the prerogatives of the inner parts, or ceded its primacy only when bulky, amorphous, and undefined mass tones came from the noisy obedience of the orchestra to ill-advised urgings of conductors. The majority of concertgoers have never heard the inner beauties of many great compositions.

There are sophisms in the technique of interpretation just as specious as the sophisms of pseudo-philosophy. The top-line sophism with its alternate, the blatant mass effect which inhibits the delineation of any however important inner contribution, has laid low, in our generation and probably earlier, not only symphonies and tone poems but great choral and orchestral movements in the classic oratorios. How often, perchance regularly, is not the "Missa Solemnis" of Beethoven shorn of essential features? When and where do the mysteries which Bach invoked for the inner parts of his "B Minor Mass," and the choral-orchestral figures of the St. Matthew and St. John "Passions" find opportunity for revelation? Have the mystical inside lines of the Mozart "Requiem" taken flight forever? Must the momentary figures with which Brahms purposed to vitalize his orchestral music be always subordinated to a false music philosophy?

The performance of *a cappella* polyphony deteriorated steadily from the seventeenth century until it reached the nadir in our generation. This deterioration was clearly foretold in the development of top-line music by Monteverdi, his contemporaries and disciples. It is my conviction that, until conductors, following Wagner's counsel, "look for the melody in every bar," top line, middle lines, or low line, the rendition of every choral and orchestral opus will share the fate of the *a cappella* polyphony. Steady deterioration is forecast. Bach, Beethoven, Brahms, Mendelssohn, and many moderns frequently seem meaningless. Those who had so much to say in their music are often robbed of intelligible speech, their utterances being inarticulate. The top-line approach to music when applied to the classics, or to other styles which draw upon the resources of the counterpoint of notes or rhythms or dynamics is disastrous. Melody must live and function and glow "in every bar" wherever it is found.

A well-known composer-conductor once asked my opinion of the rendition of one of his compositions. I answered immediately that there was altogether too much treble in the ensemble; that the top line, except in certain instances, should be considered as a canopy covering the lower parts; that its melody should never secrete inner figures; and finally, in the nomenclature of the chorus, that the treble line is the soprano line, soprano meaning the part written *over* the rest of the ensemble. His rebuttal was, "Well, many of us conductors like the treble line. Probably you have a strange aversion for it." This comment was amusing, for I had given many years of my life, energetically and with open mind, to the development of a treble quality which by its lightness and buoyancy would spiritualize and let rise to the surface the undermovements, thus permitting the concerted unit to create an aesthetic impression. The taming of the soprano choir must be paralleled in the orchestra by the disciplining of high strings, wood winds, and brass.

Top-line music minimizes the value of harmony and the timbres on associated lines; emphasis of melodic fragments will help to nullify the lure of top-line sophistry.

APPENDIX II

MODALITY

The following considerations—heretical to many readers—are set down because of the widespread false impression that each mode in Gregorian chant and *a cappella* polyphony requires special technical treatment. The simplicity of these great art forms has been obscured by the insistence of pedagogues on a vocabulary of terms which, if stripped of their archaic intimations, would have little vogue among practical musicians (cf. pages 226 *et seq.*). *Modality* is one of these almost profitless captions. The data here are assembled in answer to this question: In what measure is melody modified by modality?

The substance of melody—an orderly and rhythmical sequence of tones —is not affected by modality, but its flavor and intimations are unquestionably determined by the scale form in which it is cast. The different allocations of half- and whole-tone intervals which distinguish modes from one another are necessarily manifest in the melodies composed on their respective tonal bases. Obviously, a sequence built upon the plan of the major scale presents a tonal picture to the imagination quite different from a melody designed in the pure minor idiom. The whole-tone scale produces still another reaction, and the intervallic designs of such scales as those of the Russian Obukof and the Spaniard Esplá present the substance of melody in still another guise. The modes produce moods. For instance, the scale of C major is a plain unseasoned sequence, whereas the tonal arrangement of Esplá C, D flat, E natural, F, G flat, A flat, B flat savors of exotic spices. Melodies in both scales necessarily take on the character of their respective bases and create corresponding impressions. Perhaps the major scale usually develops single ideas in listeners while the Esplá intervals tortuously generate complex fancies.

The relationship between melody and modality is therefore a subject of psychological rather than of musical inquiry, except in so far as modality requires identification and some understanding from the conductor if he is to translate it fairly to an audience.

Discussion of the modal system naturally focuses upon the eight ecclesiastical scales of Gregorian chant and the four extra modes which the polyphonists of the sixteenth century accepted from Henricus Glareanus (*Duodecachordon*) as the logical extension of the Ambrosian-Gregorian syllabus. It is interesting to note, in passing, that Glareanus was unwilling to pursue his logic far enough to include the Locrian and hypo-Locrian modes which, extending through the octaves of B and F respectively, would allow the medieval specter (*Diabolus in Musica*) to materialize. Antonio Lotti, a century later, was among those who proved ("Crucifixus" in 6 voices) the diminished fifth, the equivalent of the "unholy" tritone, to be an acceptable and effective interval.

Broadly, however, all modes and tonal bases seem to have been guided by a single architectonic principle which urges music to create a major or minor impression.

From the experiments of Pythagoras with strings (circa 550 B.C.) the mathematical relationship of intervals lying between a fundamental and its octave were demonstrated. The octave was discovered to be divisible into two tetrachords separated by a full tone, and it was found that one semitone was required to complete the acoustical ambit of each tetrachord. The modern diatonic scale is purchased upon the Pythagorean base. Further examination of the available data discloses that the pre-Christian analysis of music recognized the controlling influence of an architectonic principle. The directive domination of this principle has been necessarily active during the progress of music through many stages of development. This principle concerns modality; it is an intrinsic coercive force which impels all the scale forms of the multitude permitted by the science of acoustics into two genetic agencies of impressionism, the major and the minor. Perhaps it is more fitting to invert the order of these agencies, since the minor seems primarily to have engaged the attention of the Pythagoreans, the Ambrosians, and the Gregorians. There are, of course, two sciences involved in the establishing of musical effects, physics, and psychology. The former deals with the mathematics of intervals, the latter with the sensitiveness of listeners to their possible arrangements.

If only the white keys of the piano are used, fifteen variously ordered modes may be played—the Ambrosian, Gregorian, those of Glareanus (including the Locrian and hypo-Locrian), and the pentatonic. With the help of the black keys seven more accepted tonal bases may be constructed—the harmonic and melodic minor, the chromatic, duodecuple, whole tone, and the scales of Obukof and Esplá. The hexachords of Guido obviously were not intended to create modes. If we avoid the terrifying contemplation of atonal and polytonal inventions (which, however, can be submitted successfully to diagnosis if not to remedy) there seem to be twenty-two scale sequences through which music has revealed itself to the Christian era.

But are there twenty-two separate and individual impressions made upon the musical perceptivity of listeners? The architectonic control of musical excitation seems to permit only two reactions, pure minor or major, although in creating these ultimate responses the vagaries of the twenty-two modes may momentarily stir up vague modifications of these more persistent impressions. The major mode, if it can be described in a word, is complete, while the pure minor mode is incomplete and restless, seemingly struggling to free itself from the uncertainty of the initial depressed third.

Pythagoras, interested chiefly in the speculative relations of sounds to mathematics, seems to have been unwittingly influenced by the inevitability of major or minor effects, because his three orders of intervals which became the basis of the Hellenic modal system, the Phrygian,[1] *defgabcd*, and the Dorian *efgabcde*, carry our minor implications, while the Lydian, *cdefgabc*, obviously constitutes our major scale. The fact that these scales proceeded downwards does not affect their modal intimations. Substitute B flat for B natural in the Phrygian scale and the pure relative minor of the key of F evolves; F sharp in place of F natural converts his Dorian mode into the relative minor of the key of G. The Lydian scale, later the Ionian scale of Glareanus (called the *modus lascivius* or wanton mode because it was the favorite of the minstrels), proved itself more adaptable to easy harmonic treatment, and perhaps for this reason became more popular—the greater or major scale.[2]

There were seven Greek modes somewhat confusedly used in the first centuries of Christianity, and the songs of the Church naturally reflected the Hellenic influence. In the fourth century, St. Ambrose undertook to bring order out of the prevailing confusion, hoping to outline a plan for a simple yet distinctively Christian music. He took the Greek material and coordinated a series of consecutive scales begin-

---

[1] The nomenclature used here is that of the Greeks.

[2] A tradition long prevailed in continental Europe, especially in France, that each of the eight Gregorian modes possessed a definite character which by its own inherence produced distinct moods. There were differences of opinion among the Gregorian musicologists as to the relation of specific modes to specific moods, but they were all probably motivated by a desire to justify the multiplicity of scale forms. Perhaps it was more than a gesture, more than the analogous effort of polyphonists to establish the ternary rhythm as perfect in honor of the Holy Trinity, but there is a certain pious naïveté involved that should interest the student. Here is a characteristic table of modal effects prepared by an early nineteenth-century professor of Gregorian chant, N. A. Janssen of Malines, Belgium:

1st tone, *lively and joyous, majestic, sad;*
2nd tone, *somber, serious, austere;*
3rd tone, *harsh, disdainful, impetuous;*
4th tone, *plaintive, sweet, tearful, slightly violent;*
5th tone, *hard, grandiose, triumphant;*
6th tone, *agreeable, conducive of gentle piety;*
7th tone, *bitter and scornful;* (named by others *Angelic!*)
8th tone, *delightful, polished, calm.*

ning respectively on D, E, F, G, the semitones variously arranged in
each, the scales on D and G only having a semitone between the same
intervals, viz., the sixth and seventh. St. Gregory, about two centuries
later, is credited with having added four modes, but as each of these
was cognate to an Ambrosian scale, they failed to contribute new tonal
flavors. The Gregorian octaves began a fourth below the Ambrosian and
were in effect only the transposition of the component sections of the
earlier sequences; thus St. Gregory placed a fourth below a fifth, while
St. Ambrose gave the more important interval the initial position. For
example:

St. Ambrose, defgabcd

St. Gregory, abcdefga

The genetic notes of the "authentic" modes (St. Ambrose) and of the
adjacent "plagal" modes (St. Gregory) were the same. The Ambrosian
forms were numbered 1, 3, 5, 7, and the Gregorian correlatives, 2, 4, 6, 8.

The genetic or *final* notes:

D 1st and 2nd modes
E 3rd and 4th modes
F 5th and 6th modes
G 7th and 8th modes

But, as in the case of the three cardinal arrangements of Pythagoras,
they can be sorted through the acoustico-psychological sieve into two
inclusive orders, the minor and major. One cannot escape the impression
that the ethos of the first four modes is minor, and that of the second
group major.

Here are the eight early ecclesiastical scales; play them on the white
keys of a piano and ascertain personally their systemic affinity with the
minor or major: [3]

1. defgabcd ⎫
2. abcdefga ⎪ minor
3. efgabcde ⎬
4. bcdefgab ⎭

5. fgabcdef ⎫
6. cdefgabc ⎪ major
7. gabcdefg ⎬
8. defgabcd ⎭

[3] The odd-numbered modes should each be played in two groups of a
fifth and a fourth, and the even-numbered modes *vice versa;* thus: 1. *defga
abcd;* 2. *abcd defga,* etc.

Although the distribution of intervals in the first and eighth modes is identical, the theory of the scales is different, because structurally the fifth D-A in the first mode comprises the important final note D, the dominant A, and the mediant F, which is clearly a minor assortment, while, in the eighth mode, G being the final note, B the original and C the later dominant, major intervals are provided, thus D-G a perfect fourth, G-B a major third, or G-C another perfect fourth. The fifth in the first mode, *defga*, implies the minor, the fifth in the eighth mode, *gabcd*, being essentially major.

The importance, therefore, of modality in music has probably even been exaggerated. The added scales of Glareanus[4] show the same eagerness for minor or major classification as the Pythagorean and Ambrosian-Gregorian modes. His Aeolian and Ionian modes are construed as the final capitulation of medieval modality to the minor and major distribution of intervals as through the modern key system. Although the composers of the later polyphonic era were giving abundant evidence of an approach to our simple modal scheme, there have appeared rather recently several neo-medievalists who proclaim that the abandonment of the Church modes has been a distinct loss in the alleged sacrifice of richer tonal opportunities than our restricted (also alleged) system provides.

The architectonic principle of music—the unity of many acoustical assortments of musical sounds in a single generic pair of psychological agencies—is restricted only by the potentialities of music itself which seem to converge in an impressionism which has but two sides, minor and major.[5]

A distinguished conductor once requested me to identify the Gregorian melody and mode of the "Confiteor Unum Baptisma" motif in Bach's "B Minor Mass." The source of the theme is a now abrogated version of Credo No. I in the fourth mode. To what extent this information served

[4] The Aeolian scale *abcde efga,* the Ionian *cdefg gabc;* their plagals are within the octaves E-E and G-G respectively.

[5] A lucid example of two modes, the Phrygian and Aeolian (nomenclature of Glareanus), used by a great polyphonist with a characteristically minor effect (with or without the *ficta* accidentals) is the celebrated "Vere Languores" of Tomaso de Vittoria. (See page 235 for the score.) The motet is candidly in the Phrygian mode, *mi fa 'sol la ti do re mi,* the semitone of the modal fifth lying between the first and the second intervals. It can be concluded authentically at measure No. 59 on the modal final note *mi;* but there is a beautiful coda attached in which the music proceeds to the Aeolian scale, *la ti do re mi fa sol la,* the semitone of the modal fifth lying (without *ficta*) between the second and third intervals. Do the Phrygian and Aeolian here stimulate different reactions? No! You find only a graceful and captivating modulation from F sharp minor to B minor (without *ficta*) or, with the accidentals, from F sharp major to B major.

any practical purpose of the conductor I never learned. Bach had clearly treated it as a theme suitable for minor harmonies, and this suitability was due of course to the minor character of the fourth mode. If Bach had expounded the theme in the free rhythm of Gregorian chant, the conductor would naturally be interested in revealing the movement as a quasi-plain-song invention, but in the absolute time-pattern grouping of the notes in Bach's score, the genealogy of the melody is of neither academic nor practical import.

However, it is reasonable to insist that conductors possess at least elementary information about the various modal structures of chant and polyphony, not only because they were the media through which music finally simplified a complexity of tonal bases, but also because such knowledge is advantageous in conducting sixteenth-century compositions in which the sharps and flats of *musica ficta* are not clearly intimated.

But the modes do not demand a highly organized technique, designed *speciatim* to reveal idiosyncrasies of each slightly varying scale form, for the variations, actually, are not sufficiently singular to be idiosyncrasies. They do not need diverse or specific treatment. The achitectonic parentage of the modes is evident in their general family resemblance. All have eyes of Aegean blue and Hellenic contours, some suggesting the traits of Dorian or Phrygian grandsires, and others those of Lydian forebears.

Pythagoras accurately analyzed a scale as a series of tones comprising the fundamental, its octave, and the intervening intervals of a fifth and a perfect fourth. Other intervening intervals, whole tones and semitones, were found necessary acoustically to fill out the skeleton form. The early Greek codification of intervals was epitomized in the three orders of the tetrachords of Pythagoras and this manner of sorting sounds gave impetus to the Ambrosian plan. It has already been noted that the psychological reactions to these tonal arrangements are not readily distinguishable from our reactions to minor and major. These reactions are energized by a subconscious attitude toward the incomplete and the complete, and by an aesthetic instinct to classify musical experiences accordingly. An instinct may be disciplined and regulated, but it cannot be eliminated or changed, for it is "a propensity prior to experience—and independent of instruction."

Curiously the ears of the ancients, the medievalists, and even of the early Renaissance musicians were not sure of some intervals. For instance, the difference between the small and large thirds was long in establishing itself. Perhaps the D-F of the Phrygian scale sounded to the Hellenes as D-F sharp has sounded to later generations. Perhaps, too, the monks of some monasteries heard tunings of the Gregorian modes not strictly in accord with the tunings in vogue elsewhere. Certainly, there were different degrees of sensitiveness to smaller or larger intervals, except of course to the mathematically fixed octave, fifth, and fourth; otherwise the confusions which were later made manifest by notation would not have been recorded. The *Tierce de Picardie* (*q.v.*) and the vigorously controverted *musica ficta* are evidence that thirds, sixths, and sevenths were frequently adjudged, perhaps by purposeful assumption, to be smaller intervals by some and larger by others.

The conductor, however, is not required to be a thorough archaist, for the most he could reasonably hope to net from much delving into fragmentary records of the formative past of music would be some highly conjectural hypotheses which could add little of value to a practicable technique.

Music, it seems reasonable to conclude, imparts a sense of minor or major. It follows as a corollary that the conductor's responsibility in this connection is to ascertain the mood suggested by a given movement, and to aim at creating that mood in his audience.

The pentatonic scale, *do re mi sol la do,* creates a minor or major atmosphere according to the sequence of intervals selected for a melody. The so-called harmonic and melodic minor scales are merely modifications respectively of the pure minor or major. These modifications do not comprise independent agencies of expression, since the modifying factors are reducible to the unsubstantial status of *accidentals* or *incidentals.* The chromatic scale, a combination of the major and the harmonic minor intervals plus a minor second and an augmented fourth, depends for its effect entirely upon the major or minor diatonic scale which it colors. Chromaticism has been promoted to puppet autonomy in the duodecuple scale, but this is equally dependent for intimations on the adjacent minor and major keys.

In spite of the absence of semitones in the Debussy octave and its partition into six whole tones, the impressionistic effect is rather minor than major. The semitones between mi-fa and ti-do are needed to give the *major* sense of satisfaction. In any event, the sequence of six whole tones is the most limited tonal basis offered to a composer, for he has at his disposal only two series of notes, one involving C and the other C sharp or D flat. Furthermore, it is generally thought to have spent its melodic resources already.

The division of the octave into microtonal intervals has been acceptable to some oriental peoples and has interested a few modern musicians. I have not had opportunity to listen to music purveyed in this strange style, but I presume the difference in effect between the semitone and the microtone to be something like the difference between G sharp and

A flat in unequal temperaments. These tonal *commas,* upon analysis, will probably be found to be inconsequential deviations from the accepted physical basis of music.

Espláism, polytonalism, and atonalism, notwithstanding their extravagant digressions from the normal routes of music, usually keep the highways in sight as frequently their footprints attest. Once in a while, the most modernistic of the *neo-mode* creators become lost in a jungle of cacophonous disorder, whereupon they make loud noises with brass instruments and rackety traps to bolster up their morale, feigning the conviction that they are unafraid of the eerie sounds. They often find the way back to charted roadways, however, to rest a while in the secure domain of major or minor.

The principles of all the arts are simple and enduring. The past, present, and future of their seemingly changing manifestations will be discovered by the sufficiently curious to be the degrees of visibility in which elapsed epochs have already revealed them and on-coming ages will make them more plain. To the incurious, each unfamiliar form in which an art presents itself is equivalent to the discovery of a new principle. This is modernism—but untutored and madcap.

The principal task of the general conductor, it may be repeated apropos of modality, is to undertake to create the mood suggested by the scale basis of a composition.

But the expert director of Gregorian chant and polyphony should know the characteristic pattern figures of the various modes in order to assure the intimacy and fluency of intervals used by the melodists.

The spontaneous reaction of a conductor to different tonal bases will necessarily influence his approach to modal melodies. Personally, I feel only the minor dominating the first four and the major the second four modes. The third and fourth modes reach out more vigorously to my temperament than the others, but their initial minor thirds prevent me from classifying them as *sui generis.*

The accepted definition of modality, in general, is *"the total character of a sensation or its stimulus as determined by the class of sensations to which it belongs or appeals."* Applied to music, modality means simply the ultimate or total sensation which specific tonal bases can stimulate. This totality of sensation involves either consonance or dissonance, the former instituting a simple and the latter a complex experience. Acousticians agree that the lowest consonance is a minor third, the greater consonances being framed by perfect and major intervals. Pythagoras discovered that the simpler the ratio the more perfect the harmony between two sounds. To quote again from Tyndall: "Why simplicity should give pleasure remained long an enigma, the only pretence of a solution being that of Euler, which, briefly expressed, is, that the human soul takes a constitutional delight in simple calculations."[6]

Thus it may be intelligently concluded that modality contributed more to the differentiations of speculative theory than to the actual content of medieval music. In practice, music was essaying to express itself without complex confusion; it was urging itself to be rid of attributes which the doctrinaires had wound around it, trying, indeed, to function as a *natural* art form. Alfred Einstein has succinctly stated the difficulties against which music was pitting its aesthetic strength.

"The Early Middle Ages made a comprehensive study of the theoretical treatment of plainsong. . . . Classical conceptions naturally played a large part in the establishment of theory. The most important of those who helped in the transmission of the legacy was, as I have already mentioned, the late Roman philosopher Boetius (d. 526); from him was derived the conception of music that dominated the whole of the Middle Ages. Creative power was ranked below theoretical knowledge; and though this attitude helped to give music its place in the scholastic culture of the time, it was bound to introduce into living creation a strain of *purely abstract* [italics are mine] *artificiality*."[7]

The key system foreshadowed in the hexachord scales of Guido, and the converging of many modes in two loosened the shackles wrought by theorists, granting music its freedom. The Church was willing to withhold this freedom through many centuries, perhaps because so emotional a force as music could easily lose its spiritual orientation and become, as it has unfortunately become in some of its adventures, only an epicurean refreshment. But it was not modality as such that so long preserved the spiritual urgency of music, for the songs of the troubadours and the love lays of the minstrels as well as the canticles of the Church were composed in the modes. It was rather the fact itself that the Church maintained a directive supervision over the expansion of the art that kept it so long and so profitably in custody. Thirteen centuries of life in the cloister have so infused music with an ascetical aestheticism that the restraints of monastic discipline must be counted the art's greatest and most fruitful experience. This span of centuries was a long novitiate for the freedom which music now enjoys, and probably the fundamental values learned during its arduous course will not be completely forgotten.

It has already been pointed out that conductors need not memorize the book of rules of that lengthy novitiate, or concern themselves intimately with the canons and criteria which evolved from the speculations

[6] John Tyndall, *Sound*, p. 411.

[7] Alfred Einstein, *A Short History of Music* (New York: Knopf, 1938), pp. 22, 23.

of early theorists. Since these have little or no significance in the general technique of conducting, they may be left securely, as genealogical records, in the many monastic archives whither they found their way after the days of Hermann the Lame at Reichenau.

A comprehensive study of all phases of modality would include an investigation of the affinity between music and color. That there is a close relationship is conceded, and many specialists have already developed interesting theories. The "Color Symphony" of Arthur Bliss is an ingenious suggestion of the reasonableness of certain hypotheses, and the more recent *visualization* of a Bach fugue by Walt Disney in "Fantasia" is a step forward. But since this aspect of modality is still inchoately envisioned, there is no adequate reason for removing it from the laboratory and making guesses about it here. Perhaps purple will require a regal scepter beat, orange a quiet upbeat, red a lively *sfzorzando*, and green a capering *staccato* in the eras to come.

Just now I'd rather look at the rainbow than hear it try to sing!

INDEX